VALUES AND EVALUATION IN EDUCATION

VALUES AND EVALUATION IN EDUCATION

Roger Straughan and
Jack Wrigley (Editors)

Harper & Row, Publishers
London

Cambridge	San Francisco
Hagerstown	Mexico City
Philadelphia	Sao Paolo
New York	Sydney

W 12853 £7.95. 780

British Library Cataloguing in Publication Data
    Values and evaluation in education. –
        (Harper education series).
        1. Educational surveys
        2. Education
        3. Values
        I. Straughan, Roger   II. Wrigley, Jack
        379′.15   LB2823

        ISBN 0-06-318137-1
        ISBN 0-06-318158-4 Pbk

Typeset by Inforum Ltd, Portsmouth
Printed and bound by
A. Wheaton & Co Ltd, Exeter

CONTENTS

PREFACE

This book is concerned with two major areas of current educational debate which are seldom looked at side-by-side – values and evaluation. The first section concentrates upon a cluster of key concepts which are of general importance to education: standards, measurement, assessment and examinations, evaluation and values are examined from the viewpoint of various disciplines, and the distinctions and linkages between these notions are explored. The second section considers different ways in which questions about educational values and evaluation arise within the teaching of specific areas of the curriculum, with separate chapters devoted to literature, language, art, history, science, and mathematics. Each section begins with an editorial introduction which identifies the main issues arising from the following chapters and the controversial questions which surround them; finally, in the editorial conclusion we reflect upon what seem to be the most complex and contentious problems to have emerged from the book.

All of the contributors are at present engaged, or have recently been engaged, in teaching and/or research at the University of Reading School of Education. This has made it possible for a considerable amount of discussion and exchange of ideas to take place during the planning of the book's structure and contents. The final product, however, is *not* intended, it must be emphasized, to represent any kind of unanimous 'party line', which lays down a clear-cut set of definitions and answers. Any attempt to achieve this sort of uniformity would be radically misconceived (if indeed possible), given the wide divergence of opinion that currently exists over all aspects of educational values and evaluation. The editors have therefore felt it their function to encourage different approaches, interpretations, and emphases from the contributors and to offer a commentary, when necessary, upon the significance of these differences, rather than to demand that all divergence and disagreement be ironed out in pursuit of compromise and consensus, which even if attainable would inevitably lack interest and conviction.

This variety of approach, we hope, will also stimulate readers to formulate their own judgements about the issues which are raised. The book is intended to be both informative and provocative, and the information which it provides should form a useful basis for any ensuing discussion of the more controversial implications of that information. The book has been written with a wide audience in mind, and to that end technical terminology has been kept to a minimum; in particular we envisage that it will be of use to students on B.Ed. and P.G.C.E. courses, and to experienced teachers with interests in curriculum development or assessment and evaluation. However, an underlying theme of the book is that questions about values and evaluation are wholly inescapable in education; if that is true, it follows that no one who is concerned with or interested in educational matters can afford to ignore the topics with which this book deals.

R.S.
J.W.

SECTION I

ASPECTS OF EDUCATIONAL VALUES
AND EVALUATION

CHAPTER 1

WHAT ARE THE MAIN ISSUES?

The claim that education must embody values hardly sounds a very daring assertion. Yet such a claim is not as straightforward as it initially sounds, for it can be interpreted in at least three different ways, and each of these interpretations carries with it different implications and requires a different sort of argument if the claim is to be defended.

Firstly, the claim could be taken as a simple statement of fact. Both individual teachers and educational institutions as a matter of psychological and sociological fact, it might be argued, *do* reveal their values all the time, whether deliberately or unconsciously, and indeed cannot help doing so. This is because any person or group of persons engaged in the business of educating others has certain aims in mind concerned with effecting changes of various kinds in those who are being educated. Value-judgements must be made in deciding what those changes ought to be, and therefore education *must* in this descriptive, factual sense embody values.

A second, alternative interpretation, however, could be that a *moral* claim is being made here. Education, according to this argument, is a supremely important activity, which has a permanent, formative effect upon children; it influences and perhaps even determines their future intellectual, social, moral, and emotional development, and thereby plays a crucial part in shaping the sort of person that the child is to become. So, if this is the case, education must not be approached in an aimless or uncommitted manner; such is its potential power that it must be used as a positive means of *improving* individuals and the society of which they will become adult members; and this can only be done if teachers and schools are seen to stand for certain values.

Thirdly, the claim could be viewed as a logical or conceptual one. The argument here would be that education must, *by definition*, embody values, and that anything which does not embody values cannot be called 'education'. The classic statement of this position is contained in the earlier work of R.S. Peters (1967), who maintained that education involves the transmission of what is thought worthwhile by morally unobjectionable means. Thus, values must enter into both the subject-matter and the methods of any activity that is to count as 'education', and if questions can be raised about the desirability of either what is being taught or the way in which it is being taught, then questions must also be raised about whether 'education' is in fact going on.

A great deal more could, of course, be said about each of these interpretations and its related argument. For the moment, however, it is sufficient to have demonstrated very briefly the variety of ways in which education might be said to be unavoidably bound up with questions of value.

Let us next ask whether it might be said to be equally bound up with questions of evaluation. The answer seems to be yes, for the same three kinds of argument which we have just looked at in connection with values can also be applied to the relationship between education and evaluation.

Firstly, many would be of the opinion that, as a sheer matter of fact, education is pretty well all about evaluation, when one considers the amount of time and effort which teachers put into testing whether pupils have learned what they are intended to learn. The importance attributed to examination results by pupils, teachers, and future employers, and the degree to which examination requirements can dictate the way that a subject is taught and presented, might be taken as further indications that education is not merely concerned with, but (some might maintain) obsessed with, evaluation.

Secondly, it might be thought that educators are under a *moral* obligation to evaluate the results of their labours, and that education accordingly in this sense must include evaluation. The justification for this claim would depend partly upon the value and importance placed on education itself; for if it can indeed exercise a powerful influence upon its recipients, then it is the duty of educators to monitor the effects of that influence and to assess whether they are in fact achieving what they intend to achieve. The huge amounts of time, money, and resources that are devoted to educational systems would add additional weight to the argument that it is wholly irresponsible not to keep a close check on what exactly is being produced by these systems. Recent demands that schools and teachers should be made more accountable for the services and alleged benefits which they are thought to provide further underline this claim that educators should be obliged to evaluate what particular goods they are delivering.

Thirdly and finally, it could be proposed that education must, by definition, involve reference to evaluation, because education is conceptually and logically linked to the notion of evaluation just as it is to the notion of values. Antony Flew (1976), for example, has argued that one cannot claim to be sincerely engaged in the business of teaching unless one is concerned about how successful one is being in trying to ensure that others master items of knowledge, and unless one takes steps to find out by means of assessment. So it might similarly be claimed that one cannot attempt to educate a child without constantly monitoring his progress to evaluate whether his understanding is indeed developing.

So far, then, we have seen that there are parallel arguments which can be used to support the claims that education must be concerned with both values and evaluation. These arguments could of course be challenged individually, but the wide range of considerations to which they appeal, even in the brief outline that has been given, strongly suggests that *some* close links of *some* kind are likely to exist between the three notions, and gives us a warrant to explore these possible links more closely.

But although various ways of seeing these possible links have now been mentioned, the discussion so far has been somewhat superficial and inconclusive, largely because no attempt has been made to get a clearer picture of exactly what we are talking about – a fundamental flaw in much educational debate. In particular both 'values' and 'evaluation' are highly generalized and complex terms, the meaning of which is by no means self-evident. Further clarification is badly needed in each case before we can even start to map out their connections with education.

This point is confirmed if we reflect upon the number of basic questions that have been begged in our account so far. What precisely is a value, and what does it mean to hold one? Are there different sorts of value, and if so, how can we classify them? What is the difference between values, aims, goals, objectives, and philosophies? Are there such things as 'educational' values? Similarly, what is evaluation? How does it differ from assessment, measurement, and examination? What procedures does it involve? How do we decide what to evaluate in education and who is to do the evaluating? Do value-judgements enter into the business of evaluation?

It is with these questions that this section will be concerned. Before looking more closely at the individual chapters, however, and the different ways in which these questions are approached, we wish to draw the reader's attention to what is an underlying theme of this section, although it is not directly discussed in any one chapter.

A sharp distinction is usually drawn between questions of fact and questions of value. For example, the question of how much food a battery hen needs to produce the maximum number of eggs is, it is often claimed, logically different from the question of whether it is right to use battery hens to supply us with eggs; the first question seeks to ascertain what *is* in fact the case and can be answered objectively by studying the empirical evidence, while the second question is trying to establish what *ought* to be done and cannot be settled simply by looking at the facts, because a value-judgement has to be made *about* the facts. There is consequently much more room for disagreement over value-judgements than over factual judgements; we know in principle how to settle factual disputes, provided that we know what evidence we want and how we can obtain it, but we have no such agreed procedures for resolving controversial questions of value. Two people may have an identical grasp of the facts about factory-farming, yet disagree completely over its justifiability, because of the different values they hold; in which case there seem to be no further, objective grounds to which either can appeal to clinch the matter.

This distinction between facts and values, however, is a disputed one, and this is not the place to plunge into the philosophical complexities of the matter. What is relevant for the purposes of this book is that most people, and that includes most teachers, probably do accept some common-sense, intuitive version of the fact/value distinction, and this will affect their view of education. Put at its simplest, the distinction could well imply an approach something along these lines. 'Education is really only a matter of deciding what children ought to learn (value-judgement), and then finding out how to teach it and how to assess it (factual study).'

What will emerge from this section, however, is that the picture is much more blurred than this. This is not to deny that a basic distinction can perhaps be drawn between questions of fact and questions of value; but in the context of education it is in practice very difficult to make such clear-cut classifications. In particular, it can be misleading, as will be shown in later chapters, to think of evaluation and assessment in education as falling entirely within the factual category and so being in some sense 'value-free'.

We have nevertheless taken note of the fact/value distinction in planning the structure of this first section and the sequence of chapters within it. A brief preview of these chapters should serve to explain this structure and also underline the main points which have so far been made in this introduction.

We take as our starting point the topical and contentious issue of educational standards. The reasons for this are twofold: firstly, the question whether educational standards are rising or falling is one of immediate and practical interest, and a book on values and evaluation should be able to make a contribution to the current debate about standards; secondly, the issue of educational standards is a superb one for the purposes of illustrating how questions of value and of evaluation can be closely intertwined. This is because disputes about standards call attention both to aims and priorities within education and also to the assessment of teachers' and children's achievements in pursuit of those aims and priorities. We also attempt in this chapter to illustrate the ambiguity of the term 'standards' and some of the methodological problems involved in trying to determine whether educational standards are rising or falling.

These problems are often underestimated. It is often thought that the simple technique of measurement is all that is needed to reveal 'the facts' about current educational standards. The following chapter by Rob Morrison is devoted to this subject, which according to the common-sense version of the fact/value distinction is located fairly and squarely on the factual side of the fence. The chapter stresses, however, that educational measurement is far from being a precise process: 'it provides us with a candle rather than the searchlight of truth to find our way in the dark.' Educational measurement is shown to be no panacea for the complex problems of evaluation; its role is relatively humble, though essential in the underpinning that it provides for broader assessments of educational achievement.

Such assessments are inevitably linked in many people's minds with examinations, and it is this thorny topic which John Wilmut discusses in Chapter 4. He emphasizes that it is mistaken to formulate an equation, 'assessment= examinations= measurement', for assessment is concerned with three areas of decision-making: what information is relevant, how to gather that information, and how to do the reporting? Thus, assessment cannot avoid the making of value-judgements, since choices have to be made about what to report and how to report it. Examinations are concerned with the information-gathering process and so do not directly involve the making of value-judgements, though the chapter shows how the various *functions* of examinations raise many controversial questions about educational values.

Moving still further from purely factual matters we next enter the area of evaluation, where values play an essential part, as Wynne Harlen argues in Chapter 5. Criteria have to be chosen by the evaluator to 'provide the framework for selecting the kinds and variety of information which will be gathered', which means that 'every evaluator chooses the clothes for the truth and it is the clothed truth – not the naked truth – which is communicated'. Thus, 'values determine the kinds of transaction or achievements which are noticed and which become the "information" on which an evaluation is based.' Evaluation in education involves reference to the subjects of the preceding chapters – standards, measurement, examinations, and assessment – but also contains a further *purposive* element, which again is value-laden; it must be intended 'for the guidance of educational decision-making with regard to a specified programme'. The focus of this chapter, then, is the 'interestingly symmetrical relationship' between evaluation and values.

This brings us to the final chapter of this section in which Christopher Ormell explores perhaps the most difficult and intangible questions of all, concerning the nature of values in general and educational values in particular. The subject is of course too vast to be comprehensively reviewed in a single chapter and the author concentrates upon a number of specific points most relevant to the concerns of this book. He underlines the practical importance of values by linking them closely with motivation: 'a person who holds certain values is imbued with certain motivations, [so] valuing needs to be seen in behaviour, not merely in a passive form of assent.' Furthermore, an interesting and distinctive feature of *teachers'* values is that they are intended to be seen in the *pupils'* behaviour.

Values also 'inform the life of an institution' and are consequently more directly related to its actual practices than are its declared 'aims' and 'philosophy'. The practical educational implications of teachers holding certain values are further illustrated within the context of various school subjects, such as science, mathematics, and history. This serves to conclude this section by directing our attention towards the need for a more detailed analysis of problems concerning values and evaluation in specific areas of the curriculum, which will be attempted in Section II.

Finally in this introductory chapter, we must draw the reader's attention to the confusion which exists with regard to the use of such words as measurement, test, assessment, examination, and evaluation. We hope that this book will clarify the distinctions, often subtle, that exist between these expressions, but nevertheless in the end some uncertainty may still remain. To some extent this is inevitable since some of the words, assessment and evaluation, for example, are almost synonymous, differing chiefly in nuance and subject to changes in fashion. As editors, we would expect that each contributor would use the word which suits his purpose best and we make no attempt to influence choice, but it is perhaps incumbent upon us to write a brief note about our view of the vocabulary.

We believe that the act of measurement underlies all the activities described in Chapters 4 and 5. Wherever one is testing, examining, assessing, or evaluating, one is measuring. Measurement is a technical activity, relatively precise in the physical sciences, but less precise and subject to a number of inevitable limitations when applied to the social sciences, and to education in particular. Rob Morrison develops this idea in his chapter, making clear the distinction between measuring physical properties such as height or weight compared with mental characteristics such as intelligence. Consider though not a mental characteristic like intelligence but an attribute such as bravery or cowardice. Most people would then be inclined to talk of the assessment of such characteristics rather than the measurement of them. So the word assessment is often used for a rather less precise kind of measurement. If we were to use a literal scale of marks, such as the very common A, B, C, D, E five-point scale, we should probably use the term assessment for that activity. To take another example, when the tax collector considers the allowances due to us before we pay income tax we designate this as an assessment. Assessment implies a form of measurement but the word is usually used in situations which allow for a less precise measure of agreement. Although we do often assess situations we nevertheless particularly associate assessment with people – for example, we often talk about individual assessment.

There is certainly a good deal of overlap between the use of the words assessment and evaluation, and sometimes they are interchangeable. Wynne Harlen makes clear the way in which evaluation is used by curriculum developers, and it has a wider connotation than any of the other words we are presently discussing. Two points worth stressing again are that (1) evaluation has a purpose and an intent, and (2) evaluation involves and is allied to the question of values – indeed this is the main theme of the

Table 1.1

Measurement underlies		
	Testing	(a) Informal and *ad hoc*, e.g., day-to-day tests in the classroom (b) Scientific and psychometric, e.g., I.Q. tests Personality tests
	Examinations	Often public and external to the school. Should be the servant of the teacher. Should in theory follow the curriculum and not influence it. In practice, backwash effects put the cart before the horse.
	Assessment	Applied to individuals. Sometimes to situations. Rather narrower in scope than the more modern term evaluation.
	Evaluation	Wider in scope and embraces all the others. Can be formative or summative and has a purpose. Has obvious links with values.

book. In our view the term evaluation is the widest of those quoted and the best for illustrating the vital connection with values.

The other two words cause less difficulty, though once again there is an inevitable overlap. Tests are sometimes informal and used by teachers in an *ad hoc* manner to measure the efficiency of the learning and teaching process. A contrast can be made between informal classroom tests and public examinations. Usually an examination is a more formal affair than a test; often it is external and public. But the situation is not susceptible to simple and logical analysis. We talk of a driving test when more logically we might use the word examination. Furthermore, there is a well-developed psychometric industry which produces quite formal tests, often standardized with national norms. Such tests are in some ways more scientific than public examinations. It is clear that the word test is used in two very different ways: (1) as an informal method in school of measuring the efficacy of learning – 'teach and test' is a slogan often heard in schools; and (2) as a scientific instrument designed to measure psychological attributes.

Perhaps of all the words being discussed examination is the best understood and has the clearest meaning. Certainly John Wilmut in his chapter makes clear the function of examinations, especially public ones like G.C.E. and C.S.E. He shows that in his use of the word there is almost a self-denying ordinance in that examiners are the servant of the public, examining the given curriculum and not attempting, at any rate consciously, to influence it. So that, in theory at least, examinations follow the curriculum. They have a less purposeful function than does evaluation in its attempt to influence curriculum development, especially if the evaluation is formative.

The table on page 10 gives a crude summary of the meanings of the chief words used.

R.S.

J.W.

References

Flew, A. (1976) *Sociology, Equality and Education*, London: Macmillan, chapter 6.

Peters, R.S. (1967) 'What is an Educational Process?' in *The Concept of Education*, London: Routledge & Kegan Paul.

CHAPTER 2

STANDARDS IN EDUCATION

Roger Straughan and Jack Wrigley

The current debate about standards in education has so far been conducted with a passion and ferocity that have tended to obscure rather than clarify the issues at stake. Probably this is because many of the antagonists have felt that the issues are already perfectly clear-cut: educational standards are either rising, remaining constant, or falling, so all we have to do is to find out empirically (or merely proclaim on the basis of intuition) which alternative is the correct one and what can be done to remedy the situation if it is thought to need remedying.

This sort of assumption, which is implicit in much of the recent controversy, either ignores or grossly oversimplifies two central sets of questions which must be asked in any discussion of educational standards, namely (1) *conceptual* questions about what is meant by 'educational standards', and (b) *methodological* questions about how such standards can be measured and evaluated. In this chapter, therefore, we shall look in turn at these two sets of questions, not with the intention of providing a definitive answer as to whether educational standards are in fact rising or falling, but rather of exploring what *prior* questions have to be asked before any such answer could be attempted. Many of the points raised will be examined in greater detail in later chapters.

Standards, in education and elsewhere, refer to levels of achievement or expectation against which people and objects can be assessed. They therefore conveniently span the two areas with which this book is concerned, for they indicate on the one hand the *values and priorities* which explain why certain levels rather than others are established (e.g., why one of the demands of the old eleven-plus examination was a high degree of proficiency in arithmetical computation), and on the other hand the existence of procedures which enable us to *measure and evaluate* on the basis of those levels (e.g., in the case of the eleven-plus again, a method of setting particular questions and marking them in particular ways which made it possible to measure the children's achievement).

This very generalized account of standards, however, does not take us very far, and in fact re-emphasizes the need to sort out the different kinds of question that have to be asked about educational standards. What sort of values and priorities lie behind the establishment of various educational standards, for example? Do standards refer primarily to achievements or expectations? How do we establish the levels against which children are to be measured? What exactly has to be compared with what before we can say that standards are rising or falling?

Let us start to clear the ground a little by considering some of the conceptual questions concerning standards. How is the concept actually used in the educational context? What different jobs does it have to perform and what different meanings and usages does it bear? What kind of confusion can the ambiguity (if any) of the term create?

Firstly, and most obviously, 'standards' is not merely a descriptive term; it carries with it overtones of value, and these can take different forms:

a   As has already been mentioned, standards reflect the values and priorities which lead to the establishment of certain levels and norms rather than others.

b   The levels and norms themselves may be concerned with questions of value, including moral value, as well as questions of fact. For example, although the current debate about educational standards has usually been concentrated upon standards of skill, competence, and intellectual attainment (e.g., are ten-year-olds better at reading now than they were twenty years ago?), concern has also been expressed about other sorts of standard – standards of behaviour, of discipline, of responsibility, of respect, of politeness, of dress, etc. (e.g., are ten-year-olds better behaved now than they were twenty years ago?). In the case of these latter standards, to decide what *constitutes* a rise or fall in them requires the making of a value-judgement, perhaps an uncontroversial one but nevertheless one which involves adopting a particular moral stance (e.g., that standards of behaviour are falling if more ten-year-olds now are committing acts of vandalism, because vandalism is a bad thing).

c   Even when we are talking about apparently non-moral standards in education (of skill, attainment, etc.), to describe a change in those standards as a 'rise' or a 'fall' carries with it some value-laden overtones of approval or disapproval. If, for example, we describe a change in children's abilities to know their tables as a fall in educational standards, there is a strong implication that we consider it a good thing for children to know their tables.

So questions about educational standards are not straightforward empirical questions of fact, and they cannot be discussed without reference being made, implicitly or explicitly, to questions of value. The second conceptual point which needs to be made, however, highlights a more direct source of confusion: the term 'educational standard' is radically ambiguous, as it can be used in several different senses:

a   It can refer to a particular method of organizing an educational system, whereby children are classified according to the level of attainment they have reached, and have their school career structured by a progression through a series of 'standards' or 'grades'. The historical connotations of this sense of 'standard' remove it to some extent from the central arena of the current debate, though it can at times be detected in arguments to the effect that too much concern for standards in schools will lead to 'standardization' and a consequent lack of flexibility and individualized teaching. The Plowden Report illustrated this view well:

We have considered whether we can lay down standards that should be achieved by the end of the primary school, but considered that it is not possible to describe a standard of attainment that should be reached by all or most children. Any set standard would seriously limit the bright child and be impossibly high for the dull. What could be achieved in one school might be impossible in another. (1967)

This passage, apart from exemplifying how the orthodoxy of one decade can become the heresy of the next, demonstrates clearly the conceptual murkiness of the notion of 'standards'. Standards are here described as 'set' which creates further ambiguity. All standards must of course be 'set', in the sense of being established, decided upon, or laid down, because that is part of what is meant by a standard. But 'set' can also mean rigid, fixed, unalterable, and it seems to be this sense that the Plowden Report is leaning upon when it goes on to talk about standards seriously limiting bright children and being impossibly high for the dull.

Standards have here been *defined* as a 'set', rigid system of standardization which will necessarily determine the organization of the school, its curriculum, and its teaching methods.

b   Standards need not of course be interpreted in Plowden's sense of organizational standardization. More commonly the term is used simply to describe levels of attainment and competence which are in fact being reached, and these levels need carry no overtones of rigid standardization nor imply any particular organizational structure. Plowden's concluding revelation – 'What could be achieved in one school might be impossible in another' – is no argument against the use of standards in this more normal sense of the term. Indeed there cannot really *be* an argument 'against' standards in this sense, for all schools *must* have these sorts of standard, even if their actual achievements are very low. The only possible argument would be that it was undesirable to conduct any evaluation or assessment in order to find out and/or publicize what the standards of achievement actually were in certain schools (perhaps because the results would be too discouraging), but that is an argument against the collection and/or dissemination of information, not against 'having standards'. Some of the problems surrounding the 'reporting' of such information will be discussed at greater length in Chapter 4.

This descriptive use of 'standards' then is not in itself value-laden to the extent that other uses are: the bald statement 'The standards of school X are a, b, c, . . .' appears in this sense to be a simple report of the facts. Yet even here implications of value-assumptions are lurking close at hand. Which achievements, for example, are being picked out as representative of the school's standards? Presumably the achievement of, say, linguistic and mathematical competence is being taken as an indication of the school's standards rather than the speed at which the dinner money is collected or the amount of fidgeting during assembly; but this selection involves the making of value-judgements, and though these may be relatively uncontroversial ones, as in the extreme example just given, it is not difficult to imagine cases where the characterization of what a school's standards of achievement actually were could raise serious problems because of the different priorities assigned to different values (e.g., the value of a low truancy rate versus that of a low 'A'-level failure rate versus that of an unbeaten school football team). Not even in the headteacher's report on speech day can *everything* that is done in a school be described, so any account of a school's standards of achievement must be selective and thereby supportive of certain values and priorities rather than others.

c   Standards may also be interpreted in a third sense, often confused with the second, which involves a much more obvious and straightforward expression of values. In this sense, standards refer not to levels of attainment which *have* actually been reached, but to levels which it is hoped, expected, or desired *will* or *should* be reached. To describe a school's standards in this third sense, then, is to specify not its achievements but its aims, goals, objectives and aspirations, and this seems to be, in part at least, the kind of standard which Plowden was objecting to in denying the possibility of describing 'a standard of attainment that should be reached by all or most children'.

Why this should be thought to be impossible, however, is not at all clear. Do not schools and individual teachers *have* to 'have standards' in this sense if they are to operate purposefully and rationally? Such standards may not be explicitly declared, but they are surely implicit in virtually everything that a teacher or group of teachers tries to do within a school. How can one set about teaching an infant to do his shoe-laces up or a sixth-former to appreciate a novel without having *some* idea of the level of skill or understanding that one is hoping the learner will achieve? Without this kind of preconception, what goes on within a school must be wholly random and aimless, and it is difficult to see how such activities could count as 'teaching' or as 'education'. Of course, a teacher's or a school's expectations and hopes may not always (or even often) be fulfilled, and they may have to be modified if found to be unrealistic, but that again is no argument against 'having standards' in this sense. One has to have a target to aim at before one can tell what chance one has of hitting it.

Whereas standards in sense (b) tend to be those of the learner (i.e., what he achieves), standards in sense (c) tend to be those of the teacher or examiner (i.e., what he expects to be achieved) – though of course it is quite possible also to talk of teachers' achievements and children's expectations. The distinction between (b) and (c) is an important one, however, which can lead to confusion if ignored. A rise or a fall, for example, in 'achieved' standards implies no necessary, corresponding rise or fall in 'expected' standards, and vice versa. A record of progressively deteriorating examination results does not necessarily mean that a school is setting its sights lower and lower; indeed its standards of expectation may be rising, while its standards of achievement are falling. Similarly, it does not follow that if a school lowers its standards of expectation, its standards of achievement will necessarily fall; a modification of unrealistic demands could increase pupils' confidence and improve their performance.

The ambiguity of the term 'educational standards', therefore, means that some exploration of its different uses is essential before any claims about rising or falling standards can be considered and before any useful discussion can get off the ground. Unless the distinction between 'achieved' and 'expected' standards is recognized, for example, any generalizations about a school's standards are likely to be radically confused.

These conceptual questions about what 'educational standards' can mean are closely related to methodological questions about how standards are to be measured and evaluated. It is not simply a matter of first defining one's terms and then finding out what the facts are. The relationship between the conceptual and the methodological questions is more complex than that. There are different ways of going about 'finding out what the facts are' about standards, and these different ways may come up with conflicting conclusions, not so much because we have not 'defined our terms' to start with as because the different methodological approaches *create* further conceptual distinctions and pose further questions about what it might mean to say that educational standards are rising or falling. Let us try to illustrate this by turning now to the methodological questions.

How can we measure educational standards? The complex issues at stake here will be considered in detail in the following three chapters, but some comments need to be made at this stage. One apparently obvious way is by looking at examination results. But immediately we find that two completely different questions about standards can be studied by this means:

i Has the number of candidates obtaining stated grades in various examinations increased or decreased?

ii Has the measure of that performance (i.e., the standard of the examination itself) remained constant?

The first question raises few methodological problems, and can be answered by producing the necessary statistics. In February 1977, for example, the Secretary of State for Education stated that the number of children leaving school with 'A' levels had gone up from 14 to 15 percent of the school population; and those passing five or more 'O' levels at the higher grades had gone up from 8 to 9 percent of the total age-group in the past ten years; there had been a dramatic improvement in the number of children getting higher grades of C.S.E. or the middle grades of 'O' level, from 14 percent in 1964-1965 to 25 percent in 1974-1975; there was evidence of a slight improvement in 'A'- and 'O'-level pass standards and a dramatic increase in average grades. If one takes an even longer time-span, the increase is even greater; so the statistics apparently show a steady rise in such standards over a period of years.

Yet the first question cannot be decisively answered independently of the second question. Increases in the percentage of children passing various examinations and improvements in the level of passes may tell us nothing about rises or falls in 'achieved' standards, if the 'expected' standards of the examiners have not remained constant; a lowering of an examination's demands will clearly diminish the significance of any rise in the number or level of passes. Unfortunately the second question is far more difficult to answer than the first. How, for instance, is one to test the calibre of candidates for examinations without reference to their graded performance in that examination? The examinees must be tested independently of the examination, the standards of which are under scrutiny, but that raises the further problem of ensuring that the standards of the independent test remain constant. One recent attempt to tackle this problem compared candidates in apparently equal grades by using an independent test of verbal and quantitative aptitude (Wilmott, 1977). This test appeared to show that the *calibre* of candiates had fallen slightly between 1968 and 1973 in both the C.S.E. and G.C.E. sectors; yet the candidates had been given almost the same grades in 1968 as in 1973 in the C.S.E. sector and slightly higher grades in the G.C.E. sector in 1973. This sort of evidence shows how dangerous it is to draw unqualified conclusions about rising or falling standards without noting the conceptual distinctions already mentioned. How can we simply maintain that standards are rising, or that they are falling, if the situation is one (as seems likely) in which more pupils are gaining more examination passes at higher grades while at the same time the average calibre of the candidates is falling and the examiners are becoming less demanding?

There are further problems also to be faced if we are to investigate educational standards on the basis of examination results. Direct comparisons from year to year, for instance, are impossible if the syllabus content is changed (as was the case in a recent Schools Council pilot study of 'A'-level standards in English literature, mathematics, and chemistry between 1963 and 1973). Subjects are not static entities, but fields of inquiry which are constantly evolving, so it is unsurprising if examiners' conceptions of the priorities within their subjects change in emphasis over a decade; yet such changes make direct comparisons between the standards (achieved and expected) of, say, 1963 and 1973 very difficult if not impossible. Even within the same year comparability of grading and consequent judgements about standards may be highly questionable, as is illustrated in the case of the various C.S.E. Modes. It seems quite possible that we may here be trying to compare unlike elements. Those teachers who elect to use Mode 3 are usually keen to prepare their own syllabuses and believe that they motivate their pupils more effectively than many of their colleagues using the more conventional Mode 1. The more extreme of these teachers may even claim that the uniqueness of their pupils' work means that it cannot be compared with the conventional work of those attempting Mode 1. Yet the examining boards have to certify the equivalence of Mode 3 with Mode 1. More will be said about Mode 3 later in this book, particularly in Chapter 4.

Generalized conclusions about rising or falling standards cannot be directly deduced from examination results for another reason also. Whose standards are we talking about? Suppose that the average G.C.E. 'O'-level mark in mathematics is 55 percent in one year and 50 percent in the next. Given that the examiners' standards have remained constant, the obvious conclusion to draw would be that the *average* 'standard of achievement' has fallen; yet possibly twice as many candidates in the second year gained over 95 percent as in the first year, in which case the 'standard of achievement' as measured by the number of 'high fliers' will have risen. Or perhaps in the second year half as many candidates as in the first year failed to gain 20 percent, in which case the 'standard of achievement' as measured by the number of 'low fliers' will again have risen. The same set of examination results can in this way be used to show that 'standards' are both rising and falling simultaneously!

Examination results do not therefore provide direct, easily interpretable evidence of rising or falling educational standards; but there are other assessment procedures available which attempt to measure qualities held to be of educational value. The main dilemma here however, to put it at its simplest, is that it is easy to measure accurately what many would consider to be narrow and relatively unimportant abilities, but difficult to assess what many would consider to be qualities of greater educational value. The national reading surveys analysed in the Bullock Report (1975), for example, were clearly using narrow, out-dated measures of reading ability. It

would be simple to continue using these straightforward, technically efficient vocabulary tests, and also to produce their analogues in arithmetic to
test children's grasp of the basic rules. But the results derived from such
methods could be misleading if they were used as a basis for drawing *general*
conclusions about educational standards. Standards must be standards of
something, though in the heat of the debate the something often goes
unspecified; there are no such things as 'educational standards' *per se*. If we
wish to assess educational standards by reference to pupils' mastery of
relatively mechanical skills, then it is essential that we realize exactly what
we are doing, why we are doing it, and what the effects may be. What we are
doing is to measure a very limited area of pupils' achievements; why we are
doing it *may* be because we rate that area to be of supreme educational
importance, but alternatively it may be because it is simply the easiest thing
to assess; and what the probable effect will be is to ensure a concentration of
teaching effort upon that limited area of skills which is being tested.

Two methodological points seem to emerge from this. Firstly, it is
unnecessary and probably undesirable to test the whole of the school
population if some indication of the general level of performance is
required. The methods suggested in the Bullock Report of light sampling
have been taken further by the Assessment of Performance Unit within the
DES, for example, which will be referred to in a number of later chapters,
especially in Section II when specific areas of the curriculum are discussed.
The more general methodological point to note here, however, is that
sampling in selected age-groups in both primary and secondary schools
should lessen the immediate and often unfortunate backwash upon teaching
objectives and methods, which has tended to characterize univeral testing in
the past – e.g., in the case of the eleven-plus selection procedures. Some
backwash, however, is inevitable, which leads us to the second and more
important methodological point: what exactly should be sampled?

A vast amount of work still remains to be done in identifying the wide
range of knowledge, skills, attitudes, and qualities which are held to be of
value in education today within all the main subject areas of the curriculum.
Obviously there will be less consensus in some areas than others, and
controversy is bound to arise generally over the ranking of priorities. But
this is no reason why the exercise should not be attempted and a rational
debate initiated. Indeed the attempt *must* be made if we are to avoid the
purely arbitrary selection of items for which children are to be tested and the
resulting, unilluminating claims and counter-claims that these tests show

educational standards to be rising or falling. The fact that it is easier to test narrow, circumscribed attributes is no justification for ascribing supreme educational value to those attributes. Decisions about what ought to be tested should not be affected by considerations of what is most easily tested. These points will be developed further in Section II of this book with reference to particular curriculum areas.

This chapter has looked at some of the conceptual and methodological questions which must be raised in any investigation of educational standards, and at the ways in which the two kinds of question are interrelated. It has also illustrated what will be a general theme of this book – the need for a combination of conceptual clarity and methodological rigour if we are to identify what we are trying to achieve in education and to know how successful or unsuccessful we are being.

References

Bullock Report (1975) *A Language for Life*, London: HMSO.
Plowden Report (1967)*Children and their Primary Schools*, Vol. 1, London: HMSO.
Wilmott, A.S. (1977) *C.S.E. and G.C.E. Grading Standards: The 1973 Comparability Study*, London: Macmillan.

CHAPTER 3

MEASUREMENT IN EDUCATION

Rob Morrison

In the previous chapter mention was made of the fact that standards 'refer to levels of achievement or expectation against which people and objects can be assessed'. In this chapter the discussion on standards will be looked at from the point of view of measurement. Any discourse on values and evaluation in education is likely at some stage to be concerned with measurement. This may be at the fundamental level of asking whether measurement itself has any value in education. Alternatively, the value of measurement may be accepted and the value-judgement focussed on some of the results of its application. It is not unusual to find acceptance for the application of statistical methods in educational research, for example, and then to find widely different value-interpretations put on the results. Has, then, educational measurement any value, in the sense of having worth? If it has, what is the particular place occupied by educational measurement in the scheme of things?

Lord Kelvin, the celebrated physicist, was in no doubt about the value of measurement in natural philosophy. He once remarked that when one could measure what one was talking about and express it in numbers, one knew something about it. He went on to suggest that a failure or inability to do this meant that one's knowledge was of a 'scant and meagre kind'. In so far as physics is preeminently a cognitive science, the emphasis placed on knowledge is probably not surprising. Certainly, it is easier, though not always easy, to measure and evaluate in the purely physical world of phenomena. It is less easy in the life sciences, and increasingly less so in psychology and sociology, areas which have come to be called the behavioural sciences. This is not due simply to an increase in the degree of variability and uncertainty as one moves from the physical to the behavioural sciences. It is due also to a broadening of the focus of attention to areas other than the purely cognitive. The study of man, and by implication the study of education, involves us with affective and spiritual matters as well as the cognitive.

It might be worth considering at this point a similar state of affairs which exists in the scientific field. The application of scientific method has not only increased our understanding and awareness of the natural universe, it has also led to discoveries which have been applied in our everyday lives. If the disinterested pursuit of science to increase our understanding is amoral, the application of science or technology immediately raises moral issues. When Rutherford split the atom, he was motivated by the natural curiosity to find out more about the nature of matter. In due course this discovery made a contribution to the emergence of a number of applications which have proved to be mixed blessings as far as mankind is concerned. Radioactivity can be used to heal in medicine, to kill in atomic and nuclear warfare. The internal combustion engine has brought benefits to easing transport; it has also brought pollution and death. Increased understanding would be regarded by many as being a desirable and worthy pursuit by man, but since man can use such understanding for good or evil, it would appear that the real value-judgement rests with the nature of this use. If science is amoral, technology is not. In the same way, the disinterested methodology employed in educational research to increase our understanding may be used out of context for reasons of a more doubtful kind. Reichmann has illustrated convincingly in his book *Uses and Abuses of Statistics* how, in the field of statistics, this same problem of worthy and unworthy application takes place. Cognitive pursuits inevitably present man with a choice when the area of application is reached, and this choice is inextricably bound up with values.

It has been observed by many writers and thinkers in philosophy that questions of value are not finally answerable by the collection and assessment of factual evidence, nor settled by the deductive procedures of mathematics and formal logic. This could be because questions of value cannot be considered purely within a cognitive framework. It is possible to describe the standard of achievement expected of, say, a fourteen-year-old pupil studying geography in reasonably specific cognitive terms. It is also possible to assess the standard reached by such a pupil in reasonably meaningful terms. The question as to whether the study of geography itself has any value cannot be appraised in quite the same kind of way. It is a more complex situation for, while value-judgements may be described in apparently cognitive terms, they often include noncognitive factors. The attempt to rationalize feelings referred to by psychologists shows how a cognitive description may be of a very different nature to the affective state which gave rise to it.

The value, if any, of measurement in education cannot be decided until one has a reasonable appreciation of its nature, scope, strengths, and weaknesses. What is the nature of measurement? Fundamentally, measurement is a comparative process. This is to say that measurement is not possible without some clearly defined or appreciated standard which can be used as the basis for comparison. It is not simply a quantitative process involving the manipulation of numbers according to strict rules of logic. The measurement of length, for example, is not possible without a standard of length. The statement of a length as being ten metres means we are dealing with a very different concept to that of pure number. The figure ten conveys no appreciation of length until the standard of length is known, and ten metres is very different from ten inches. We can see, therefore, that measurement involves us with something more than the concept of number and numerical calculations.

A further feature of measurement is that it involves error. This error may be small, and for all practical purposes may not be significant. However, the existence of error requires knowledge of its magnitude before any meaningful interpretation of measurement can be made. In this respect measurement differs from counting, which is a purely quantitative process involving neither standards nor error; assuming of course that one can count! The number of pupils in a class is capable of precise description and does not involve measurement. The height of a pupil or his level of attainment in a history test are both measurements in that a standard serving as the basis for comparison is required.

The difference between measurement in the physical sciences and measurement in education lies in the nature of the standards used for the basis of comparison. It is possible in the physical sciences to have objective standards which, as far as one can judge, are invariant, such as the wavelength of cadmium light to serve as the standard of length. However, there is no similar standard for, say, ability in geography for fourteen-year-olds, kept under prescribed 'temperature' and 'humidity', as it were, at the Department of Education and Science! Apart from the error inherent in any measurement process, there is in educational measurement a source of variability which arises in trying to define an acceptable standard. The situation is rather like a dressmaker who is given an elastic tape-measure with which to produce a useful garment.

The absence of absolute standards, however, does not mean that measurement in education is not possible. Societies over the centuries have devised their own standards of measurement, and to this day many of them are different. This has not prevented bridges being built or successful commerce being undertaken. A problem arises only when the societies need to work with others and comparisons have to be made. It then becomes necessary to relate one standard with another. A satisfactory conversion is required or a new definition arrived at.

Because of the presence of variability and uncertainty, statistical methods are needed to interpret observations made and information collected. Here again, it is necessary to be clear as to what is meant by statistics. One sense in which the word is used is in the sense of pure description, and here it is often used loosely to mean the presentation of measurements in some ordered way. The output figures for a factory, the height distribution for children in a certain age-range, the number of teachers in training in any one year – these are some examples of descriptive statistics. However, this is not the only function of statistics, any more than the collection of weather measurements is the sole function of meteorology, or the production of a balance sheet the sole function of a business company. They are but the raw material on which to work, to frame hypotheses, or to decide policy. The collection and ordering of data is a necessary prerequisite to statistical analysis, i.e., a method for interpreting measurements and for inferring significance or pattern, or the absence of it.

Sometimes a precision is assumed which is not present. The language of statistics is probability, not certainty. The idea that statistics can afford proof in the sense of a Euclidean proof is quite false. It is this misunderstanding or ignorance of statistical method which leads many a politician or advertiser to speak of certainty where none exists. It is perhaps this realization which led Disraeli to remark that there were lies, damned lies, and statistics. There is no doubt that many think that statistics is a technique for presenting misleading information. All this misunderstanding betrays an ignorance of what statistics is and what statistical methods aim to achieve. Unfortunately, statistics has been so misused and misapplied, so arbitrarily employed to lend weight to a particular point of view, that the Disraeli witticism has come to occupy a lasting niche in the English language.

What then is the nature of the statistical method which has found its place in educational research? First, it is a method which acknowledges variability and uncertainty, and can express them in definable, measurable terms. For example, the standard deviation is a statistic. It is a statistic which quantifies the concept of the range of variability which exists within a group. If a class of thirty pupils all got the same mark in a test, there would be no variability, and the standard deviation is found to be zero. If, however, the marks for the pupils were well spread out over the mark scale, the standard deviation has a finite value. The larger the standard deviation, the greater the variability within the group. The standard deviation is therefore a useful statistic which tells us something about the spread of the measured characteristics of a group. Other statistics perform a similar function in that they define numerically what has been observed conceptually.

Secondly, statistics is a method which can be used to test hypotheses and to assess observed differences in terms of the language of probability. Whereas the first aspect of statistics is concerned with definitions, the second aspect is concerned with applied logic. This important function of statistics may require some clarification, because it is the safeguard against taking measurements or observed differences in measurements at their face-value and so creating the situation which Disraeli referred to. It is also the safeguard against the kind of abuses which Reichmann has mentioned.

If one considers numbers at the arithmetical level, then we should agree that the number 57 is greater than 53. Is the situation any different in the case of a group of pupils who average 53 percent in a test one term and then average 57 percent when taking the test again the following term? Can we conclude that, because 57 is greater than 53, the group has shown an improvement? Unlike the arithmetical situation, we are no longer concerned with pure numbers but with measures. Further, we are concerned with averages. Because we are concerned with measures, we need to remember that each measure involves an error, and this error needs to be known before we try to interpret the situation. To interpret an improvement simply because 57 is greater than 53 would be to oversimplify the situation completely. Further, an average mark involves a further error. This error is based on what is known as the error of sampling. Without being technical and pursuing this further, it is sufficient to appreciate that numbers cannot be taken at their face-value if those numbers are assigned to measures or statistical derivatives from them.

It might help, to emphasize a healthy distrust of numbers taken at their face-value, to consider a more familiar situation. Is a bath containing water at 68° Fahrenheit hotter than one containing water at 20° Celsius? If one based one's judgement purely on the arithmetical level, the answer must be yes, because 68 is greater than 20. We are again dealing with measures, in this case measures of temperature, and these measures go beyond pure numbers and involve a definition of standards. The Fahrenheit standard for the basis of comparison is different from the Celsius standard. Only when the question 'How are they related?' is asked, can we make a meaningful interpretation of the question posed. We then find that 68° Fahrenheit and 20° Celsius are equivalent measures of temperature, so that the water in each bath is at the same degree of hotness, which temperature purports to measure. In science, the distinction between number and measure is appreciated, yet often in education it is not. A mark of 68 percent is just as much a measure as 68° Fahrenheit and needs to be interpreted accordingly.

Fundamental to interpreting significance in variable or uncertain situations is the concept of chance. By definition, an observed event is unlikely to be significant if there is a high probability of it occurring by chance. Statistical methods enable us to formulate the chance situation, and this can then be used as the basis for comparison with the observed situation. Here we have a similar methodology to the one we have in measurement, i.e., the need for a yard-stick or basis for comparison. If an observed situation can arise by chance on one in every three occasions, it is less likely to be significant than one which can arise by chance on one in every thousand occasions. One would have more confidence supporting a hypothesis linked with the latter evaluation than with the former. The chance 'pattern', as it were, needs to be known before any statement of significance can be made. Even then, it must remain a statement of probability rather than one of certainty.

The concept of probability which arises when variable and uncertain situations are being considered takes us further away from the arithmetical concept of number. It takes us further away from precision and certainty. To proceed with a reasonable degree of confidence instead of certainty is all we can expect, but such is all we may reasonably expect when coping with variable or uncertain situations. To know that the success rate for a particular operation in surgery is one in three is a more reassuring situation than one for which the success rate is only one in a thousand, albeit far from perfect. Neither situation guarantees certainty, but the former gives more confidence. There is a close parallel between the fields of medicine and education and the statistical techniques used to advance both. If a teacher tries to explain by one method and twenty out of thirty understand, this is better than a method where only five out of thirty understand. Because of variability and uncertainty, some of the surgeon's patients are going to die and some of the teacher's pupils will not understand however good the technique. Perhaps this is not surprising, as the focus of attention in both cases is that variable and uncertain creature *homo sapiens*.

A comparative situation need not always be a chance situation. Sometimes we may wish to compare with another formulated situation. How do this year's students compare with last year's? Has form 4 shown an improvement in performance since the beginning of term? The philosophy of approach embodied in the methodology of educational research and measurement remains the same. Some formulated basis for comparison is required before any meaningful evaluation can be made. The absence of such a formulated basis often leads to misinterpretation and false conclusions. Consider a statement to the effect that '65 percent of drivers under the age of twenty-five have one accident a year'. Such a statement made in isolation may sound impressive. If published as a newspaper headline, we might be forgiven for thinking that young drivers have the most accidents. Perhaps they do, but this can only be determined in a comparative sense. We must have a basis for comparison. What if 65 percent of drivers over the age of twenty-five also had one accident a year? The hypothesis that younger drivers have a higher accident rate cannot be decided by confining attention to younger drivers alone. The basis for comparison is the accident rate of older drivers.

The successful application of measurement techniques is dependent upon the ability to define what is to be measured in specific and unambiguous terms. Experience has shown that the measurement of educational achievement is more reliable in areas such as mathematics and the physical sciences than in art and the writing of compositions. The more specifically structured the area to be assessed, the more reliable becomes the measurement process. In less tangible areas, however, any attempt to concentrate on more specific aspects may result in improved reliability at the expense of validity. It has been found, for example, that the marking of written compositions may be made more reliable if attention is confined to such aspects as spelling, punctuation, and the use of capital letters, i.e., to mechanical accuracy. In doing this, however, something different is now being measured. In ignoring the less tangible aspects such as style and imagination, a different kind of achievement is being measured. The limitation of science in the broader field of philosophy is that it extracts from reality that which can be measured. A similar limitation exists for educational measurement in the broader field of education as a whole.

This need to define what is to be measured in specific and unambiguous terms applies equally in educational research. This may be illustrated by two simple examples. Do older teachers prefer to teach in rural as distinct from urban schools? Do older people make better citizens? In the first example, age and preference need to be measured. In the second example, age and good citizenship need to be measured. Of all the factors needing a specific statement, good citizenship is the least tangible and most likely to have widely different interpretations. As a result, more confidence may be placed in testing the first hypothesis than the second. The language used in the specification of what is to be measured needs to be precise, and where this is not forthcoming it would be misleading to proceed. Even with precise definitions, as we have seen, the results of measurement techniques are associated with probability rather than with certainty.

Further caution in using and interpreting measurement techniques in education is needed when sampling is carried out. If anything significant is to be said about a population from which a sample has been taken for the purpose of research, then the sample needs to be selected in a special way. The sample needs to be representative of the population and free from bias. Failure to observe this means that any findings may only be applicable to the particular sample and not generally applicable to the population as a whole. Even when care is taken in the choice of a sample, no two samples will be alike in every respect and this gives rise to sampling errors. Such errors are calculated to give an estimate of the confidence we may place in the observations made with the sample. Such errors need to be appreciated in the same way as errors in the measurements themselves.

It has been said that the method of science is to extract from reality those aspects which can be measured. In so far as areas in education are capable of measurement, the scientific method may be applied. It is to be hoped that enough has been said to show that this is far from being a precise process. Nevertheless, it is a useful process and can assist in our thinking when faced with variable and uncertain situations. It can help us to discern a pattern or trend, or aspects of likely significance, thus contributing towards a better appreciation of what are and what are not relevant factors in the situation being studied. It provides us with a candle rather than the searchlight of truth to find our way in the dark. In the absence of such a searchlight, it is *a* way and perhaps better than nothing.

Surrounding the areas of measurable activity are vast areas which are immeasurable and may always be so. Some of the insight, caution, and humility gained from the study and application of measurement in education, however, may be of value in discourse in these other areas. One might recall the words of John Henry Newman when discoursing on the scope and nature of university education, when he warned of the dangers inherent in the cultivation of one method of thought to the exclusion of all others: that it can degenerate into error when carried beyond the point where it requires interpretation and restraint from other quarters; that it can be employed to do what is too much, inasmuch as a little science is not deep philosophy. Newman was, of course, using science in the sense of knowledge. He goes further in his *Discourses on the Scope and Nature of University Education*:

> We refer the various matters which are brought home to us, material or moral, to causes which we happen to know of, or to such as are simply imaginary, sooner than refer them to nothing; and according to the activity of our intellect do we feel a pain and begin to fret, if we are not able to do so. Here we have an explanation of the multitude of offhand sayings, flippant judgments, and shallow generalisations with which the world abounds. . . . We cannot do without a view, and we put up with an illusion when we cannot get a true one.

Education is not simply psychology, or sociology, or communication theory, or even philosophy. It is not confined to the cognitive, or affective, or psychomotor, or even the moral domain. Education embraces all these things, and probably much more besides. Each has a part to play, a contribution to make, whether that be in its own unique specialism or in its restraining function as outlined by Newman. A worthwhile evaluation is unlikely if measurement, psychology, sociology, or any other –ology takes on the role of the philosopher's stone and comes to assume the measure of all things. This need for a broad evaluation which considers all the evidence and aspects which have a bearing on the subject being studied is essential. Too often, sadly, only the evidence in support of a theory is given any weight. Perhaps the educational value of the study of history and science is that the habit of carefully weighing all the facts before coming to a conclusion is an essential part of these studies. As Karl Popper has observed in his *The Logic of Scientific Discovery*:

The wrong view of science betrays itself in the craving to be right; for it is not his *possession* of knowledge, of irrefutable truth, that makes the man of science, but his persistent and recklessly critical quest for truth.

This critical quest involves looking for evidence which does not fit a theory as well as looking for evidence which does.

In education at the present time there is much activity and there is no shortage of ideas. When, however, did we last pause to reflect on the situation and attempt an appraisal? Such an appraisal is difficult without standards by which to judge, and this age would appear to be less unanimous in agreeing on satisfactory standards than any which has preceded it. It would be difficult to find a single general aim of education to which all might give assent, and to which we might refer for the purpose of appraisal. Sir Richard Livingstone in his *Education for a World Adrift* observed:

> We must look beyond (without overlooking) science, technology, economics, sociology, handicrafts, subjects with a vocational bias, and recall and extend a statement by A.N. Whitehead that would probably surprise many English people: 'Moral education', he says, 'is impossible without the habitual vision of greatness'. It could not be put more strongly . . . 'impossible', 'habitual' vision. Outside Plato there is no profounder statement about education. A 'habitual vision of greatness' is necessary not only to moral education but to all education.

Here is excellence in education, a total concern for the first-rate, expressed not simply as an attitude, but as a vision. This goes far beyond the cognitive domain of definable standards. It becomes the criterion by which one may distinguish the inspired teacher from the competent one, the job well done from the second best, love from do-gooding. Perhaps it is a counsel of perfection, but man has a disconcerting habit of becoming engrossed with what is beneath his feet if he does not look up.

This looking beyond, of which Sir Richard Livingstone speaks, also takes us beyond any one area or discipline of education albeit philosophical in nature. This is now the region of values with which this book is concerned. In so far as measurement is more involved with specifics and is more a technique than a philosophy it occupies a place on the periphery of this region. It is there, on the side-lines as it were, waiting to contribute as soon as specific and tangible entities emerge. Besides this contribution in its own right, measurement has its restraining function also. It can test hypotheses which arise from any area in education and where possible assess their significance. In these ways educational measurement makes its contribution to the philosophical debate.

References

Ebel, R.L. (1972) *Essentials of Educational Measurement*, Englewood Cliffs, New Jersey: Prentice-Hall.

Livingstone, R. (1944) *Education for a World Adrift*, London: Oxford University Press.

Newman, J.H. (1915) *The Scope and Nature of University Education*, London: Dent.

Popper, K.R. (1959) *The Logic of Scientific Discovery*, London: Basic Books Inc.

CHAPTER 4

ASSESSMENT AND EXAMINATIONS IN EDUCATION

John Wilmut

Everyday conversation in education uses the word 'examination' to describe several different processes, relying on the context to distinguish one meaning from another. In this chapter, which attempts to review the roles of examinations within secondary education, we must first make it clear how we are to use this word.

Entrenched within most education systems is the assumption that we must periodically formally report the achievements of individuals within the system. At this stage it doesn't matter very much why we need to do this, although the reasons for, and consequences of, this reporting will be discussed later in this chapter. It is sufficient to recognize here that the process exists and involves three major decisions. The first is a decision on what information is relevant, the second a decision on how to gather the information, and the third a decision on how to do the reporting, and to whom.

The term 'examination' is applied to the information-gathering part of this process and it includes all situations where assessments are made of a pupil in order to report his or her progress in a subject studied in school. We shall only briefly discuss assessments made for diagnostic purposes, and we shall exclude assessments which do not deal with performance within the curriculum. Within this arbitrary definition we can include examinations originating internally or externally (to the school), those using written tests or other means, and those concerned with cognitive or other elements.

We must assume that *assessment* is concerned with all three parts of the reporting process and is not simply the measurement phase; otherwise, we will isolate the assessment from any relevant and useful context. Not all assessments are made for the purpose of reporting achievement, and therefore not all assessments involve examinations. Where it exists, an examination can be regarded as the 'hardware' of assessment, or the mechanism used to carry assessment decisions into effect. Thus, whilst we can regard assessment as having values and standards (since it involves processes of decision about what performances to report, and at what levels these are to take place), examinations do not, of themselves, possess these values or standards.

There is therefore no equation:

$$\text{assessment} = \text{examinations} = \text{measurement}$$

but rather processes placed in a hierarchy with measurement embodied in examinations and examinations sometimes embodied in assessment. It is convenient to avoid the word 'evaluation' here, not because it is wrong or irrelevant but because it is confusing, frequently being used to describe a much wider process than that involving examinations. This process will form the subject of the following chapter.

Given these descriptions we can embark on a discussion of examinations in the secondary school context, but remembering that the use of the word 'examination' does not now imply simply traditional external written tests, but is being used to describe all information-gathering processes within the context of assessment for formal reporting purposes.

Functions of examinations

It is important at the outset to distinguish the roles of examinations from their stated goals (Moore, 1975; Holmes and Dryland, 1965). The traditional goals have been to provide criteria against which individual students can judge their performances, to provide a framework of incentive for both teachers and students, to act as selection mechanisms; inevitably they have assumed other roles, and some of these may have undesirable overtones. The extent of this undesirability will be judged by each observer according to his own values, and could, for instance, involve considering examinations as a means of evaluating school and teacher performance, perhaps making each accountable to a wider social or political demand. Similarly, the goal of the examination as a selection mechanism may be undesirably extended into a role as part of the process of social engineering through education.

More subtly, examinations also have a distinct role within the curriculum, although it may be more truthful to speak here of the wider role of formal assessment. Stenhouse (1975) identifies 'objectives' and 'process' models of curriculum, and links examinations firmly to the former, regretting that education as a process is damaged by the need to push pupils through examinations. He comments:

> This tension between educating and examining is, of course, at the centre of most teaching from the third year of the secondary school onward. Conflicts have to be resolved by compromises. The quality after which the process-based curriculum reaches is to some extent sacrificed by the acceptance of the public examination as a legitimate social objective, though it is recognised as an arbitrary educational goal. (p. 96)

However, it is not clear whether Stenhouse is rejecting all assessment for reporting purposes (which we can call 'formal assessment'), although he hints at a strong preference for assessment within dialogue between teacher and pupil. As will be seen later, this may not be possible to integrate into more formal assessment, and so we must presume that, through a rigid process approach to education, a teacher may exclude the possibility of formal assessment. However, we can be left in no doubt that formal assessment frequently comes into conflict with curriculum aspirations and therefore promotes a series of constraints within which much school curriculum decision-making must take place. We should bear in mind that it is conflict between the needs of the teaching and the assessment which is the fundamental problem, since it is with decisions about *whether* to assess that curriculum processes can conflict; examinations are themselves only a surface feature of the assessment process. Examinations are seldom away from the centre of educational controversy. There is a lobby (stronger in some countries overseas than in the UK) which would abolish public examinations altogether and place the whole responsibility for assessment in the hands of teachers. This is an attempt to remove the conflict, but it frequently fails to recognize that the formal reporting would still exist and it is this which is the problem, rather than the external nature of the examinations themselves. I would like to come back to this problem later in this chapter.

Examinations are also frequently cited as sources of 'proof' for rising, static, or (most often) falling educational standards, as has been illustrated in Chapter 2. It is often pointed out that they predict almost every aspect of subsequent performance very badly. They are accused of placing stress on a limited set of skills in a limited range of academic subjects and assessing in these areas with only a limited precision.

There is some irony in this situation. In general, examination boards are responders rather than innovators; that is, they do not seek to manipulate the curriculum or teaching styles, nor do they see themselves as intruding upon education to any greater extent than schools will allow. Further, the boards claim only a very limited task for examinations – that of measuring attainment. They do not seek a role of predictor, nor do they see examinations as monitors of standards in education. In other words, examinations assume a humbler role than they are publicly given. The irony is even stronger than this. The introduction in 1965 of the Certificate of Secondary Education (C.S.E.), bringing with it the school-based syllabus and examination (Mode 3), opened the door for greater control of assessment by teachers. To those who value the role of the teacher as both curriculum innovator and assessor, Mode 3 has been a considerable success. For those who doubt the ability of teachers in making assessments, or who value the external objectivity provided by Mode 1 (the traditional external examination), there are many reservations about Mode 3. Whatever the viewpoint, it is interesting that Mode 3 has not displaced Mode 1 by as much as might have been expected, accounting for only about 12 percent of all examination entries at sixteen-plus, though with almost all of these in C.S.E., within which there is a considerable variation between boards. Even where it is being used, 'continuous assessment' (that is, assessments made at intervals during a school year and accumulating to a total) is not usually the major part of the Mode 3; one would have expected teachers to use this method of assessment more extensively (Smith, 1976). We seem then to have a situation where there is considerable conservatism among teachers, with the traditional external examination, terminal to a course, as entrenched as ever.

It is important to make some distinctions between the two sectors of the present examinations system. The General Certificate of Education (G.C.E.) Boards, with a longer tradition and closely linked to universities, regard themselves as custodians of standards of qualifications, clearly relating these to the requirements of education beyond the secondary level. They have only limited direct contact with schools; those in England are 'national' boards in that entries are accepted from any school or college, and from individuals, and most have some entries from overseas. These boards are very much a part of institutionalized British education. The C.S.E. boards are, in contrast, much smaller, regional in nature, and therefore closer to their schools. They exercise something which is almost pastoral care over these schools, laying less emphasis on conferring qualifications and more on providing a means of assessment suitable to the school curriculum, especially for those pupils of moderate or lower ability. This philosophy was first stated for C.S.E. in the Beloe Report (1960) and emerged again in a later report on sixteen-plus examining (Schools Council, 1966). Here, then, Mode 3 has come to be very attractive, with schools creating courses suitable to the needs of particular groups of pupils, yet retaining the opportunity to provide those pupils with certificates of attainment under the name of an examining board. The biggest single growth occurred in 1974 when the school-leaving age was raised from fifteen to sixteen, and schools used Mode 3 to provide examined courses for pupils in this last year of formal schooling. Mode 3 also allows flexibility in curriculum planning which exists in the G.C.E. system by virtue of the free choice between Mode 1 syllabuses offered by the different boards; this is something which is valued by the G.C.E. boards.

A scrutiny of these functions

What then are the real purposes and functions of assessment in our education system? It is first important to remember that we are considering the whole area of pupil assessment for certification (reporting), and not simply the external examination. It is also important to distinguish this assessment from the informal (diagnostic or formative) assessment which is a part of teaching and often a part of curriculum evaluation. Indeed, a conflict is likely to develop if an assessment process is used both as a diagnostic tool and as a formal judgement of pupil attainment. This point will be considered later in more detail.

The first purpose of formal assessment in schools is to establish a measure of each pupil's *attainment*. Secondary school examinations are not intended to measure ability, nor to predict future performance. The attainment will be defined within a subject area and will almost certainly have many facets, though it will almost always be finally expressed on a single-grade scale. It follows that the judgement of the pupil's attainment will be against a series of attainment criteria; these are statements of expected performance within the subject and appropriate to it. Although it does not necessarily follow from this that the criteria are to be wholly cognitive in type, it is generally true that noncognitive performance is seldom part of formal assessment. Black and Dockrell (1979) point out that many teachers frequently make assessments in the affective domain and are glad to do so, but that there is

uncertainty about the propriety of some assessments and about their validity and reliability. Certainly such assessments find only a very limited place
in formal assessment, mainly occurring in the assessment of things like
project work where the classification and explanation of affective processes
frequently reduces them to a trivial status.

An essential consequence of this view of formal assessment is that we are
concerned with the relation between a pupil's performance and a number of
stated criteria, rather than his or her performance measured against the
performance of others (sometimes known as 'norm-referencing'). For this
reason we must be cautious in our use of some aspects of the classical
theories of testing, particularly as these are applied in the field of psychological tests.

The importance of referring examination candidates' performances to a
number of related criteria seems to lead to a rejection of single, undimen-
sional scales of attainment. However, since we report examination results
on a single-mark or -grade scale we seem to accept the existence of the
single-attainment scale (such as 'attainment in mathematics' or 'attainment
in English'). The paradox has led to considerable research and much
controversy, and examinations are unlikely to escape from this in the
immediate future. It is possible to foresee the eventual emergence of
multiple-reporting of pupil performance in examinations (e.g., of profile-
reporting), and this may go some way towards recognizing the proper
emphasis of the individual parts of the assessment. In the meantime, we
concentrate on the production of a final assessment (mark or grade) which
most reasonably combines a number of discrete performances whose interrelationships are not perfect (and should not be so).

Single, unidimensional scales of attainment have led us into a consideration of 'latent trait' models for educational tests. The best known of these
models is the Rasch model (Willmott and Fowles, 1974) and, though not
currently in use in examinations boards, this model is forming the basis for
the construction of national banks of objective items, and for some of the
work of the Assessment of Performance Unit. The use of the Rasch model
has had many critics and there seem to be good reasons for not using it in an
examinations context since there is a need to emphasize the criteria of
assessment rather than the statistical test homogeneity which the Rasch
model demands. Some critics go further and reject this and other latent trait
models for all educational tests (Wood, 1978; Goldstein, 1979).

The controversy over the latent trait concept has accompanied a much more critical view of examination processes. We now have a better aware-ness of the approximate nature of examination results, and the extent to which an individual grade represents a valid and reliable description of an individual's attainment. We have also greatly extended the range of assess-ments that are commonly in use, and questions and mark schemes are far more carefully constructed now than fifteen or twenty years ago.

We have also begun to take a more realistic view of comparisons between examinations; experiments making these comparisons are known as com-parability studies. The concern has been to see that standards applied in equivalent situations are similar, and examinations boards and others have conducted studies to compare examination standards from year to year, from subject to subject, from board to board, and from mode to mode. Some of these studies have had methodological shortcomings and we are now recognizing that some comparisons might be futile. Although some studies have shown variations in standards, it is not possible to say whether these are of any major or long-term significance, and it is certainly no basis for assertions about falling educational standards. A good review of some comparability studies is given by Bardell et al. (1978), and this review includes a good discussion of the methodological problems that have been encountered in comparability studies.

Examinations boards are (probably rightly) extremely cautious about the use of their grades for judgements about educational standards. It is very difficult to assert comparability of grading standards over time (perhaps considering one subject over a ten-year interval), and quite obviously impossible to make direct and exact comparisons between boards in any one subject (since syllabuses and candidate entries are not identical). Compari-sons between modes of examining and between subjects are probably almost irrelevant because of the intrinsic differences between the things being compared.

Using examination evidence to compare standards is therefore dangerous unless there is a proper recognition of the approximate nature of examina-tion grades, as was pointed out in Chapter 2. Moreover, to use examination results as a commentary on the nature of the curriculum, or on pupils' behaviour within it, may be downright misleading. This is particularly the case when one recognizes that examinations are wholly subject-based and subject interrelationships (in the context of a curriculum design) simply do not exist in examination terms.

The second major function of formal assessment leads to examinations which act as *selection* mechanisms. This suggests that there is competition between candidates for some scarce resource, usually some higher level of education or some specialized employment. The earliest examinations, in Imperial China, were established for the purpose of selecting entrants to the civil service, and the element of competition was extreme. Although modern UK secondary school examinations do not attempt to produce order of merit lists, but rather assess attainment against specific criteria, the element of competition cannot easily be eliminated, since candidates know that their future social position depends to a great extent on examination performance (Holmes and Lauwerys, 1979).

In a wide-ranging review of educational assessment, Ingenkamp (1977) observes:

> Educational criticism is aimed chiefly against the direction of assessment towards selective practices, and its educationally undesirable side-effects, and also against adverse effects on the pupils' personality due to stress, examination anxiety, the notion of competition, cheating, frustration and the falsifying of educational objectives through orientation towards competitiveness and efficiency. It is argued that the only assessment that is educationally justifiable is that which promotes the individual learning process. Measurement for this purpose is objective- or criterion-referenced, and is formative not summative. (p. 14)

This selection function might be acceptable if the results of school examinations were known to be good predictors of subsequent performance; it is known that this is not the case. Many studies have attempted to relate G.C.E. 'O'-level or C.S.E.-level performance with that at G.C.E. 'A'-level or in some specialized occupational tests, or to relate 'A'-level performance with that at degree level, and most have reported poor predictions unless some other factors are also entered into the prediction. Examinations boards rightly point out that their examinations test attainment, and therefore only indirectly imply ability or aptitude. The use of examinations results as criteria for selection is thus a doubtful process since we can never be sure that we are selecting those who will, in the long term, perform best in a higher level of education, in an apprenticeship, training, or employment. Further than this, since there is no single path through school to employment, no examination alone is able to at as a predictor of success. This would be to reverse the trend of the last two or three decades, during which school examinations have been seen as general commodities, terminal to one phase of education, rather than as a bridge between one phase and *one* other.

In fact, the reaction to this problem has been to attempt to increase the quality of prediction either by substituting occupational entrance tests, or by supplementing examination result information by other assessments of the pupil. Thus, in the first case, many industrial concerns subject potential entrants to their own batteries of tests and interviews, whilst in the second, the universities also rely on the teachers' information in the U.C.C.A. report, plus an interview.

It is interesting to reflect on a further aspect of school examinations in relation to adult society. Examinations can be seen as a bridge between childhood and adulthood, selecting people for different roles in later life. Firth (1969) argues that examinations can be seen as a ritual initiation process, and draws parallels with the initiation ceremonies of many cultures. She concludes:

> My view is that in a society which tends to break education into a number of discontinuous processes, to detach people from their background and to train *elites* at various levels, examinations can also be seen as rites which serve to validate the process of exclusion, as well as to demonstrate the grounds of inclusion, for those permitted to be initiated. From a sociological viewpoint, however faithfully or unfaithfully they reflect knowledge or ability, they also serve as a charter for the broad patterns of our manpower selection. (p. 242)

The third function of formal assessment creates examinations which provide *incentives*. This has to be seen in the light of the two functions already discussed. It has long been argued that pupils will be galvanized into desirable activity because they know that some work is to be assessed. This view appears in one of the earliest reviews of school examinations in the UK (Board of Education, 1911) which states:

> The good effects of the examination on the pupil are (a) that they make him work up to time by requiring him to reach a stated degree of knowledge by a fixed date; (b) that they incite him to get his knowledge into reproducible form and to lessen the risk of vagueness; (c) that they make him work at parts of a study which, though important, may be uninteresting or repugnant to him personally; (d) that they train the power of getting up a subject for definite purpose, even though it may not appear necessary to remember it afterwards – a training which is useful for parts of the professional duty of the lawyer, the administrator, the journalist, and the man in business; (e) that in some cases they encourage a certain steadiness of work over a long period of time; and (f) that they enable the pupil to measure his real attainment (i) by the standards required by outside examiners, (ii) by comparison with the attainments of his contemporaries in other schools.

Quite clearly, if the examinations are to be a basis for selection, there is an in-built incentive for pupils to work towards examinations, not as ends in themselves, but in terms of what can be gained by those who possess certificates. It may be regrettable that learning cannot be undertaken for its own sake, but if this is an unrealistic goal then examinations have to serve as targets towards which pupils will be pointed, and it is quite clear that many parents and teachers direct pupils' thoughts through examinations to the prizes that await the successful.

It is here that the concept of 'qualification' emerges most strongly. Providing that the assessment is recognized as being to a suitable standard, most people would regard the examinations as simply conferring passports to the future. Although it is possible that some sections of British youth have rejected the conventional climb through schooling to employment, the steady increase in examination entries over the last twenty years seems to indicate the difficulty in getting off the 'qualifications' treadmill.

Examinations and the curriculum

So far we have looked at some aspects of the operation of assessment within our educational system, noting a number of clear anomolies and a number of ways in which the results of examinations might be misinterpreted. In one sense these problems are a reflection of the profound interaction between assessment, school curriculum decisions, and societal expectations. It is not uncommon for teachers to complain of the constraints which examinations impose upon them. They feel that, if there was no examination at the end of a course, they would be free to interpret their subject in a more proper way, perhaps more in keeping with some concept of the nature of the subject. This complaint is perhaps most noticeable from teachers of literature, music, art, history, or geography, but it is not unknown in other areas.

Teachers also complain of the pressures from parents whose hopes for their children centre on examination results. These results are seen as conferring 'qualifications', these being passports to the future. There is also the feeling that the school curriculum is in danger of being reduced to the study of examinable material, and that which is not to be examined is neglected (often by pupils as much as by teachers or parents).

There is little doubt that most of these complaints are justified in that schooling has become caught in the pincer of conflicting expectations and demands. To fix the blame for this situation on examinations is probably wrong, though to be expected. Although it is true that each school curriculum is manipulated by the demands of assessment, it is probably also true that this is the way that most people expect it to be. If we regard the examinations system as a 'service' to education, much as a manufacturer of desks or a publisher of books provides a service, then it is possible to see change only by a manipulation of assessment within the curriculum, and not by a simple manipulation of examinations.

It is perhaps surprising that attempts to 'free' the curriculum by putting assessment in the hands of teachers have not been wholly successful. Although there may be very good reasons for asking teachers to assess pupil attainment (as an alternative or complement to the external examination), it is doubtful whether the curriculum is thereby under any less severe a constraint. Fundamentally, it seems to be the presence of *assessment* which has an effect on the classroom, assuming that the assessment is known by pupils and teachers to be for purposes of certification. This knowledge shapes the attitudes of all concerned; they are forced to view the material entered into the assessment as important, and all other material as secondary, perhaps to be minority time interest or to be removed from the curriculum altogether.

If there is here a 'trap' in education, it is therefore an assessment trap and not an examination trap. At its most fundamental the issue is whether to assess, not how to assess. Of course, we can do a great deal to bring assessment processes into a closer harmony with curriculum objectives, and much of the development of the last fifteen to twenty years can be traced to the increased involvement of teachers and others in the work of examinations boards. This has sprung from two, not unconnected, sources. The advent of C.S.E. in the mid-1960s, with the deliberate policy of making assessment strategies the responsibility of teachers, represented on examinations boards' committees, did a great deal to close the divide between curriculum planning and assessment influences. This coincided with a large commitment to curriculum development projects and, more recently, some curriculum evaluation projects. The effect of these upon the examinations boards has been profound since, in order to keep pace with changing teaching strategies in schools, they have had to review and revise existing syllabuses and introduce new ones. In doing so they have often involved those who led the curriculum projects in a deliberate attempt to harmonize assessment with the project objectives.

If examination entries are any guide, this has been a successful process. The number of candidate entries continues to rise each year, and this reflects both an increase in the number of candidates and an increase in the average number of subjects taken. This general rise in entries has some interesting aspects. Originally, the G.C.E. boards designed 'O'-level examinations to cater for the top 20 percent of the sixteen-plus ability-range (roughly corresponding to the population of the old grammar schools), whilst C.S.E. examinations catered for the next 40 percent. It is now generally agreed that both of these ranges are greatly exceeded, so that, between the two sectors there is probably coverage of 70–80 percent of the school population, with the boundary between C.S.E. and G.C.E. now extremely blurred, and lower than the 80th percentile cut-off level. We thus see an increasing number of 'fail' or unclassified grades being issued by both sectors. In the easier economic climate of the late 1960s it was common for a candidate to be entered for both a C.S.E. and a G.C.E. examination in a subject, in the hope that he or she would gain a G.C.E. grade, but with C.S.E. as a fall-back. This gave impetus to the movement for a common examination at sixteen-plus, something that will now almost certainly happen at some future date, although a harsher economic régime has now drastically reduced the double-entry phenomenon. In retrospect, the double entering of candidates did little good to the image of assessment in schools since it imposed an unnecessary strain on both pupils and teachers.

The increase in the assessment by teachers over the last fifteen years has been one important way in which schools have sought to reassert their control over assessment. The channel for this activity has chiefly been through Mode 3 examinations. Control over Mode 3 has always been stronger in G.C.E. boards, partly because this type of assessment was born within the C.S.E. sector with some obligation on these boards to accept Mode 3 proposals from schools. To some extent the G.C.E. boards have compromised with the wider use of a teacher-assessed component in an otherwise external (Mode 1) examination, although in these situations the decision about what to assess remains with the examinations boards. The effects of teacher assessment on the schools are not well understood in this country. The issue has been clouded by a feeling that the diagnostic use of assessment can be merged with its formal use, provided that both are in the hands of the teacher. In other words, since assessment is a continuing, though often informal, process, frequently used as a feedback device for the teachers' information, some have argued that it is logical to extend it for purposes of certification. Further than this, some have seen all assessment as one part of a curriculum evaluation process. Thus we might expect to get information about the suitability and presentation of material by assessing the pupils' understanding of that material, and to expect that this can be the same assessment as is used for certification.

Evidence from overseas suggests that these assumptions are false. The central issue is the pupils' knowledge of the purpose of the assessment process. Pupils seem to be quite willing to accept the normal question-and-answer dialogue of the classroom as part of teaching, even though the teacher may be using this diagnostically or for an evaluation of teaching. They also seem willing to accept the classroom test or the assessment of homework in the same light, and expect some fairly immediate feedback from both, seeming to recognize these as teaching rather than assessment devices. Although they may note that the results of such assessments are recorded, and recognize that this might contribute to an end-of-term or end-of-year report, this does not seem unduly to trouble them. Once it is known that assessments will contribute to certification, pupil behaviour seems to change quite radically, though understandably. A piece of work which is to contribute to the final assessment is given greater priority (by the pupils) than one which is not. We then begin to see the work of a class building up to the assessment, then dropping back again when that assessment is complete, thus breaking the continuity of the work (Campbell and Campbell, 1978).

We also see the emergence of a quite disturbing pupil-with-pupil competition. If the teacher has charge of the assessment it seems to be quite clear to each pupil that he or she is competing with others in the class for the high marks. Although, in a strictly criterion-referenced assessment this should not be so, it is almost impossible to convince pupils of this and, of course, if marks (or, more properly, grades) refer one pupil's performance to that of his fellows (norm-referencing), the competition is fostered by the system. In summarizing this distinction between the two uses of assessment, Evans (1976) speaks of evaluation for guidance (diagnostic assessment) and evaluation for selection (formal assessment):

> Evaluation for guidance is more likely to be concerned with the skills of getting and using knowledge, with attitudes, values and human relationships. There would be also interest in the student's knowledge of facts and principles. Evaluation for selection might also be concerned with these qualities but it is more likely that the need for comparability might restrict what is assessed to matters of fact, verbal statements of principles and procedures, or routine application of rules. (p. 25)

Of course, there is never a guarantee that any assessment process will stand the test of time. What may be started by a teacher as an imaginative process of assessment can very easily become stereotyped, and it takes a determined teacher to see that this is not the case. An observation that might well be included in all commentaries on Mode 3 is quoted by Elley and Livingstone (1972):

> The internal examination does not remove the evil of bad examining . . . it removes it only one stage further from the public gaze.

All of the foregoing dicussion neglects a problem which certainly preoccupies many examinations boards. Given that there are good arguments for using teacher assessment, at least as part of a wider spectrum of assessment, what guarantees are there that the results are any more credible than those produced by the external examination? Certainly it can be argued that, by acting both as teacher and assessor, one person can more closely integrate the assessment with the purposes of the school course, and probably place the emphasis where it should lie, that is, in the classroom rather than in the examination room. This is a powerful case which is used when proposing assessment by teachers, and there is no reason to doubt its truth.

However, many people will then want some assurance that the quality of measurement is at least reasonably comparable to the measurement on which examinations are based. We should notice here that we are becoming concerned with *how* performance is being assessed, not with *what* is being assessed; the latter has been taken for granted.

There are varying degrees of examination board control over teacher assessment. We have already noted that G.C.E. boards frequently ask teachers to make some assessments, but reserve to themselves the right to specify the criteria for those assessments, and to moderate the marks given by the teachers. At the other extreme there is the view that, since teachers are doing the teaching, and setting the tasks upon which testing is to be based, they should also have absolute control over the testing itself. At this extreme the boards might apply the lightest of monitoring to the process, but usually only with a view to getting some general uniformity of standard across schools or between comparable examinations. The fundamental responsibility is in the hands of the teacher.

We might note here that, were the schools to issue the certificates, we could remove even this light monitoring and approach a system operating in some other countries where syllabuses are accredited by an external authority, but assessment is entirely in the hands of the teacher. The desirability of this process depends upon your point of view; is the responsibility for 'standards' to rest in the school or in an examination authority? Some would argue that it always rests in the school anway, whatever measurement system is used, and that examination authorities reflect the standards desired by the schools rather than originating those standards. Certainly, in their day-to-day working the present British boards accept the standards given to them by teachers and others sitting on their subject committees and working on grade-awarding panels.

We have some evidence that teachers' assessments are sometimes partly based in constructs other than those expected by examination boards. Wood and Napthali (1975) offer six such constructs likely to be used by teachers in differentiating between pupils' achievements:

(a) The involvement of the pupil in the learning situation.
(b) The ability the pupil has in the subject.
(c) The overall ability of the pupil.
(d) The behaviour of the pupil.
(e) The quality and tidiness of the work presented.
(f) The interest displayed by the pupil in the subject. (p. 159)

The authors also note differential assessment between the sexes, and say

. . . the worry is that mediocre but compliant girls may attract better ratings than more talented but difficult boys.

These areas of uncertainty are obviously extended when teachers are making assessments of project work, creative writing, design or art work, etc., although it is quite clear that work of this kind may be of great importance in the subject but cannot be assessed externally to the school. Several solutions to this problem have been presented. There is clearly a need for teachers to be better trained in assessment methodology, something that is largely absent from many initial teacher-training courses. There is also a strong case for creating opportunities for teachers to meet one another to discuss methods of assessment in particular areas, whether such meetings are used for moderation or not. Finally, there is a clear need for assessment criteria to be spelled out as clearly as possible, and in terms which relate pupil performance to recognizable behaviour patterns.

A further problem also exists. Mode 3 examinations frequently contain a terminal component, usually conventional examination papers, but set and marked by the teachers. We are, in general, fairly ignorant of the criteria for setting 'good' examinations although the examinations boards are slowly accumulating a great deal of empirical evidence, which has enabled them to formulate some principles controlling the quality of examination papers. Although there is no reason to believe that this wisdom is confined to examinations boards, it is probable that the quality of written papers set in Mode 3 situations is not as high as those set in Mode 1, unless the controlling board is able to operate an advisory (or even monitoring) service. Teachers tend to rely heavily on old examination papers (usually those of a comparable Mode 1 examination) or textbooks, and there is always a danger of stereotyping which is ultimately destructive of any examination scheme.

We have therefore a confusing dilemma in Mode 3. There is little doubt that it is an important strand in modern British examining, and represents a way of closing the gap between curriculum and assessment in schools. However, it is subject to several effects which will cause it to degenerate quite rapidly and, perhaps, cause it to fail as an alternative to Mode 1. It is probable that it needs continuous servicing by the examining authorities, particularly as it must not become a 'second-class' qualification.

Users of examinations results

This last point leads us to a further issue in our consideration of examinations. The credibility of an examination can be established in three distinct areas. Firstly, it has to pass scrutiny in the examinations boards which are concerned with the overall *quality of the measurement* to which they are putting their names. Secondly, it needs to be credible in the schools, in which teachers will judge it primarily on *what is being assessed*. Finally, it will have to satisfy the external world, included in which are employers, further education institutions, parents, etc. For this last group credibility exists in terms of the *hardness of the currency*: how useable is the certificate?

It is in this last area that C.S.E. and Mode 3 have suffered, and where G.C.E. examinations carry a much higher credibility. This is, of course, partly because the G.C.E. examinations are aimed at higher ability groups, and also has something to do with the association of G.C.E. examinations with university interests. It is also a reflection of the conservatism of the external users of examination results and the extent to which each of them is perhaps less concerned with previous attainment and more with future performance. Nevertheless, there is a residue of suspicion about C.S.E. examinations in general and Mode 3 in particular, and it leads us to wonder how credible a wholly internal assessment scheme would be. Perhaps the heart of the matter lies in the old concept of a 'qualification'; whilst employers and others are looking for qualifications they are unlikely to be easily satisfied with the emphasis on continuous school-based assessment which would follow a wholesale use of Mode 3.

Since the evidence for changing standards in education is scanty and largely impressionistic, the linking of C.S.E. and Mode 3 to 'falling educational standards' is probably unjust. A great deal has changed in the last twenty years, altering the patterns of employment of school-leavers and the nature of their schooling. Whilst it may be reasonable to ask whether the State gets value for money out of its educational systems it is unreasonable to assume that it is not doing so simply because of a mismatch between the activities of the schools and the expectations of employers. Assessment is likely to remain in the middle of this controversy for the forseeable future, and it is difficult to see whether, in the long term, it can ally itself more closely to internal school demands or external social demands. It probably cannot do both.

The forseeable future

In this chapter we have looked at a number of issues connected with assessment in schools. A great deal has been omitted, particularly matters which deal with the technologies of testing. The reader can get a great deal of information on these matters from the wide variety of examinations literature, perhaps starting with the Schools Council series of publications on examinations (e.g., Deale, 1976).

At the time of writing the future of school examinations seems likely to change in the next ten years. Following the exercises mounted by the Schools Council which resulted in the Waddell Report, the Department of Education and Science (1978) has proposed a common examinations system at sixteen-plus. Although the proposals for the common sixteen-plus system seem radical (doing away with the G.C.E. and C.S.E. sectors and the large number of examinations boards), it is likely that the fundamental effects of assessment in the schools will then be much the same as they are now. We are also unlikely to see radical changes in the nature of the measurement methods being used, and to this extent the prospective changes are another stage in the slow evolution of assessment within British education, rather than the revolution which some would want. Indeed, a great deal of the initial enthusiasm for C.S.E. examinations (the last major change in the system) has evaporated as the distinctions between these and the older G.C.E. examinations have become less and less clear.

A final strand for the future comes from the establishment of the Assessment of Performance Unit whose role has scarcely been considered in this chapter (Kay, 1975). This is chiefly because its impact on the examinations scene has as yet been slight, although it is possible that, if it becomes a reputable and acceptable part of the education system of this country, we shall see a closer linking between examinations, performance measurement, and accountability of schools to society. There are some who regard this as a disturbing possibility (Galton, 1978), and there is little doubt that this and other aspects of assessment will thus continue to attract considerable attention.

References

Bardell, G.S., Forrest, G.M., and Shoesmith, D.J. (1978) *Comparability in GCE*, Manchester: Joint Matriculation Board.
Black, H.D. and Dockrell, W.B. (1979) 'Assessment in the Affective Domain – do we, should we, can we?', Paper presented to 1979 Annual Conference of the British Educational Research Association.
Board of Education (1911) *Education in Secondary Schools*, Report of the Consultative Committee, London: HMSO.
Campbell, W.J. and Campbell, E.M. (1978)*School Based Assessment*, ERDC Report No 7A, Canberra: Australian Government Publishing Service.
Deale, R.N. (1976) *Assessment and Testing in the Secondary School*, Schools Council Examination Bulletin No. 32, London: Evans/Methuen Educational.
Department of Education and Science (1978) *School Examinations*, (The Waddell Report), London: HMSO.
Elley, W.B. and Livingstone, I.D. (1972) *External Examinations and Internal Assessments*, Wellington: New Zealand Council for Educational Research.
Evans, G.T. (1976) 'Reflections on the Campbell Report and the Radford Scheme' in McMorrow, J.F. (ed), *Moderation – at the Crossroads?*, Brisbane: Queensland Teachers' Union.
Firth, R. (1969) 'Examination and Ritual Initiation' in Lauwerys, J.A. and Scanlon, D.G. (eds), *Examinations*, World Year Book of Education, 1969, London: Evans.
Galton, M. (1978) 'Accountability and the Teacher: some Moves and Countermoves' in Richards, C. (ed), *Power and the Curriculum*, Driffield: Nafferton Books.
Goldstein, H. (1979) 'Consequences of using the Rasch Model for Educational Assessment', *Brid. Ed. Res. J*, 5.2, 211-220.
Holmes, B. and Dryland, A. (1965) 'The Role of Examinations in an Expanding Education System' in Holmes, B. (ed), *Aspects of US and UK Examination Systems*, London: Association of Technical Institutions.
Holmes, B. and Lauwerys, J.A. (1969) 'Education and Examinations', in Lauwerys, J.A. and Scanlon, D.G. (op. cit.).
Ingenkamp, K. (1977)*Educational Assessment*, Council for Europe, Slough: NFER.

Kay, B.W. (1975) 'Monitoring Pupils' Performance', *Trends*, 2.

Moore, W.E. (1975) 'Some Functions of Examinations' in Dunn, S.S. (ed), *Public Examinations*, Adelaide: Rigby.

Schools Council (1966) *Examining at 16 +*. Report of the Joint GCE/CSE Committee, London: HMSO.

Secondary School Examinations Council (1960) *Secondary School Examinations other than the GCE*, (Beloe Report), London: HMSO.

Smith, C.H. (1976) *Mode III Examinations in the CSE and GCE*, Schools Council Examinations Bulletin 34, London: Evans/Methuen Educational.

Stenhouse, L. (1975) *An Introduction to Curriculum Research and Development*, London: Heinemann.

Willmott, A.S. and Fowles, D.F. (1974) *The Objective Interpretation of Test Performance*, Slough: NFER.

Wood, R. (1978) 'Fitting the Rasch Model – a heady tale', *Brit. J. Math. Stat. Psychol*. 31, 27-32.

Wood, R. and Napthali, W.A. (1975) 'Assessment in the Classroom: What do Teachers Look For?' *Ed. Stud*. 1.3, 151-161.

CHAPTER 5

EVALUATION IN EDUCATION
Wynne Harlen

Perhaps the fact that there are so many differing views about the meaning of evaluation in education and about how it should be practised is the clearest indication that it is a subject influenced by personal values, ethical principles and political stances. It is not so much technical issues which divide evaluators into different camps as matters of overall policy. These differences are reflected in the variety of models of evaluation which have been defined and which can be found well represented in the literature on evaluation (e.g., Scriven, 1972; Tawney, 1976; Hamilton et al., 1977; Lewy, 1977).

This chapter, however, is not about models, which are frameworks or guidelines for how evaluation should be carried out; it addresses the question of what evaluation *is* rather than how to do it. Any discussion of evaluation must concern both its meaning and its practice, since the overall conception of what evaluation is necessarily affects how it is carried out. The present discussion, however, is at a more general level than that of particular approaches or methods. It concerns the issues raised when attempting to clarify the concept of evaluation as it appears both in theory and practice.

Since the word 'evaluation' contains the word 'value', there would seem to be little need to make out a case for their connection; indeed it would appear that one should be defined in terms of the other. The more important relationship, however, which represents the major underlying theme of this book, is interestingly symmetrical – values play an essential part in evaluations and vice versa. In everyday life people's values develop as the result of certain objects or experiences being evaluated as more worthwhile or satisfying than others. Thus the process of evaluation plays a part in developing values. At the same time values have an unavoidable influence on the process of evaluation. This is shown in the following diagram, which attempts to represent what evaluation involves.

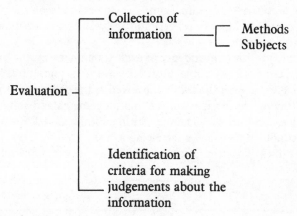

The proposition expressed schematically here is that evaluation comprises not only the collection of information but the identification and use of criteria for making judgements about that information. This explicitness of criteria distinguishes evaluation from the notion of 'pure' reporting of information, from the making of judgements when criteria are not made explicit, and from the falsely claimed 'objectivity' of information expressed numerically.

The choice of criteria is clearly an aspect of evaluation which involves values. Where the choice is a free one the point is not difficult to illustrate in the everyday context. One person may praise a particular holiday accommodation as being 'perfect', but another may be well advised to inquire further before committing himself to spending his holiday there. 'Perfect' for one may mean bingo, bars, and bathing pools, whilst for another it may mean temperance, tranquillity, and table tennis. In an evaluation, it can be argued, the position is very different; the evaluator does not choose the criteria freely, but, according to the above, 'identifies' them. The evaluator should use the appropriate criteria and these may not be his own. But how does he 'identify' these? They will not be found neatly listed and agreed by all concerned; they will instead have to be inferred from people's writings, actions, and speech. There will not be consistency between different people involved nor between criteria which can be inferred from what people do and what people say. Inevitably the evaluation will take more account of some criteria than others, perhaps because they are more attractive or understandable to the evaluator, perhaps because some are less visible though not necessarily less important; for whatever reason the evaluator will select as well as identify criteria and the resulting evaluation will be affected by this choice.

In order to avoid this dependence of evaluation on the evaluator's selection of criteria some (for example, Stufflebeam, 1971; Hemphill, 1969) have proposed that evaluation should be conceived as the collection of information only, leaving the business of making judgements and statements of value to decision-makers. Though Stufflebeam's model for decision-making does not ignore values as an element in the process, it takes account only of the values of decision-makers, not those of information-collectors:

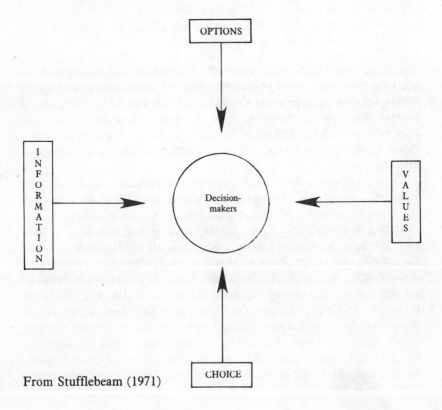

From Stufflebeam (1971)

Although the evaluator may be involved in helping to identify options and clarify values, there is an assumption here that 'information' can somehow be neutral, a true reflection of 'what is'. Stake also came close to this position when, in 1967, he wrote that an evaluation 'tells what happened'. Later, however, he wrote 'I have lost the sense that there is any "the way it is". *What is* only seems to be.' In this case he was writing of measurements but the point is true of any kind of information. 'My measurements are not the first approximations to truth; they are choices I make as to how to clothe the truth. It is another case of the Emperor's clothes – with the minor switch that it is the Emperor who is invisible and it is only the clothes that are seen' (1972). Every evaluator chooses the clothes for the truth and it is the clothed truth, not the naked truth, which is communicated.

Evaluation involves unavoidable decisions; to report this, but not that, to measure these things, but not those, to question these people, but not those, and so on. Neither the artist nor the scientist can observe everything in a scene or event, giving equal weight and no special significance to particular points. If they could do so, their minds would be cluttered with details and denied the ordering which preconceptions bring. People are trained by experience and by formal education to filter observations and there is no way of avoiding this filter. Thus it is necessary to accept and acknowledge its influence. One way of working with this reality, rather than against it, is to make the selection, the filtering, public. This means making clear the basis for examining one thing rather than another and brings us back to the need to make the criteria explicit. Greater weight is now added to this point since the criteria used in 'filtering' are the same as those used in judging information. That is, we choose to find out about certain things, both because we feel they are significant and because what leads us to consider them significant will be the basis on which we make judgements.

The meaning of 'criteria' emerges as something combining certain aspects of both values and standards. If we take values to be the underlying principles which are considered to be desirable and of utility at a particular time, then these provide the framework for selecting the kinds and variety of information which will be gathered. This does not mean that an evaluation will look only for what is thought to be good and useful; it will also look for anything else which affects the presence or absence of these things, but the search will be along these dimensions, set by the values which they reflect. Values thus determine the kinds of transactions or achievements which are noticed and which become the 'information' on which an evaluation is based. Standards, as suggested in Chapter 2, 'refer to levels of achievement or expectation against which people or objects can be assessed'. Whilst values determine the qualitative nature of criteria, standards determine the quantitative aspects.

There is a further point to be considered here, as to whether the qualitative and quantitative features of criteria are in fact separate. It would be reasonable to suppose that it is the qualitative feature which influences the choice of information to be collected or sought, whilst the quantitative feature operates later, at the point of judging the information. This is not so and if it appears to be it may be that too simple a view has been taken in making a sharp distinction between the qualitative and the quantitative. In reality the fact that it is thought worthwhile to look for certain *kinds* of achievements generally means that these are looked for *in a certain degree*. Thus the expectations, or standards, affect how the information is sought and not only how the information obtained is judged. For example, an expectation that children of a particular age should have some knowledge of their surroundings could lead one to gather information about this, but the fact that certain levels are implied in the expectations would lead one to gather the information in such a way that the degree of achievement of these can be evaluated. Or, to take a different and real example, when the National Science Foundation of the USA set up a project to give them 'a portrayal' of current conditions in science classrooms from kindergarten to grade twelve, the project directors (Stake and Easley) chose to provide the information in the form of a series of case studies. Each case study was a description of the circumstances and events in a particular group of schools reflecting the different perspectives of those involved, from teachers and pupils to administrators and parents. This method of gathering and conveying information was chosen because the expectations were that the problems of science teaching and learning would be complex and involve subtle interactions, which could be less easily tackled by other methods, but also because of the desire to find out not only what influences were operating but also the degree to which each was important.

To complete discussion of the schematic definition of evaluation on page 53 let us turn our attention to the variety of methods and subjects which it covers. The word 'subject' is used here as it is in speaking of the subject of an inquiry, that is, it can concern objects, persons, events of all kinds. Thus, in education evaluations can be of such things as pupil performance, teachers or teaching, school conditions, community influences, the effect of policy decisions or new curriculum materials. Clearly what is being said here does not go along with the distinction between assessment and evaluation in terms of assessment being about pupils whilst evaluation is about other things. Such a distinction confuses the subject of the information with the process of gathering and using it. Assessment is just one way of gathering information, which involves some attempt at measurement; it can be part of evaluation but it is not an alternative process simply concerned with pupil achievements rather than other things. One can assess or measure such things as teacher performance, school provisions, even the efficiency of educational administrators, providing there is 'some clearly defined or appreciated standard which can be used as a basis for comparison' (see Chapter 3). What makes assessment and measurement different from other ways of gathering information is that the use of standards is part of the method. These are standards *of* measurement, however, and not the standards by which the results of measurement are judged in the process of evaluation. Thus, an evaluation involving measurement demands the use of 'standards' of different kinds at two levels, once in collecting the information and once in relating it to criteria reflecting expectations of the level the measurement might reach.

It is the insistence on explicitness about criteria which distinguishes evaluation as used here from the 'everyday' use of the term. We do not have to go out of the educational scene, however, to find examples of 'evaluations' which can only be described as such in the everyday use of the term. A headmaster produces an 'evaluation' of his school which praises all the old traditions, deplores the loss of some of them, and disapproves of all new ideas introduced by young teachers. Clearly these are his opinions; there is no attempt to provide the facts and to indicate how he reaches his judgement of them. Opinions expressed in this way do not count as evaluations.

Often care is needed to distinguish such nonevaluations from evaluations which use criteria which are considered inappropriate for some reasons or too narrow. One may wish to dismiss the conclusions of both but for different reasons; in one case because one cannot know the basis of the judgement and in the other because one may not agree with the basis. Bennett's (1976) research into formal and informal teaching in the primary school is an example of an evaluation where the criteria used may be challenged. One may claim that it is not fair to have made judgements on progress in reading and arithmetic without having information about other areas (e.g., creative arts, science, personal and social development) which might be set against a low rate of progress in what was measured. One might – theoretically, though probably not in practice in this instance – be prepared to apply different standards to what was measured and perhaps to judge that what was achieved in informal classes was indeed good enough, or alternatively to say that what was achieved in either type was not good enough. The point here is that it is possible to disagree with the criteria used both in selecting and judging the information because these are made explicit. The study fulfils the requirements of an evaluation and this sets it apart from other statements which present conclusions whose bases cannot be challenged because they are unknown.

There is a further element in the concept of evaluation which is difficult to show in the scheme on page 53: evaluation is purposive. Unless it serves a clearly defined purpose requiring decisions or judgements to be made, then the gathering of information does not constitute evaluation. Thus a pre-evaluation activity is to examine decision possibilities or information needs and if none exist then there is no setting for an evaluation. Whether or not there are options which are considered worthwhile can, of course, be a matter of contention. An interesting example of a situation where opinions on this may have differed is given in Christopher Ormell's chapter on mathematics. Advocates of the early 'new mathematics' materials did not consider evaluation necessary 'because there were no other candidates in the field'. Thus, on the view that there were no decisions to be made about the materials, no evaluation was required. This illustrated the point that an evaluation must be seen to have a purpose, though in this particular case it could be reasonably argued that there were in fact decisions to be made and hence an evaluation was necessary.

People's activities are not purposeless and indeed it could be said that no information is ever gathered without a purpose, be it only to satisfy idle curiosity. Clearly there are particular purposes in mind which form part of the concept of evaluation and the best way to describe them may be through examples. Whilst working with an evaluation project in Australia (Hughes et al., 1978) the author was involved in studying a number of evaluations carried out in schools, some by teachers and some by outsiders. Part of what was being examined was why an evaluation had been undertaken and what purposes it had served. Several groups of purposes could be identified. In some cases a decision had to be made and would be made, one way or another, whether an evaluation was carried out or not. Such decisions might concern the rearrangement of options at various points in the school, or the continuation or abandonment of an experimental use of new materials; several such examples could be given where the decision would be to continue with things as they were or to change, and, if so, what change to make.

There was a different group of studies undertaken in fulfilment of an obligation to 'evaluate' some sponsored innovation. When money was provided to support the development of new things in schools it was part of the contract that the recipient of the grant should produce an evaluation. Apart from fulfilling this contract, the report also served the purpose of clarifying the advantages of the innovation. It was not common for the disadvantages to be given equal attention and the 'evaluation' report was often a justification for using the money spent, even though no decision about the grant depended upon it. For the providers of the money these evaluations might help in making decisions about further applications of the same kind; for the recipients the evaluation would enable them to decide whether the advantages of the innovation were such that they would wish to continue to finance it out of resources taken from elsewhere.

There were also groups of evaluations carried out in response to dissatisfaction felt either within the school or by parents or more generally in the community. Where this was directed at specific points, such as home-school relationships, for example, the evaluation showed up areas of misunderstanding and suggested changes which might reduce the dissatisfaction. Where the unease was more diffuse, however, transmitting a general view that 'schools are spending too much and producing too little', the evaluation was a response to a request for a school to give an account of itself. In some cases a school took up the challenge to examine its own working, to see how well it was achieving its own intentions, and to find out where improvements could be made. By so doing the results of the evaluation were used both for internal decisions about changes found to be desirable, and as a basis for explaining to outsiders what the school achieved, what it attempted to achieve, and the constraints under which it worked. Unfortunately, the processes and outcomes of evaluation were not in all cases viewed so positively by those involved. Sometimes the evaluation was perceived as externally imposed and was carried out unwillingly by those in the school and, far from being seen as of benefit, was regarded as a bureaucratic burden. This brings into focus the issue of who should benefit from evaluation – those who receive information or those who supply it? It would seem reasonable to propose that, to be perceived as a benefit, the evaluation must be seen to serve the purpose of providing information for which there is a need and on which there is a possibility and a willingness to act.

Another group of so-called evaluations were carried out for the purposes of advancing the status or qualifications of individuals. Apart from work for higher degrees, which is more correctly described as research according to the distinction to be drawn later, there were the activities of evaluation 'bandwagoners' and those who sought to impress others. A librarian might 'evaluate' the use of the library in order to improve its function as a resource, but could also do so to show other people what a good job he or she was doing. Where no decision is to be taken which can be affected by the information – and this is clear from the inception of the work – then it does not seem appropriately described as evaluation.

This argument is in line with the definition of evaluation given by MacDonald (1975):

> Evaluation is the process of conceiving, obtaining and communicating information for the guidance of educational decision-making with regard to a specified programme.

Here two important features of evaluation are stressed: one, its purpose, just discussed; the other, that it involves the 'conceiving' of what information is relevant. This brings us back to the selection of information which, it has been argued, will be based on the same criteria as are used to make judgements about the information. When these two are put together – the purpose and the selection of information – it is obvious that the information gathered should be seen as relevant to the purpose. Differing views on what is relevant have been largely responsible for the proliferation of models. These tend, however, to be generated in a process of generalizing from a very small number of instances (if indeed more than one) and can very rarely be applied as 'off-the-peg' solutions to problems which require a bespoke evaluation. It is generally, then, those carrying out the evaluation who decide what is relevant and this must vary according to the values of those involved.

Take an apparently straightforward example of a school wanting to improve its communications and image in relation to its parents. It engages an evaluator to gather data and report on the state of things as they are and to suggest where change is required and where they would do best to leave well alone. If they engage evaluator A they are persuaded that the relevant information will come from interviewing parents, from trying to understand what it is like to be outside the school. This evaluator will also interview pupils, since it is largely through them that the parents' image of the school is formed. He will be informal in approach, though use of a tape-recorder will mean that his information-gathering is efficient. From miles and miles of tape he will gain insight into the complex mixture of past and present personal experience, ambitions, prejudices and mis/understanding which forms parents' attitudes to schools in general and this school in particular. He will probably write a lengthy, anecdotal report, supporting his generalizations with specific examples and including more than a hint that the school will improve its relationship with parents if it takes the trouble to look at things from the parents' point of view.

Alternatively, they will engage evaluator B, who will convince the school that the relevant information can be gathered by questionnaire. By discussion with the staff he will find out what kinds of questions to ask and will probably probe the nature of the home background in his instrument. From surveying the literature on home-school relations he will find out what factors are likely to be influential variables, and will make sure that he includes all the questions found relevant in previous work. He will send out his questionnaires, meticulously code and analyse the responses, and impress everyone with a smooth and professional job. His report will be partly statistical, partly descriptive of his method, and his conclusions will probably hint that the school could hardly expect to communicate well with its parents considering their low socio-economic status.

Evaluators A and B both do a good job in their own terms, but these are very different terms. They probably reflect considerable differences in the way they view (and value?) education. Evaluator A takes the position of the recipients; for him education is a process which should take as much account of the learner as what is to be learned. Evaluator B starts from, and maintains, the point of view of the educators; he keeps at a distance from the recipients. One can hypothesize that he regards education as a process of transfer of knowledge from teachers to taught. Thus A and B, because of their different value-positions, conceive of what is relevant information in quite different ways, produce findings which, while not in contradiction, are certainly oblique in relation to each other, and which lead to different conclusions. It is not necessary to argue which is the more worthy evaluator in order to appreciate the importance of the decisions they take and that there is no 'right' and 'wrong' about their actions.

It is partly for this reason and for other reasons now to be introduced that the way an evaluation is conducted becomes relevant to what it is. 'The way it is conducted' does not mean the technical methods used but rather the principles governing how it is carried out. Those involved in evaluating the situations, achievements, or products of others enter, as part of their job, privileged positions. They take information from various sources and as a result come to know more about a situation than any single one of these sources. They bring together data, see patterns in it, test out hypotheses in relation to it, which no one else has done before. They hear confidences (particularly if they work to form friendly, relaxed relations with people, as for example evaluator A would do), they gain insights into people's views of each other, they see evidence of shortcomings, of failure, as well as of good and bad personal relationships. All this places a great burden on evaluators which they do well to carry carefully. People who give others information also give those others a degree of power over them and the information is given in trust that this power will not be abused. This is true whatever kind of information is concerned and however it is gathered, but the issues it raises assume greater urgency consequent upon the increased use of information-gathering methods such as case study (see page 56), unstructured interview, and anecdotal records of observation. It is not only the closeness of evaluator and information source but also the diffuse and unstructured nature of the information, clearly requiring selection to give it any form, which immediately draws attention to 'subjectivity' and unavoidable 'bias' in the data. Pointing out that subjectivity and bias are present in all information-gathering does not remove the obligation to provide safeguards.

Proposals for safeguards have been made by Lovegrove (1978), Simons (1979), Kemmis (see Simons) (1979), among others, and there is an interesting agreement between workers approaching this problem from differing starting points. What appears to be emerging is the suggestion of a form of ethical code which would govern evaluators' activities. This would involve negotiation between givers and receivers of information as to the use to which the information would be put, thus putting control of the information in the hands of those who provide it (and therefore own it?) rather than in the hands of the evaluator. Any change in the intended audience for the information or in the use to which it will be put would have to be renegotiated with the providers. Simons claims that negotiation does not only ensure a balance between the 'public's right to know' and the individual's 'right to be discreet' but also 'encourages people to participate; gives them room to contribute equally and fairly; improves the impartiality of the account by inviting checks on biases and improves the reliability and validity of the accounts'.

The activities of the evaluator and the researcher have, on the surface, much in common but there are important distinctions to be made in terms of purpose and in terms of involvement in value-judgements. MacDonald (1976) has written one of the most interesting discussions of the connection between research and evaluation, from which he concludes that research would be better regarded as a branch of evaluation rather than vice versa, which is often taken to be the case. He points out that a researcher can choose his area of inquiry to suit his own interests, the tools he has available or can devise, and he is at liberty to exclude from his work areas which he cannot tackle. So, for example, a researcher can choose to examine the effect of certain learning activities in science on the development in the pupils of the relevant concepts without being obliged to find out what effect these activities might have on other aspects of their development.

An evaluator, on the other hand, does not have this freedom. In Mac-Donald's words he must never 'fall into the error of answering questions which no-one but he is asking'. The evaluator has to define his questions but the overall problem is not for him to decide, and he is obliged to look at all parts which he or others consider important. This means he may not have the tools available and will have to do the best he can within the often pressing constraints of time and manpower imposed on his work. He will not be able to spend the time that the researcher can on refining methods and instruments but neither can he afford to ignore certain questions because the tools to answer them do not exist. Moreover, since he has to clarify the purpose of the evaluation, deciding whose questions are most important and what information is relevant to their answers, he is involved in judgements which must reflect his own values. MacDonald concludes that 'the involvement with values is so much greater than that of the researcher that it amounts to a difference in kind. It also makes explicit the political dimension of evaluation studies.'

The final section of this chapter looks in more detail at the gathering of information. This is not the place to describe methods and techniques; what is attempted is a discussion of the factors which may influence selection of methods and subjects for data-gathering. The subject of the information, the object or person the information concerns, may also be the source, as when a pupil responds to a question which elicits statements of his attitude, but often the source is different from the subject, as when a teacher may provide information about the pupils' behaviour from which their attitudes are inferred. The choice of subject in an evaluation study reflects the judgement that certain data are more relevant or important than other data and the emerging report is clearly dependent upon this judgement.

Methods of gathering information range from those which can be described as attempts to measure, that is, some forms of assessment, to those which attempt only to describe, to portray, and not to summarize or place against a standard of measurement. It is very difficult to make a clear distinction between what is assessment and what is description and these are better thought of as words which describe the ends of a continuum of methods. There is an obvious difference between the extremes. At one end are methods of assessment which have been refined to reduce the inevitable errors as much as possible. These generally involve test situations where variations in conditions which would increase error of measurement are reduced as far as possible. At the other end are methods which attempt to reproduce in some condensed form a picture of some event or behaviour or achievement without putting it against a scale or replacing it by a score or mark, as is done in measurement. In between are methods where, for example, events or performances may be compared against descriptive criteria. Some would call this a kind of assessment, taking the term to cover any attempt to compare one thing against criteria. In this interpretation a frown or a smile on a teacher's face can be called an assessment of whatever behaviour provoked it, since the teacher had compared the behaviour with some expectation, the criterion, in order to arrive at the judgement which led to the nonverbal response. The point is not, however, to find the spot at which assessment ends and description begins, but rather to realize that, in their different ways, methods at both ends of the dimension are dependent on subjective and value-based judgements. How the results of a standard test are marked and scored may not be a matter of judgement – the process can be fully mechanized in some cases – but what goes into the test must be a selection of what might have been put in. Even if items are selected mechanically from a bank, the result of the process is entirely dependent on what items are put into the bank in the first place. At the other end of the dimension a 'pure' description of an event attempts not to measure or judge or sum up so that others can use their own criteria in evaluation. But again there has to be a selection from all the possible features and details of the event which could be reported and the filtering of the eyes and mind of the observer is inescapable.

Methods and subjects have to match, but there is always a range of methods which could be used to gather information. In education the choice is not by any means always obvious and neither will it always be agreed. Often it is not, as it were, a matter of choosing between using a tape-measure and a pair of callipers, but more akin to choosing between a ruler and a pair of scales. Methods in educational evaluation yield different kinds of information, not merely different degrees of precision of the same thing, and the choice of one method will mean that judgements will be made on that basis and cannot be made on the different kinds of information which alternative methods would have produced. Some examples that follow illustrate this and also clearly show that what determines the choice one way or another is not an innocent preference for particular methods but more of an ideology of education.

The first example concerns the pupil as the subject of information-gathering. The case is a first school involved in an argument about the number of its pupils described as in need of remedial teaching by the head of the middle school it feeds; this head says the pupils are not 'up to the standard' when they transfer to his school. The middle school head gives standard reading tests to the pupils when they reach his school and for him the results prove his point. The first school staff deplore the narrowness of the information on which the middle school judges the pupils' learning and indeed disputes even the results of the standardized test, saying that testing children in the first few days at a new school and after a long holiday does not give a fair indication of what they can do. Instead the first school points to the detailed records they have kept of individual children which show development in cooperation, responsibility, inquiry skills, aesthetic appreciation, and so on. These records are offered to the middle school, but rejected as being 'too subjective' to be worth taking into account. Here we have a not uncommon clash in methods used to evaluate pupils' learning by these two heads. Each claims that the methods used by the other lead to inadequate information. It is as if one uses the scales and the other the tape-measure.

The second example concerns the school as the subject of information. For many years schools in the USA have been more publicly evaluated than has been the case in this country. It is not uncommon (Stokes, 1978) for 'league tables' of local schools' test scores to be published in American newspapers, and recently the possibility of the same thing in this country has been widely discussed. The purpose of gathering and publishing such information is not only so that schools can be held accountable for the performances of their pupils but also so that changes intended to improve these performances can be made. Whether or not changes forced through this kind of publicity are always improvements is an arguable point, but it is necessary to believe that this is the intention. Many LEAs in this country have now introduced programmes of regular testing of pupils and, whilst not publishing results, it must be assumed that they consider the testing ultimately enables improvement to be brought about in the education in these schools. But this is only one method of getting information for this purpose and is in sharp contrast with two other methods, one of long standing and one relatively new.

HMIs have inspected and reported on schools for as long as government money has been used to support schools. Their reports have been strictly private and based on descriptions of events observed during the inspector's visits. Apart from the period of 'payment by results' when pupils were tested and schools rewarded for getting them through the test, the methods used by inspectors have been to observe transactions and conditions in the schools and make reports on the standard of work they have seen being carried out. It is assumed that the experienced eye sees more than can be seen in the results of tests posted to schools and that in judging a school there is more information to be taken into account than measurable learning outcomes.

Inspectors' reports have been kept secret not only from the public but also from the schools, and a third method of gathering information about schools, to be contrasted with both of the others, involves the staff of the school in reviewing its own work. After a series of meetings between the ILEA staff inspectors and some headteachers, a booklet describing itself as 'a method of self-assessment for schools' has been made available. The foreword explains the nature and purpose of the document:

> It is presented as a basis for the development of a school's own form of self-assessment, to be modified and extended to suit the intentions and interests of the individual school. The object of applying some form of systematic self-appraisal is to assist in the clarification of objectives and priorities, to identify weaknesses and strengths and ensure that due attention is given in time to all aspects of school life. (ILEA, 1977)

This proposes that the method is one for teachers for their own use, but the suggestion is also made that the outcomes could be discussed with members of the inspectorate. Schemes of this kind are already operating in North America (Alberta Teachers' Association) and in Australia (Queensland Department of Education, 1977). If this were to be done more generally it could be the beginning of school evaluation where data is provided by the schools, reviewed by a body of outside moderators, and drawn together by education authorities to provide the picture they want of the performance of their schools.

In the third example the information focus is the national system. The Assessment of Performance Unit in this country provides an example of one method of gathering information at this level. This involves testing the performance of a sample of pupils in schools across the country and correlating these results with a rather small number of sampling variables such as size and location of the school and age and sex of pupils. A similar exercise has been in operation in the USA for a decade, carrying out its first survey in 1969 and reporting at regular intervals since that time so that trends in performance over time can be revealed. In the USA, however, this national assessment has existed side by side with a project which exemplifies an alternative method of providing data for a picture of education in the nation's schools. This is the Case Studies in Science Education project (already mentioned on pp. 56). A balanced sample of eleven campuses, each comprising a high school and its feeder schools, was selected from across the whole country and a research worker was sent to each for a period of four to fifteen weeks' field work. Each field researcher then wrote a case study of his or her observations and this was supplemented by information from a questionnaire survey and visits by a separate team to each campus. From the set of case studies a series of conclusions was drawn by the project team about, for example, the aims of science education, the curriculum, student learning, the teachers, and the schools in relation to the community.

What these examples serve to show is not only that there are very great differences in the ways of gathering data about pupils, schools, and the national system, but that these different ways provide different kinds of data. In all three examples one of the main issues which distinguishes one method from another is the degree of dependence upon the evidence of measurable learning outcomes as against the examination of processes, conditions, and learning transactions. Underlying this issue are different views of the processes and products of education.

The position that measurable outcomes are the only worthwhile information reflects a view of education as a process of producing well-defined changes in pupils' abilities and knowledge. Moreover, this view assumes that what is well taught is learned and conversely that what is not learned has not been taught or not taught well. In other words, it accepts that the pupils' learning is a direct product of the teaching and so can be taken as a measure of the quality of the teaching. Generally the process is seen as beginning with a statement of behavioural objectives which indicate the measurable outcomes to be expected. It is then assumed that the process of education is one of translating objectives into curriculum transactions and thence into learning outcomes.

An alternative position combines views about the product and process of education which are quite different from these. In the first place it regards education as a very complex matter, of which few outcomes can be precisely defined and measured. It holds that aesthetic and affective development, which often have long-term effects, are as important as the more immediately measurable cognitive development. It also challenges the assumption that outcomes can be used as indications of quality of transactions and of objectives. It points out the many reasons why intentions may not be translated into practice and why the provision of learning opportunities does not always lead to learning outcomes. The C.S.S.E. project provides support for this view:

> The effectiveness of science programs is not indicated by the measures of student outcome in any district we visited. Some test performances had declined . . ., some level performance trendlines were proudly displayed . . ., but it is questionable to attribute either change or no change to the quality of instruction. (Stake and Easley, 1978)

The consequence of accepting this view is to adopt methods of data-gathering which look directly *at* transactions, at processes, and not at the learning outcomes only, since it is pointed out that these outcomes are the product not only of the curriculum but also of the effect of factors such as home support, previous learning, attitudes developed elsewhere, and the interaction of these factors with the learning opportunities provided at school.

The choosing of both methods and subjects in evaluation is inevitably affected by the beliefs and values of those who make the choice. If we add to this the decisions which have to be made in evaluation, about what information is relevant, what criteria should be used, who should control the data, what audiences should be informed, the involvement of evaluation with values is striking. This leads to two final points, the first being simply that awareness of this position is perhaps long overdue and the most important initial step in encouraging responsible evaluation.

The other point is summed up in a slightly facetious question: 'is evaluation too important to be left to evaluators?' Who should carry out evaluation is made a more serious issue by recalling the emphasis which has been placed upon evaluation being a purposeful activity. Results of evaluation have to be used and thus have to be fed back to those who have to decide upon and implement changes. This is often very difficult to do and various methods have been tried – from shock publicity stunts (the announcement of a fall in science scores in American schools was made dramatically on television by an astronaut) to threats and punishment (payment by results in various modern guises). The uncertain process of feedback can be avoided, however, if those who have to act on the results are also involved in the evaluation. To say it would be an improvement would be to make a claim which, like so many others in education, could not be proved. Clearly the evaluation of different approaches to evaluation would depend in a multiple manner on judgements as to what changes can be called improvements, what information is worthwhile, and what things are of value.

References

Bennett, N. (1976) *Teaching Styles and Pupil Progress*, London: Open Books.

Hamilton et al. (eds) (1977) *Beyond the Numbers Game*, London: Macmillan.

Hemphill, J.K. (1969) 'The relationship between research and evaluation studies', pp. 189-220, in Tyler, R.W. (ed), *Educational Evaluation: New Roles, New Means*, Chicago: University of Chicago Press.

Hughes, P. et al. (1978) *Teachers as Evaluators Project, Policy Paper*, Canberra College of Advanced Education, Canberra, Australia (mimeo).

ILEA (1977) *Keeping the School under Review*, ILEA, available from Public Information Bookshop, Greater London Council, County Hall, London.

Lewy, A. (1977) 'The nature of curriculum evaluation', in Lewy, A. (ed), *Handbook of Curriculum Evaluation*, New York: Longman, and Paris: UNESCO.

Lovegrove, E. (1978) *The Role of the Outside Facilitator in School-Based Evaluation*, paper presented at the Tasmanian High School Principals' Association Annual Conference Workshop (mimeo).

MacDonald, B. (1975) *The Programme at Two*, (evaluation report on the National Development Programme in Computer-assisted Learning), Centre for Applied Research in Education, University of East Anglia.

MacDonald, B. (1976) 'Evaluation and the control of education' in Tawney, D.A. (ed) *Curriculum Evaluation Today: Trends and Implications*, London: Macmillan.

Queensland Department of Education (1977), *Cooperative School Evaluation: a Guide for Queensland Primary Schools*.

Scriven, M. (1972) 'Prose and cons about goal-free evaluation', *Evaluation Comment* 3 (4), 1-4.

Simons, H. (1979) 'Suggestions for a school self-evaluation based democratic principles' in *Classroom Action Research Network Bulletin No. 3*, Spring 1979, Cambridge Institute of Education.

Stake, R.E. (1967) 'The countenance of educational evaluation', *Teachers' College Record*, 68, No. 7, pp. 523-540.

Stake, R.E. (1972) 'Comments and conjectures: the seeds of doubt', *The Educational Forum*, January 1972, pp. 271-272.

Stake, R.E., Easley, J., et al. (1978) *Case Studies in Science Education*, Vols. I and II, Government Printing Office, Washington, D.C.

Stokes, H. (1976) 'Should exam results be public property?', *Where*, February 1978.

Stufflebeam, D.L. et al. (1971) *Educational Evaluation and Decision-Making*, Itasca, Illinois: Peacock.

Tawney, D.A. (ed) (1976) *Curriculum Evaluation Today: Trends and Implications*, London: Macmillan.

CHAPTER 6

VALUES IN EDUCATION
Christopher Ormell

It is evident that different conceptions of education as interpreted at different times, and by different cultures, embody different values. These values are near the heart of the educational enterprise. Change the values a little and the education which emerges (i.e., the kind of qualities and capacities the children possess when they leave school) changes a lot. This is why it seems to be important to try to bring modern conceptual-clarification methods to bear on the subject of educational values. If values in education are as important as this, at least let us be clear what we are up against.

There are various questions we seek to answer:

What is a value?

What are the standard types of values with which we are concerned?

When is a value educational? How do educational values relate to other values?

How do educational values relate to educational philosophies and aims?

What values have been thought to be educational?

From where do changes in the values expressed in education arise?

How are values transmitted to the child?

How much emphasis on a specific set of values is it reasonable for a teacher or an institution to display?

To what extent does the curriculum embody values? Do values apply only to certain subjects?

To what extent do examinations embody values?

It is often said that values are the essence of education: that if one can get the values right, the rest will follow. This proposition does seem to be broadly true. The famous expression of this thought was the Jesuit principle that if a child had been initiated into a close-knit set of values by the age of seven, whatever happened to him after that would hardly matter: the values he had acquired would, in a word, probably 'stick'. This is a measure of the importance of values in education.

On the other hand, the topic of values has suffered an amazing degree of neglect. As Popper says (1976) '. . . few scientists and few philosophers with scientific training care to write about values'. And he adds the reason. 'The reason is simply that so much of the talk about values is just hot air' (p. 193). This is a measure of the difficulty of the subject.

What is a value?

It is evident that human beings value things: this is a general characteristic of the human species. A person who values a thing X shows this when he takes *risks* in defending or securing X, and when he expends *effort* and makes *sacrifices* on its behalf. Many parents value a good school, and are willing to put up with less than satisfactory jobs, to live in neighbourhoods they would not otherwise want to inhabit, to fetch and carry their children over distances, etc., in order to secure this commodity: 'education for their children in a particular school'. The fact that people value their friendships, their footballs teams, their music, their political affiliations, their privileges, etc. is shown by the fact that they are willing to take risks, put themselves out, expend effort, and make sacrifices in order to try to gain and secure these things.

But it is evident at once that not everything that a person values would count as 'one of his values'. A man may value his wife, his key to the executive washroom, and his 450g steak, but it sounds odd to say that these are 'his values'. It is hard to imagine an obituary in *The Times* which claimed that a deceased man's values were 'his first wife, his key to the executive washroom when he worked for ICI (1972-1978), and the 450g steak he ate on January 1st 1980'!

Clearly then, to say that V is 'a value' is to claim more than that certain people do, or have, valued V. The question is: how much more? What are the extra conditions required?

One hardly needs an elaborate proof that it is not correct to say that a material object such as 'a 450g steak', or a person such as 'his first wife', is a 'value'. For a thing to be a 'value' it has to possess considerable generality and also universality, in the sense that one must be able to envisage that *anyone* could hold it. The archetypal values were beauty, truth, and goodness, and it is to qualities of this level of generality that we look when we are presented with a new claim that such-and-such is a value.

It also seems quite inappropriate to say that things like favours, gifts, privileges, sleep, warmth, sex, eating, or drinking are 'values'. Values are rather things which one has to work at, to strive for, to expend effort in living up to.

The next thing to say about values is, perhaps, that a person who holds certain values will be imbued with certain motivations. This follows, of course, from the fact that values are valued qualities and conditions; but it is important to realize that this valuing needs to be seen in behaviour, not merely in a passive form of assent. Indeed it is expected that a person who holds a value V will also from time to time actively encourage others to acquire a V-oriented motivation. This is particularly important in the case of teaching, because to say that a teacher expresses a value V in his teaching is mainly to imply that he encourages V-oriented motivations to develop in his pupils: teachers are busy people engaged in the process of encouraging and discouraging others (i.e., children) and are not always very active as agents in their own right.

The valuing motivation, then, implies a motivation to motivate others in the same direction. We might call this 'motivation to motivate others' in a given direction an *'exomotivation'*. The idea behind the concept of 'exomotivation' is partly that it is a case of *exporting* a motivation which one has oneself to others. It is a motivation which operates outside a person's direct behaviour.

In general, to talk about values in the educational context is clearly to talk about motivation and example: the rhetoric of scorn and admiration, of encouragement and discouragement. For example, the person doing a given job may change – say, the headmaster of a school – and yet we say things like 'Roger left, but John who took over has exactly the same values' – meaning that he appreciates human actions, qualities, and products in the same way. He encourages the same kinds of things, and he raises his eyebrows at the same kinds of things.

Notice the extent to which we see the new head in cases like this in terms of his *public* personality, his exomotivations. We are hardly concerned at all in the educational context with what he does in his spare time. In the educational context then, the exomotivation towards V is often much more important than the motivation towards V.

The next step in our analysis of what it is to hold a value V must be to observe that simply to possess a motivation, and the corresponding exomotivation, towards V is not enough. Certain qualifications have to be met. Briefly, both the motivation towards V and the exomotivation towards V need to be long term, consistent, stable, effort-intensive, and reasonably justified, before we are likely to recognize their occurrence as constituting a 'held value'. We shall look at these essential qualifications in turn.

Consistency and stability are evidently required before we are willing to concede that a certain person (a teacher, say) holds certain values. A teacher who encouraged her pupils to be creative and expressive on Mondays and Wednesdays but who (intentionally) discouraged this on Tuesdays and Thurdays would certainly *not* be credited with holding the values of creativity and expression. (But such cases need to be judged in context. The work allocated for Tuesdays and Thursdays might be concerned with acquiring mechanical facility in basic skills: and so the encouragement of creativity and expression might be simply inappropriate in this context. Many curriculum experts advocate an alternation of work requiring more and less creativity. (See, for example, Chanan and Gilchrist, 1974.)

Effort-intensity is needed to exclude the cases considered earlier: favours, sleep, etc.

Reasonable justification was partly, though not fully, implied in our previous observations about the need for universality. We are not saying that for George to hold the value V, *George* must be able to give a reasonable justification of his V-oriented motivation; but a reasonable justification must exist. It must be possible to give a reasonable defence of V-oriented motivation. To say 'George holds the value V' implies, *inter alia*, that V is reasonably justified as a motivation.

What counts as 'reasonably justified'? The general tendency seems to be to accept justifications or alleged justifications fairly tolerantly. But this tolerance does not stretch indefinitely. A person who had a long-term, consistent, stable, effort-intensive, allegedly reasonably justified motivation and exomotivation to murder to child-molestation would not be said to hold the 'value' of murder or child-molestation. No civilized person would accept that motivations of this kind were 'reasonably justified'.

Nowadays, people are said to have 'values' of a much wider variety – and sometimes of a somewhat less serious moral complexion – than was customary in the past. For example, it might be said that a man's values were 'football, driving fast cars, and jazz'. One would expect him or his friends to be able to give a reasonable justification for these motivations and the associated exomotivations; we would also expect them to be long-term, consistently held, and stable. Many people might be shocked at such nonserious items being cited as 'values', but that people do possess such motivations, and exhibit them in a way similar to that in which their grandfathers clung to the traditional virtues, is a fact of the modern world. If one is shocked by this, one is shocked by the modern world; it is not really the localized idiom in which we speak of these as 'values' which is responsible for this response.

The important point is that when we say that Jim holds values X, Y, and Z, we do give a certain limited recognition to X, Y, and Z as being socially accepted motivations, though not necessarily ones which we ourselves hold. This is a fairly sophisticated point of view, embodying a generous measure of democratic-liberal tolerance. One would not find it in an ideologically monolithic society; and it seems probable that the ordinary man-in-the-street in Britain boggles, too, at the full breadth of such moral relativism. Nevertheless, it is customary in educational circles to presuppose this agreed plurality of values.

Another aspect of values which may be noted at this point is that a value is a consistent, reasonably justified, effort-intensive motivation (and exomotivation) in relation to which the person who holds it *is ready to stand up and be counted*. Hitler may have claimed during 1939-1945 that his values were the establishment of Nazi hegemony and of German military supremacy, but he was careful not publicly to claim *genocide* as one of his values. Knowledge of the gas chambers may have circulated by word of mouth, but it was never officially admitted by the state propaganda machine.

One can interpret this in two ways: *either* by saying that genocide was one of his values, because he was willing to stand up and be counted within a small circle of sycophants, *or* that it was not one of his values, even in the context of the Nazi State, because he did not think he could justify it in the eyes of the German people. It was certainly a consistently held and terrible irrational motivation. ('Irrational' because founded on a fantasy about the Jewish minority's influence on the State, and because it led to the exit of many of Germany's most able scientists.) This implies that in a secretive society the values people are perceived to hold are relative to the social context, namely the social group in which they are prepared to justify the motivations involved.

In an open society such social relativity of values virtually disappears, and a person will be said either to hold or not to hold certain values in that society. This does not imply, however, that it is impossible to make mistakes about a person's values; or even that a person may not make mistakes about his own values. A person may claim to have certain values X, Y, and Z and yet close observation of his behaviour may lead one to see that these are not his real values. In other words, when it comes to the crunch, these are not the bases on which he makes his decisions. We might say that he 'thinks' that X, Y, and Z are his values and that these are the things on which he is ready to stand up and be counted, but that really there are other things U, V, and W which count more with him though he does not readily admit this. I think we have the same choice here as in the Hitler example: *either* we can say that U, V, and W are irrational motivations below the level of recognition appropriate to 'values', *or* we can say that, given a slight push, he would be willing to stand up and be counted on U, V, and W. If he does, in fact, base his decisions on U, V, and W instead of on X, Y, and Z, he already does stand up to be counted – in a certain sense – on U, V, and W, and once this is widely publicly perceived (and assuming that U, V, and W can be reasonably justified in the society), I think we would want to say that U, V, and W were his 'real values'.

Thus a person's real values are those stable, consistent, effort-intensive motivations, etc. which, it becomes clear, as a result of analysis or the pressures of life, underly his behaviour. They are rather like the basis of a vector space. Given these motivations, we can work out what his attitude to many things is likely to be: by mixing them in various proportions a great variety of different responses may be deduced. (Another analogy would be that they are like the *ingredients* of a cake, behaviour itself being the cake.) Najder (1975), in an excellent discussion, speaks of values as being 'the strongest or ultimate motivational factor' in a person's behaviour.

A person's values, then, may be seen as the basic motivational constituents of his intentional behaviour and in view of which it may be explained. It is as a consequence of this fact that people try to use values as touchstones for settling disputes about the relative worth of things. Where people share the same values, it is supposed that such disputes will always be capable of resolution, in principle, by reference back to the basic values.

(In the kind of diverse society which we have at present, it is easy to forget this socially cohesive aspect of values, and it was, paradoxically enough, equally easy to forget it in the past, when it was taken so much for granted.)

Of course, values, once consciously identified, have a tendency to consolidate motivation. As Kluckholm (1951), quoted in Najder (1975), says, '. . . values canalise motivation'.

Values, then, are, as it were, established currencies in things about which people care. A school which claims that its values are discipline, character-formation, and physical hardiness aims to please parents and others who share these values. By saying that its values are discipline, character-formation, and physical hardiness, it declares the currencies in which it deals. The intellectual values of a classical syllabus may be mental-training, discipline, knowledge of words, syntax, and verbal accuracy. An institution which adopts such a syllabus aims to please those who care about these things. On the other hand, a rival scheme may claim that its values are awareness of our Graeco-Roman heritage, imaginative reconstruction of the past, classical poetry and legend, and an appreciation of the great ideas of the ancient world. No one is in any doubt that this scheme operates with different currencies from the other. It aims to please those who care more about the cultural content of a classical education and less about its form.

The negative side of such caring is that people often feel worried and guilty at the absence of certain things. A teacher who is teaching Latin using the former scheme may feel that she is offering her girls too little of the values embedded in the latter scheme: she may feel that they are 'missing out' on this, as we say nowadays.

A teacher teaching science as an authoritative body of verbal and spatial knowledge may wonder whether his pupils are really getting the 'feel' of science: perhaps they, too, are 'missing out' on something here? So he may adopt a new science scheme, in which youngsters are encouraged to formulate their own hypotheses, to design experiments, to carry them out, and finally to interpret the results. Such a scheme clearly embodies new values. One might say that it is more 'educational' because it achieves a better balance between encouraging the passive absorption of answers and fostering an active participation in asking questions. When he changes his scheme in such a way the teacher adopts new exomotivations. He encourages his pupils to think more, to ask more questions, to construct explanations, to envisage (and do) experiments. He discourages them from merely reading it all in the standard textbook – or even in another pupil's workbook! He ends up encouraging a different kind of mental development from the one he encouraged before. And it is not merely different in technical ways: people really do feel strongly about these things. (Perhaps they feel that it is a *misuse* of science education merely to cram facts, or perhaps that these 'fun' schemes are all right where teachers have to keep their classes amused, but that 'they do not deliver the grades at 'A' level'.) This is the kind of thing that issues concerned with values in education are all about: *delivering* cognitive and other kinds of personal development of a type which the child, its parents, heads, advisers, authorities, examiners, higher teachers, etc. will, one hopes, appreciate.

In general, new values in education seem to derive from new perceptions of the nature of society and of the individual's role within it.

Types of values, including educational values

That values come in types is of course a truism. We speak of 'moral values', 'social values', 'spiritual values', 'aesthetic values', etc. And here we encounter our first problem: are 'educational values' another subspecies of values, distinct from the moral, social, spiritual, and aesthetic values mentioned above? If so, does this mean that education is not concerned with the moral, the social, the spiritual, and the aesthetic? This is a very curious conclusion; for the trend at present is for commentators to say that education should not concern itself only with moral, social, spiritual, and aesthetic values, but should do something about technological, industrial, and economic values, too.

At first it might seem that the answer is quite simple: that all values are automatically 'educational values'. Such a solution will, however, hardly do. It might be possible to argue that 'football' is an educational value, but it is not at all plausible to maintain that 'driving fast cars' and 'jazz' are educational values!

It is evident that values tend to be held, not as individual items, but in sets. Certain values have an affinity with other values. Such values 'go well together' in the sense that they minimize the occurrence of behavioural contradictions and of agonizing choices of action.

We might roughly characterize the provinces of some of the main types of values as follows:

Moral values are values to which we appeal in judging the worth of actions and products which affect the life-energy and welfare of others and oneself.

Aesthetic values are values to which we appeal in judging the worth of actions and products which affect the total impact of a situation on the senses.

Social values are values to which we appeal in judging the worth of actions and products affecting the manner of life in groups and communities.

Spiritual values are values to which we appeal in judging the worth of actions and products which do, or claim to, help people to see a purpose or 'meaning' in life as a whole.

Intellectual values are values to which we appeal in judging the worth of actions and products which do, or claim to, help people to achieve a coherent mental picture of parts of the natural, man-made, and human worlds.

Using the same form of words we might enunciate the following definition: 'Educational values are values to which we appeal in judging the worth of actions, programmes, and products which are, or claim to be, conducive to the education of the child.'

It may be noted that educational values are almost coterminous with educational aims. There is an ambivalence associated with theorizing about educational aims, in that something which is listed as an 'aim' in relation to a five-year-old will, we hope, have been achieved by an eighteen-year-old. In a word, what has hopefully been achieved is that the eighteen-year-old has acquired the *value* corresponding to the aim. (It may be noted here that when educationalists write on the subject of the 'aims of education', for example, Whitehead in his famous lecture of 1912, they are often concerned with the discussion of new, as yet little implemented, values. These are primarily 'aims' for schools or education systems rather than for the average child who is moving through the system.)

It is interesting at this point to look at the contrasting ways in which we speak of values, aims, and philosophies in the context of an institution. To identify the values inherent in the work of a given educational institution is evidently a fairly analytical enterprise. And having identified these values, one is apt to feel that one has got to the root of the matter: 'This is really what makes them tick!' By the same token, to convey the conclusions of such an analysis to others is a condensed way of telling them a great deal about what the institution in question is like.

On the other hand, it is usually *too* condensed to appeal much to the institution itself: it reduces a way of life to a mere list of words, *sans* justification, *sans* charisma. An institution is much more likely to want to put out a condensed statement of its 'educational philosophy', or, if still greater brevity is required, of its 'educational aims'. So what are the main demarcations between the roles of statements of 'educational values', 'educational aims', and 'an educational philosophy'? The three statements seem to lie in a kind of sequence expressing the degree of commitment which obtains to a certain sort of education. We use the terminology of 'values' when we wish to convey that the institution in question has the sort of education it offers *in its bones* – when the way of life it projects has been deeply assimilated. Values inform the life of an institution, not merely the verbalizations which its members interchange.

The terminology of 'aims' suggests a serious motivation to do well, but there is no guarantee that these aims will be met, partially met, or even closely approached. We make statements like 'This institution has very good educational aims, but it does not always succeed in achieving them.' An educational institution may officially adopt a set of new aims, whilst still exhibiting, in practice, many of the old values.

The terminology of educational 'philosophy' (so-called) is altogether more cerebral than the terminology of aims and values. To say that a given institution has a certain 'educational philosophy' suggests that a lot of intellectual justification is being done. One expects a lot of talk in the direction indicated; but doubts may remain about whether this talk has been fully condensed into agreed aims, not to mention accepted values.

As a preliminary to looking at the question 'When is a value educational?', it is salutary to recall some of the things which have been variously advocated under the heading of 'educational aims' or 'educational values'. A list of values/aims which were formerly strongly supported might include: religion, character-building, personal advancement, learning, traditional culture, manners, socialization. Of these, religion, character-building, learning, traditional culture, and manners have tended to receive decreased emphasis in recent years. A list of values/aims which have risen in prominence in recent years might include: nontraditional culture, doing your own thing, creativity, independence of judgement, thinking, expression. In effect, these are new *motivations* which parents and educators have perceived to be important in present-day society and which it is probably desirable to encourage in the child if he or she is to be able to lead a worthwhile life in the future. This change of values results, therefore, ultimately from social and technological changes in the complexion of society itself.

I have advocated the view elsewhere (Ormell, 1975) that there are two overriding imperatives which tend to operate in education. The first is the imperative to conservation and stability in the life of the community; the second is the imperative to innovation and change. The first imperative was formerly dominant in the schools but has now been replaced in many places by the second. In certain places, where innovative educational methods have come spectacularly unstuck, there has been a limited reversion to the first imperative. These imperatives are, as it were, superordinate values; and the changeover from the first to the second is reflected in the changes of emphases noted above.

One may doubt, however, whether either imperative or the values which express it is truly 'educational'. Neither conservation for the sake of conservation nor innovation for the sake of innovation can be regarded as a very satisfactory superordinate value in schools. If the main purpose of education is to prepare children for a worthwhile form of life in the future, the condition that the value-system they acquire should reflect the *priorities* of the future is fairly obvious. To let them acquire a value-system which is fundamentally at odds with the priorities of the future is a fairly certain way of ensuring that they will be *ill* prepared to live a worthwhile life in the future. It is quite evident that the priorities of the future will involve a mixture of conservation and innovation. Innovation will be present in strength but it will not be the only sentiment. One cannot simply discard three thousand years of civilization without destroying the very foundations of the social edifice.

This is, of course, in essence, a negative point: namely, that there is no simple identification to be made between 'educational values' and those implied by the imperatives. But it is much harder to answer the question 'What is an educational value?' positively. The essence of the difficulty seems to reduce to the question whether educational values are simply a subset of other values, or whether there are some characteristically 'educational' values.

The best way to tackle this question is probably boldly to list at the beginning the kind of values which *may* have a plausible case for being considered to be characteristically 'educational' values. Such a list might include: *encouragement* of wholeness, balance, life, coherence, comprehensiveness; general varieties of understanding, awareness, constructivity, creativity, expression, thought, and problem-solving capacity. There is no doubt that such values are, in fact, appealed to when people judge the worth of 'actions, programmes, and products which are, or which claim to be, conducive to the education of the child'. The only question, therefore, is whether these values have been already classified under one of the headings 'moral', 'aesthetic', 'social', 'spiritual', and 'intellectual'. It is not difficult to exclude the first three categories; but there is a real question about the relationship of these values (a) to spiritual values and (b) to intellectual values.

That there is a link with spiritual values is evident enough, in that a teacher's relationship to his pupil is, as experienced by the pupil (at least in the case of a wise and sympathetic teacher), in a kind of analogy to the relationship between God (as postulated) and man. This of course explains the kind of emphasis on spiritual values in the writings of the previous generation of educationalists, e.g., James (James, 1945; White, 1978). But this having been said, it is certainly not the case that the values listed above, as potential educational values, coincide with the standard spiritual values of reverence, openness, humility, etc.

In relation to intellectual values the position is somewhat less easy to disentangle. It appears at first that the twelve values listed above are directly intellectual values, viz., values to which one might appeal in criticizing or praising a new intellectual work, such as a theory or an exposition. But what is meant by 'wholeness' here is not simply the unity of an intellectual artefact. We are concerned here with the wholeness of the child embracing the gamut of moral, social, aesthetic, and intellectual values. This is a second-order 'wholeness' compared with the first-order intellectual variety. Similar remarks apply to balance, life, coherence, comprehensiveness, etc. ('Life' in an intellectual context would be shown by vigour in drawing inferences, discussing cases, considering alternatives, etc.; in the second-order educational context it embraces all this and much more, namely vigour in fielding the full gamut of moral, social, aesthetic, and intellectual values.)

So I conclude that the kind of values listed above are, indeed, educational values. They form a distinct category of stable, consistent, effort-intensive, reasonably justified motivations and exomotivations – ones relevant to the teacher-child relationship. Such a relationship is quite unique, and it is the perception of this fact that leads one to a degree of confidence in the judgement that this category of values is distinct from the categories of moral, social, aesthetic, spiritual, and intellectual values, Occasionally one may find an example of a similar relationship; e.g., Diaghilev and Louis B. Meyer may have exercised the exomotivation of encouraging creativity. I think the educational paradigm is sufficiently strong to say that, in so far as they did this, they were 'educators', albeit in a highly specialized, adult, and artistic context. And if they were 'educators' when they did this, there is no strain in saying that the values they were exhibiting in this connection were 'educational' values.

Educational values distribute over ordinary values

We have already remarked that the values of encouraging wholeness, balance, life, coherence, comprehensiveness, etc. apply across the gamut of ordinary, first-order values. But how wide is this gamut? Although moral, aesthetic, social, and intellectual values have usually been taken to encompass the task of education, there is a tendency currently operating towards recognition of certain new values as fit for inclusion in the educational process. These new values are chiefly those of economics, national development, technology, and industry. Can one take 'educating the whole child' seriously as a slogan if it turns out that no serious intention exists to offer the child economic, national developmental, technological, or industrial values? I have argued elsewhere that one cannot (Ormell, 1974, 1976). If the task of education is to prepare children to lead worthwhile lives in the future, it is essential that they should be prepared for life in the world as it is, not as educators would prefer it to be. Now it requires no great degree of epistemological insight to see that there are three major worlds of human experience: the human world, the natural world, and the man-made world. To distribute our educational values over the familiar quartet of moral, aesthetic, social, and intellectual values is, in effect, to cover the human and natural worlds, but to leave the man-made world alone. How can one justify such an exclusion of the man-made world, in the current state in which we find ourselves – namely of massive, far-reaching, revolutionary technological change? If we intend to educate seriously, we need to wake up to the world as it *is*, and to distribute the educational values across the three spheres which children will later actually experience.

In saying that the educational values should distribute across ordinary values, we do not however commit ourselves to any particular set of first-order moral, aesthetic, social, economic, or technological values. The agonizing difficulty remains of choosing a particular combination of moral, aesthetic, and social values which will be appropriate to an essentially plural society. In other words, we need to make first-order choices of values in each area, to inform the total educative process which youngsters will undergo. And it is hardly possible to adopt a neutral attitude to such values in general. One reason is that the school is a community, as well as an educational establishment. It is composed of individuals, whose life-energy and life-hopes can be bruised in all the usual ways; so a healthy moral atmosphere is needed. It is a community; so social relationships need to be nurtured, and social justice needs to be seen to obtain. It is composed of visually, aurally, and kinaesthetically sensitive individuals; so the prevailing aesthetic judgements which are made by the school will weigh heavily on those who prefer opposing styles.

Different first-order values contradict each other: for example, to take the most dramatic example, the value of chastity contradicts the value of sexual freedom. Similar contradictions may be found in every area. Even in the area of intellectual values, there are some who emphasize the power of generalization, and others who condemn generalization as a scholarly vice. One man's rigour is another man's pedantry.

Thus, getting clear about the role of educational values, in general, does little to reduce the difficulty we face in treading through the minefield of ordinary, first-order values. Alan Bullock, in an address to the Mathematical Association in 1965, referred to the difficulty of trying to educate in an age which lacks consensus on many of the crucial issues of personal life, social life, politics, education, etc. There is little doubt that this permanent lack of consensus and the consequent weary, endemic clash of contradictory first-order values is rather debilitating for education. (For the intellectual child, clashes of values may stimulate curiosity and challenge the child to seek more profound reconciliations. But for the average child they all too often simply cancel out, leaving a 'demotivated' feeling in the child's mind.) The damage inflicted by these value contradictions may be seen, even in the microcosm of intellectual values, as embodied in rival approaches in science and mathematics education. In mathematics, for example, there are two broadly contrasting schools of thought. One party stresses an inward-looking interpretation of mathematics, operating in splendid isolation, whilst the other stresses the outward-looking interpretation of the subject, linking its perceptions with those of ordinary life, science, and technology. The educational values of encouraging wholeness, balance, coherence, and comprehensiveness seem to point in favour of the latter school; but some mathematical educators prefer to distribute these values only *within* an isolationist mathematics. (See Chapter 13 for more details.) Here too, as in the case of the neglect of the man-made world in education, the problem is essentially about the *distribution* of educational values, not about the educational values themselves.

The general answer to lack of consensus about first-order values seems to be the encouragement of parental choice and of diversity of educational régimes. It is better that children should travel a little farther, and go to a slightly less well-equipped school, if they and their parents are happy about the set of first-order values accepted there, rather than go to a closer, glossier establishment whose values constantly contradict their own familiar judgements. When a school is operating with an harmonious set of values (e.g., a Catholic, Jewish, or Marxist school), one expects, and usually finds, a gradual rubbing off of these values onto the average child. If we permute the categories of acceptance, acquiescence, and adoption against motivation and exomotivation we obtain six logically distinct stages in the taking up of a given value:

1 Recognition that the motivation is socially acceptable

2 Recognition that the exomotivation is socially acceptable

3 Acquiescence in the motivation through group responsibility

4 Acquiescence in the exomotivation through group responsibility

5 Active adoption of the motivation

6 Active adoption of the exomotivation

Such stages, however, are not the only developmental landmarks which have been noted by psychologists in their studies of the process of taking up a value. Piaget, Bloom, and Kohlberg each offer a slightly different set of partition points along this path (Piaget, 1932; Bloom, 1964; Kohlberg, 1970).

It should be emphasized that, in a situation of conflict between different value-systems, and particularly in situations where values are scrambled in a confusing way, there is no automatic progression of children along this route from 1 to 6. Where contradictory values are circulating simultaneously, their tendencies to be taken up are all too likely to cancel out.

In the next three sections we look briefly at the role which educational values (and other values) play in teaching, in the curriculum, and in examinations.

Educational values in action: the teacher and the schools

There are two main questions in relation to the role of values in teaching which we shall attempt to answer:

1 What is the status of so-called values like punctuality, neatness, and manners in the classroom?

2 How much emphasis is it appropriate for the teacher to give to personally accepted, first-order values in the classroom?

The set of so-called values we are concerned about in the first question includes speech, handwriting, accuracy, hard work, work completion, quietness, paying attention, personal appearance. The chief question is whether we should regard these values, too, as 'educational' values, and if so, what their relationship is to the rather different kind of educational values considered earlier. The main reason for calling them 'educational' values would be that many teachers believe that these values are conducive to – or at least preconditions of – education. The main reason for not calling them 'educational' values would be that they receive virtually equal emphasis in other, noneducational contexts such as military life and industrial work: and that they have little direct connection with the major aims of education. Another version of this argument is that these are not 'values' proper, but 'manners'. People who believe strongly that these things are conducive to education usually base their case on the premise that these are, in themselves, necessary for the individual to lead a worthwhile life. (In other words these alleged values are conducive to education, because acquiring them constitutes a part of the aims of education.)

It is evident that the question whether such a thing as 'punctuality' or 'neatness' is a value, or simply a variety of manners, is largely a semantic question. There seems little harm in describing it as a mini-value; but the important question is whether the link with education is sufficiently strong and sufficiently unique to justify the description of these mini-values as *'educational'* mini-values. The answer seems to be that it is not. These are values which are brought into play whenever one individual is working for, or under the jurisdiction of, another. There is very little educational gain, as such, if a youngster copies out her notes in a neat, rather than in a ragged, form, provided that the degree of raggedness is not such as to render them confusing or illegible. The same applies to the other mini-values listed above. One might describe such mini-values as values appropriate to any work situation. They are essentially connected with the work-and-social aspect of social life, rather than with its educational function. One is not saying that they are unimportant, but only that they are in a different case from the educational values considered earlier.

On the degree of emphasis which it is appropriate for a teacher to give to his or her own first-order value system in the classroom, the basis for the answer may be found in the previous section. In the first place, a given school has a particular set of presupposed social, moral, and aesthetic values, and if an individual teacher's values seriously contradict these presupposed values, he would probably be ill advised to advertise this fact, still less to emphasize it. In fact it is highly questionable whether he should be teaching in that particular school at all, since, given time, some manifestation of the value-contradiction will almost certainly occur.

In the second place, where a teacher refers to, or is asked about, his own personal moral and social values, he should always make it clear that the values in question are simply personal ones; otherwise zealous, one-track-minded teachers would be given a *carte blanche* by society to indoctrinate their classes.

But having said this, there remains a considerable area of leeway in the teaching of subjects vis-à-vis values. I have observed elsewhere (Ormell, 1977) that a subject like mathematics can act as a carrier wave for various unusual value systems. Similar remarks apply to other subjects. The main rule which it is desirable for teachers to observe is that any special, personal kind of indirect value emphasis they are accustomed to placing in the classroom should be broadly consistent with the prevailing educational value-system of the school, as well as with the school's presupposed first-order social, moral, and aesthetic values. If this rule is not observed, the work of such a teacher, if lacking in vigour in any way, is likely to be ineffective (because cancelled out by values being more vigorously propogated elsewhere in the school). On the other hand, if it is vigorously promoted, its success may be at the expense of work being done elsewhere from the opposite point of view.

It should be pointed out that any influence exerted by a teacher through the expression of his or her first-order moral, social, or aesthetic values in the classroom is unlikely today to be a direct one. Modern discussive teaching methods, curricula, and examinations set a style of work far removed from anything approaching Jean Brodie-like indoctrination. Because value transmission occurs, if at all, by this indirect (carrier-wave) mechanism, some teachers may be hardly aware that they *are* exerting a specific influence in favour of certain first-order moral or social values. There is a role here for the self-evaluation procedures developed by Adelman (Elliott and Adelman, 1973) and others, for until one is aware of one's personal value influence, one is hardly likely to be able to correct it.

On the question of the degree to which it is reasonable for a school to develop a specific value-system, the same factors apply. A school which tries to contradict some of the values taken for granted in the surrounding community sets itself an uphill task. Of course, there is no sharp dichotomy between values which are 'taken for granted' and values which are not, so there is quite a lot of flexibility in the situation. Some values seem to have a kind of latent credibility. They may be socially dormant for long periods, but they are capable of being restored to active use in a thriving school; and they will then often achieve a fair degree of acceptance in the local community too. In general, where there is parental choice (e.g., in the case of private educational régimes), there is more freedom for schools to set up distinctive value-systems than there is where parental choice does not exist.

Educational values in action: the curriculum

In general it seems to be safe to say that the curriculum is a much less potent source of values than the teacher. However, it does exert a peculiarly subtle influence through its prior definition of what the subject is, what counts as knowledge in this subject, and, in particular, in the cognitive scale employed. (The analogy is to maps. One could study a country, say Greenland, on various levels of scale.) It is to Bernstein that we owe the perception that these factors in the curriculum operate through the influence of 'classification' and 'frame' (Bernstein, 1971). (The 'classification' adopted in an institution determines how the different subjects on the timetable are composed: e.g., 'molecular sciences' is a different classification from 'natural philosophy' and both may cover ground fairly similar to 'chemistry'. 'Frame' is concerned with the shape and size of the parts of the subject on which emphasis is placed: which are specifically taught and are expected to be specifically learnt or mastered. Frame alone has surprisingly subtle implications in terms of the *size* of the youngster's role vis-à-vis the teacher and, indeed, the size of his eventual role in adult society.) In a traditional curricular context these factors are hardly noticeable, since there is no active choice involved in either classification or frame. But in an educational institution fully under the influence of the imperative for innovation, the curriculum becomes a kaleidoscope capable of being rearranged in an infinite variety of different nontraditional ways, and in this kind of fluid curricular situation the two factors noticed by Bernstein obviously do come into play (notwithstanding the criticisms of Pring, 1978 and Gibson, 1978). SMP (the School Mathematics Project, the leading UK project) uses different classifications and a somewhat different type of frame from so-called 'traditional mathematics'; whilst in applicable mathematics the classification of the subject itself is radically different and the frame used (the standard modelling problem) is quite different from that of both SMP and traditional mathematics. History taught with a sharp empirical focus is a totally different subject from history taught with the broad sweep of human affairs in the forefront of attention. An English curriculum chosen by F.R. Leavis will tend to differ markedly from an English curriculum chosen by C.S. Lewis. Similar differences may be seen between an old-fashioned political-based geography syllabus, and one based on tracing the all-pervasive effect of economic influences.

The central question is really this: does the effect of changes in classification and frame on the values implied by a curriculum operate via the first-order, or via the educational, values?

A typical case would be history, where the modern type of syllabus emphasizes the values of accurate expert inquiry, whilst the older type of syllabus emphasizes the cultural dimension of the subject, and the development of a general understanding of social and political psychology. The former tends to project a clinical detachment from value-judgements about the events of the past, whilst the latter often fed the political prejudices of its age. Arguments about the educational implications of this difference often tend to concern the question whether the new 'balance' is more or less educational than the old, rather than being concerned with the particular first-order moral and social values involved. There is, however, a distinct difference in emphasis on first-order intellectual values too: from the relatively synoptic values of understanding broad trends to the more myopic values of accuracy, evidence, and verification. (See Chapter 11 for a further discussion of the role of values in historical education.)

Do values apply to only half the curriculum?

It is sometimes said that questions of value only arise in the arts subjects (and perhaps occasionally in social biology): in other words, that they do not normally arise in the physical sciences, in technology, or in mathematics. This assumption seems to embody a serious misconception. Of course it is a truism that the *content* of the physical sciences, the technologies, and mathematics as taught in schools often does *not* include any discussion, or even mention, of human values. (This value-neutral approach to teaching in the predominantly cognitive subjects is, I would urge, a mistake. If physicists are financed by society – as they are – on a greater scale than other types of scientist, it is because both the destruction, and the survival, of civilization probably depend mainly on their efforts. The human implications of technology are always the chief reason for doing it. And mathematics, presented as an innovation-previewing discipline, is vastly more interesting to the average youngster than mathematics as mental embroidery.)

Nevertheless we must recognize that the value-neutral teaching of the cognitive subjects is common; that is, that in many schools human values are never included in the content being taught or discussed in these lessons. Does this mean, then, that values have no part in the process of teaching in these subjects? Or that issues involving values hardly arise?

The answer is, of course, no. Even in the most neutral curriculum context, the job of teaching is intrinsically bound up with values: with intellectual values obviously enough, but also with moral values (like telling the truth about why the homework wasn't presented on time), social values (like supporting one's team in a spelling bee), and aesthetic values (like admiring the stellated icosahedron). Good teachers go into teaching situations values-first. How else can one 'get through' to the average child?

We have already seen in this chapter that there are certain deep controversies about teaching, curriculum content, and form in the predominantly cognitive subjects. Of course in the arts subjects there are greater opportunities for the imaginative consideration of the human condition. And it is probable that the development of *imagination* in this way is the main factor which is likely to lead youngsters towards civilized and humane points of view, which, then, one hopes will mature into firmly held values. Bringing human-world values into the cognitive subjects (as suggested above) can, however, greatly improve their educative effect too.

Educational values in action: examinations

The channel through which values probably exert their greatest influence on education is that of the system of national and local examinations. Social convention allows that the examining boards may issue pieces of paper called 'certificates', on which appear summary judgements on the work of the individual concerned in various subjects. These assessments have great social significance, perhaps mainly because they have little credible competition. If a youngster can wave a piece of paper signed by the secretary of an examining authority saying that he has an 'A' grade in ancient history, or Latin, or even English literature, who is to gainsay it? There is virtually no competition, no independent verification, no second channel of information. It therefore acquires that kind of heightened, slightly artificial credibility which only a totally unchallenged authority is able to enjoy.

However unrepresentative of true merit, or capacity, or understanding an examination result may be, it has the enormous advantage of social reality. It becomes a kind of glittering prize, and in taking on this role exerts a massive influence on the schools, in *favour* of certain values, and in *opposition* to others. It motivates behaviours of one kind (which are likely to lead to candidates gaining marks) and inhibits behaviours of another kind (which are likely to lead to candidates losing marks). In particular it exerts a massive pressure in favour of memorization of facts and process drills. By this means the first-order intellectual values of knowing your facts and knowing how to do it receive an enormous emphasis, to the detriment of the more intrinsically important values of thinking, problem-solving, and understanding.

The main reason for this disproportionate emphasis is quite simple: these items are comparatively easy to test in a way which can be shown to be both valid and reliable, whereas the items of thinking, problem-solving, and understanding are extremely hard to define, still less (reliably) to detect. Nevertheless, the phenomenon is a relative one, in which various shades of grey occur as well as black and white. Certain kinds of thinking, problem-solving, and understanding are undoubtedly testable. And there is a body of fairly intuitive examining practice which attempts to test mental qualities like 'capacity to marshall rational arguments', 'critical evaluation', 'discursive survey', 'informed appreciation'. (For a more detailed study of ways in which values are implicit in examinations, see Chapter 4.)

The problem posed by the extreme social importance of examinations is not confined to the comparatively simple distortion in favour of factual recall and drill skills. Everything which is perceived in the schools as being tested in examinations is, potentially, a source of influence on the schools. It is hardly satisfactory that such potent sources of value-emphasis should operate on the schools in a largely hit-or-miss, unanalysed way. This has led to the idea of analysing the behavioural objectives actually implicit in existing examination practice. The question is: what specific behaviours are the examiners really looking for?

In attempting to answer this question there are two main prerequisites: a method of analysis (behavioural) and a vocabulary of basic elements (of behaviour) into which the raw material (what the examiners are looking for) may be analysed. In effect a vocabulary of such elements largely determines the method, since once we know what we are looking for, we hardly need a body of special expertise to tell us how to find it. Such a system is called a 'taxonomy of educational objectives'. Of these, Bloom's (Bloom, 1956) is the best known, but many local variants of Bloom's taxonomy have been developed too, and taxonomies of a different type have been produced by Guilford (1967), Gagne (1965), and others.

In theory such taxonomies should provide an efficient, accurate way to monitor the potent effect of the values implicit in a curriculum or an examination. The trouble is, however, that a taxonomy of objectives is yet another classification, which tends to impose its own bias *towards* certain values and *away* from others. It simplifies the educational reality and, in doing so, risks caricaturing it. There is also the basic difficulty of founding a taxonomy on a philosophically valid account of the aims of education. Such an account has to take fully into account both the social function of education and the intrinsic nature of the knowledge-cum-understanding-cum-creativity aimed at; and all this in addition to the usual constraints of psychological development. This is a huge problem. It is immediately evident that Bloom's taxonomy is mainly a product of psychological expertise, and that it virtually ignores two-thirds of the criteria which it ought to be at pains to fit. This is the drift of criticisms of the taxonomy as being 'epistemologically naîve' (Pring, 1971; Socket, 1971) and 'ill tuned to the needs of modern society' (Ormell, 1974).

New, more sensitive taxonomies will, undoubtedly, be devised: taxonomies are here to stay. It is unlikely that educationalists will cheerfully revert to a state of self-imposed ignorance about the values implicit in a curriculum or an examination. On the contrary, the topic is one of great social importance, and there is a rapidly growing awareness around the world that this is so. Everyone is interested in these values, because it is these values which largely determine what teachers teach and what children learn.

It may be noted that Flew (1976) argues that an intention to assess (not necessarily via national examinations) is intrinsic to the intention to educate. This is consistent with the view expressed in this chapter of the educational values as being essentially *distributive*. How can one tell whether children are achieving balance, wholeness, life, coherence, etc. (i.e., the aims implicit in the educational values) except by assessing them in some way?

Summary

A value is a particular type of motivation, which may be characterized as being long term, consistently expressed, stable, effort-intensive, and reasonably justified. Associated with the motivation is an exomotivation, i.e., a motivation to motivate others in the appropriate direction. An *educational* value is a second-order value which does, or should, *distribute* over ordinary first-order values, including moral, social, aesthetic, and intellectual values, and perhaps (if current trends of opinion prevail) over industrial, economic, developmental, and technological values too. An educational value is capable of having this 'distributive' action over ordinary values because it operates through the medium of the teacher-pupil relationship. What happens is that the teacher encourages the youngster to achieve qualities like balance, coherence, understanding, creativity *across* the first-order motivations. Unlike ordinary values, educational values are primarily expressed in, and through, the holder's *exo*motivations. It is only in the case of the so-called 'self-educated man' that the motivation side predominates.

The point of talking in terms of 'values' is that it enables us to reduce a consideration of very complex behaviours to a fairly small set of basic motivational ingredients.

Changes in the prevailing set of values in education are brought about by changes in our perception of the nature of society, and of the individual's relation to it. In other words, as society changes, some motivations come to play a larger part; and it may begin to seem to be appropriate to initiate children into the expression of these new motivations, or at least not to place barriers in their way. Other motivations may diminish in significance, relative to the total set. However, it is surprising how few values have become totally obsolescent: most of the old values are still needed somewhere, though perhaps in a diminished role.

Three potent sources of first-order values in schools are ideologically active teachers, the perception of what count as 'subjects', and the influence of external examinations. Each of these value-inputs is a potential source of imbalance of first-order values, and there are various kinds of checks and balances which may be operated here, in order to try to correct this tendency. In the end, however, it is to the characteristically *educational* values that we must turn in order to ensure that the overall mixture of motivations we transmit to the child will make sense in relation to the modern world.

References

Bernstein, B. (1971) 'On the classification and framing of educational knowledge' in Young, M.F.D. (ed), *Knowledge and Control*, London: Collier-Macmillan.

Adelman, C. and Ellott, J.H. (1973) 'Reflecting where the action is; the design of the Ford Teaching Project', *Education for Teaching*, November.

Bloom, B.S. et al. (1956) *A Taxonomy of Educational Objectives I*, London: Longman.

Bloom, B.S. et al. (1964) *A Taxonomy of Educational Objectives II*, London: Longman.

Chanan, G. and Gilchrist, L. (1974) *What School is For*, London: Methuen.

Flew, A.G.N. (1976) *Sociology, Equality and Education*, London: Macmillan, chapter VI.

Gagne, R. (1970) *The Conditions of Learning*, (2nd ed) New York: Holt, Rinehart and Winston.

Gibson, R. (1978) 'Chimerical concepts in educational research . . .', *British Educational Research Journal*, 4, 2, 91-96.

Guilford, J.P. (1966) *Fields of Psychology*, Princeton, N.J.: Van Nostrand.

James, Eric (1949) *An Essay on the Content of Education*, London: Harrap.

Kluckholm, C. (1951) 'Values and value orientations in the theory of action . . .' in T. Parsons and E.A. Shils (eds), *Towards a General Theory of Action*, Cambridge, Mass.: Harvard University Press.

Kohlberg, L. et al. (1970) *Moral Education: Five Lectures*, Boston: Harvard University Press.

Najder, Z. (1975) *Values and Evaluation*, Oxford: Clarendon Press.

Ormell, C.P. (1974) 'Bloom's Taxonomy and the objectives of education', *Educational Research*, 17, 3-18.

Ormell, C.P. (1975) 'Towards a naturalistic mathematics in the sixth form', *Physics Education*, 10, 5, 349-354.

Ormell, C.P. (1976) 'On the balance of the content of education', *Educational Research*, 18, 3, 163-173.

Ormell, C.P. (1977) 'Is there a hidden curriculum in mathematics?', *Power and the Curriculum*, Nafferton Books, 109-116.

Ormell, C.P. (1978) 'La manipulacion de los objetivos en la educacion', *Editorial Adara*.

Piaget, J. (1932) *The Moral Judgement of the Child*, London: Routledge & Kegan Paul.

Popper, Sir K.R. (1976) *Unended Quest: An Intellectual Autobiography*, London: Fontana/Collins.

Pring, R. (1971) 'Bloom's Taxonomy: a philosophical critique 2', *Cambridge Journal of Education*, 2, 89.
Sockett, H. (1971) 'Bloom's Taxonomy: a philosophical critique 1', *Cambridge Journal of Education*, 1, 23.
White, John P. (1978) 'The aims of education: three legacies of the British idealists', *Journal of the Philosophy of Education*, 12, 5-12.
Whitehead, A.N. (1929) *The Aims of Education*, London: Benn.

SECTION II

VALUES AND EVALUATION IN SPECIFIC AREAS OF THE CURRICULUM

CHAPTER 7

WHAT ARE THE MAIN ISSUES?

The first section of this book has dealt with matters of a necessarily generalized kind which we claim are relevant to *all* levels and areas of education. The points which have so far emerged, however, concerning the nature of educational values and evaluation and the interrelationships between them are also highly applicable to more specific areas of the school curriculum and to the practical business of 'teaching a subject'.

Clearly, in any form of teaching, decisions and choices have to be made at some level about *what* is to be taught and *how* it is to be taught; and equally clearly, such decisions and choices will reflect particular emphases and priorities which indicate the holding of certain values. Likewise, decisions about how to evaluate pupils' knowledge and understanding within any area of the curriculum must also involve the making of value-judgements. It might be said that to teach any subject successfully one needs first to be clear about the values which the subject stands for, and secondly, to be able to evaluate whether those values are in fact getting across to the pupils.

But where exactly do these values come from, how are they to be identified, and how do they influence the teaching and the testing of a subject? These are the general questions with which this section will be concerned, and we shall see how different answers are offered by different subject-specialists. One common factor of crucial importance, however, can be isolated at this point before the reader embarks upon the following chapters.

Interpretations of any subject vary. This may sound an obvious and unexciting claim, but it lies at the heart of most disputes about educational values and evaluation. Nor is it in fact so universally accepted as one might suppose, even among teachers. A history teacher will, one hopes, be aware that there are differing views among historians as to the precise nature of history and the procedures of historical inquiry, but he may well never have considered that the same situation exists within science or mathematics; we tend to feel, if we ever think about it, that other subjects about which we know little are less problematic and controversial than our own.

Different views about the nature of a subject, then, produce different sets of values, and it will be seen in the following chapters that this is the case not only in a subject like art (where Fraser Smith classifies various stereotypes of art teacher, such as 'High Priests', 'Technocrats', and 'Social Workers', each of which exhibit distinctive clusters of values), but also in areas like mathematics (where Christopher Ormell describes two schools of thought within the subject, claiming that it is 'the coexistence of these rival views of mathematics itself which gives rise to conflicts of values in the classroom'). An important element, therefore, in most of the chapters in this section will be an examination of the nature of the subject under discussion and of how this can be differently conceived.

The values associated with a subject on the school curriculum can be of varying types, and these will all be illustrated in the following chapters. They may, for example, be intellectual values, such as concern for truth, validity in argument, respect for evidence, and critical appraisal, to which Raymond Davies refers in his discussion of history; or they may be moral values of the kind that Raymond Wilson claims for great literature, which 'habituates the learner to the virtue and nobility it portrays'; or they may be instrumental values, like the 'strong emotional satisfaction' which some art teachers see as a therapeutic effect of their subject; or they may have overtones of social appraisal and approval such as the 'appropriateness' and 'correctness' of language, which Desmond Vowles discusses.

So do values enter in these ways into all subjects? It is commonly assumed that this is not the case, and that some subjects, notably science and mathematics, are in some sense 'value-free', but this view is strongly opposed in Chapters 12 and 13 which deal with these two subjects. A parallel assumption is that measurement, assessment, and evaluation are much easier and more 'objective' in the sciences than in the arts, because there is greater agreement about how to test the truth of statements in the former than in the latter. This assumption will also be questioned at times and discussed at greater length in our concluding overview. However, these twin assumptions, false though they may be, suggest a structure and sequence for this section, which may help the reader to see the various curriculum areas in the form of a continuum, stretching from what are often thought to be the most value-laden, 'subjective', and unassessable provinces of the arts, through the intermediate no man's land of history, towards the allegedly value-free, 'objective', easily assessed territory of the sciences. The section accordingly begins with chapters on language, literature, and art, then considers history, and concludes with accounts of science and mathematics. Some further comment on the obscure notions of 'subjectivity' and 'objectivity' will be made in our overview.

This structure explains to some extent the selection of subjects for this section but something must be said at this point about its inevitable limitations and omissions. We are not claiming that these subjects hold any particular, distinctive status, other than that they represent a reasonable spread of the arts and sciences and are in practice major components of most school curricula; had space allowed, other subjects could have been included (e.g., music, religious and moral education, geography, physical education) and analysed in the same kind of way. Nor should it be assumed from the contents of this section that we are advocating a 'subject-based' form of curriculum rather than an 'integrated' one; even the most 'integrated' of curricula will presumably contain elements of science, history, mathematics, literature, language, and art, and the issues discussed in the following chapters are thus applicable to the basic ingredients of any curriculum, however those ingredients are mixed and served up. Nor do we wish to maintain that values can be expressed and transmitted only through the medium of teaching a subject, for this would be to ignore the obvious and potent influence of the 'hidden curriculum'; clearly children can be influenced by the values of individual teachers and of educational institutions in numerous indirect, informal ways, but it would need another book at least to deal adequately with these kinds of interaction.

Finally, before letting the reader loose on Section II, we want to underline and expand two points which were made in the Preface. Firstly, all the following chapters are intended to be suitable reading for all teachers or prospective teachers. Although each chapter will probably be of greatest interest to someone who is or will be concerned with teaching that particular subject, it should be possible for any intelligent reader without specialist knowledge of the subject to follow the thread of the argument and grasp the essential points; indeed, in view of the book's overall emphasis upon the interrelationships between values and evaluation throughout education, it is vital that teachers should realize that the same sorts of problem and issue arise within all areas of the curriculum. Secondly, the perceptive reader should notice that the contributors do not aim to present a totally united front, and some disagreement is evident at times (compare, for example, the accounts of the nature of science given by David Malvern and Raymond Wilson). Such disagreements, when they occur, serve to highlight the most contentious issues; they are also an invitation to the reader to probe the values which lie behind the conflicting positions and to form his own evaluation of the arguments.

R.S.
J.W.

CHAPTER 8

LANGUAGE
Desmond Vowles

'Times change: values don't': so the billboards proclaim in a recent series of advertisements. A more relevant juxtaposition for our discussion would be: 'Times change: language must'. Yet this apparently simple aphorism, which professional linguists would take as commonplace, creates an astonishing emotional blockage in the minds of many of those whose everyday job it is to evaluate language in the classroom and in the exercise book.

The two words most often used in this connection are 'intelligibility' (applied to speech) and 'correctness' (more frequently applied to written language). It will be necessary to examine each of these concepts in turn, in order to see how social and professional attitudes have changed towards them in recent years. But first, an important distinction must be made, as Jeremy Warburg makes in a valuable little pamphlet, *The Best-Chosen English* (Warburg, 1961), between language as meaning and language as vehicle.

To quote Warburg,

> English may be considered well-chosen or badly-chosen. In either case, such views may be based, wholly or in part, on an evaluation of the choice of *meanings* which English reflects in a given instance: the language is good or bad, that is, because it is thought that the sayer has used it to communicate good (valuable) or bad (valueless) meanings. On the other hand, such views may be based on the choice of *means* in a given instance: the language is good or bad, that is, because it is thought that the sayer has used good (successful) or bad (unsuccessful) means to communicate whatever meanings he or she intended to communicate.

In this short chapter, emphasis will be placed on language as *means* – 'the effectualness with which one communicates whatever meanings one chooses to communicate' – as it is this aspect, the externals of language as it were, with which teachers are most immediately and often obsessively confronted. Language is clearly more – much more – than vehicle: recent attempts to communicate with young chimpanzees and to teach them not only vocabulary but also linguistic structures show all too clearly what mankind would have been if its utterances had been limited to 'Roger Washoe Tickle' or 'Sarah take jam-bread' – and these were the results of two years' intensive training! (Gardner and Gardner, 1969).

Yet to evaluate the language we ourselves use is to attempt the impossible: we inhabit our language as we inhabit our physical selves. Although it is possible to look critically at these words as they create themselves on paper before the writer's eye, or to listen dispassionately to one's own voice on a tape-recording, this is far from being an exercise in evaluation. For the disembodied voice and the stylized lines of print are no more the totality of language than the ordnance survey map is the countryside or the townscape which it attempts to represent.

But ironically the process of evaluation of the language of others – a process which implies necessarily the assumption of values – is a process which, certainly as far as the *spoken* language is concerned, every Englishman is daily, even hourly, engaged upon with a mixture of fascination and distaste. Unlike the average American citizen, who is generally content to receive aural information about the regional provenance of any other American, and to leave it at that, English men and women are never wholly at ease with one another until they have placed all those they encounter not only geographically (and this sometimes with great precision as between one town or village and the next), but also socially, economically, and educationally. For this process the Englishman is equipped with a pair of linguistic antennae which respond to the smallest nuances of pronunciation, intonation, and stress.

In the famous 'Paddington Station' experiment, carried out by the Oxford University Institute of Experimental Psychology (Sissons, 1971), the effects of language on others (though unfortunately coupled in this case with physical appearance) were shown all too clearly. An actor wearing middle-class commuter clothing, and using the appropriate accent and style of address, approached a variety of respondents on Paddington Station, asking them for directions to Hyde Park. The experiment was then repeated with the same actor in working-class clothing (denim jacket and slacks) again simulating the appropriate accent and speech-pattern. Thirty interactions were filmed, and respondents were approached and asked to furnish information about their own social class.

Correlations were made between the amount of 'smiling time' (as a measure of friendship) and the social class of respondents, showing, as might have been expected, that 'friendliness' was most manifest where there was a match in social class between the actor and his respondent; and also, perhaps more surprisingly, that 'working-class respondents do not smile much of the time to either class of the actor'.

A more interesting evaluation would have been to study the effects of a mismatch between appearance and voice, a situation we are all familiar with when the elderly 'gardener' raking the leaves in soiled corduroys and dirty cap turns out to have the voice of the retired Army officer which he in fact is, or the television commercial in which the soignée debutante figure has the give-a-way accents of an unregenerate Eliza Doolittle. Indeed, it is often forgotten how far ahead of his time Shaw was, in this as in other things, when he stated in his preface to *Pygmalion* 'an honest slum dialect is more tolerable than the attempts of phonetically untaught persons to imitate the plutocracy'. This, at a time when the Society for Pure (sic) English was gaining the support of such notable men of letters as Robert Bridges.

This, the Pygmalion myth, that phonetic drills can effect social change, still dies hard: a generation or so ago 'elocution' lessons were *de rigeur* in independent girls' schools. There remains within the teaching profession a strong feeling, certainly predating the Bernstein era, but strongly reinforced by his work, of the inherent inferiority of working-class speech and of dialectal variants of received pronunciation. By the time that Bernstein's original research had been assimilated second-hand at the training colleges, and purveyed third-hand to classroom practitioners, the linguistically descriptive terms 'restricted code' and 'elaborated code', far from being, as their progenitor no doubt intended, value-free, had become associated respectively with the idea of narrowness, confinement, even imprisonment on the one hand, and with fullness and exactness on the other. Thus working-class speech has been consistently devalued, and a degree of (no doubt unconscious) discrimination against its users has been practised.

There must be every sympathy with the view that any interference (however well-intentioned) with the home language of a child is a direct and explicit attack not only upon the individual, but upon the values of that home. To put it more explicitly: if a 'middle-class' teacher criticizes adversely the spontaneous utterance of a child, he is driving a linguistic wedge between that child and his parents. This may on occasions be necessary: it should always be handled with tact and with a full understanding of its social and personal implications. At the same time it must not be forgotten that the five puny periods a week in which English is being 'taught' contribute merely a drop to the language-bath of home, street, and playground, in which the child is immersed for the remainder of his waking hours, for the teacher is *not* a parent, still less a member of the peer-group; and although many teachers now accept that they are no longer raised above the children they teach on a platform of correctness, a deep division of opinion is emerging between the 'cherishers' and the 'improvers'.

This debate is currently finding expression in the pages of *The Use of English* magazine, where a sympathetic review of Peter Trudgill's book, *Accent, Dialect and the School* (Trudgill, 1975) (itself a by-product of the influential Schools Council *Language in Use* project), called forth an angry response from A.C. Capey (himself the co-author of another Schools Council English project) under the heading *Fair Attitude(s)?* (Capey, 1978).

The basic confusion here is that Trudgill is writing as a linguistician and making (or attempting to make) value-free statements about the nature and use of language-variants which are in his terms unexceptionable. But Trudgill is writing for practising teachers and it is when he moves from the rational, linguistically descriptive statement, 'There is no way in which one variety of language can be considered superior to another', to the apparent prescriptiveness of 'children should not be asked to change or even modify their accents', that he is in deep trouble, and has called down upon himself the wrath of the 'improvers'. For it is one thing to assert – as Harold Rosen and his disciples do – the validity of urban working-class speech, and quite another to claim that it is adequate for all social purposes: 'any subject can be dealt with in any dialect' (Trudgill).

To take but one dialectal example drawn from a rural area: if we examine 'Gloucestershire English', we find that the common form of greeting between acquaintances is 'How bist?' The verb 'to be' is here declined in its weak form: I be, thou beest, he be, we/you/they be. There is good historical and regional precedent for this – it is 'correct' and it is totally unambiguous. But it is a variant from the accepted norm as gross as those grammatical forms with which we are familiar in Caribbean English, 'The man die after he had drank the poison', or in Asian English, 'Yesterday this man is telling me I am not filling in form correctly'.

For in spite of the widening of range (and of the tolerance of the speech of others) with which television has made us aware through such programmes as *When the Boat Comes In*, *Coronation Street*, and *Crossroads*, there is still a remarkable degree of conformity in the aural media to the norm of southern English received pronunciation, as witness national newsreaders and even disc-jockeys. Male or female, young or old, they talk within a comparatively narrow range of pronunciation and intonation patterns. The wartime experiment (on radio) of permitting Wilfred Pickles to read the national news in a modified version of his northern accent has never been repeated, and even the occasional West Indian and Asian reporters who appear on the television screen today betray no trace of dialectal variation. (It is true that local radio has done something to counteract this trend; but this is merely reinforcing local speech-patterns, not making them available nationwide.)

All, therefore, that Trudgill appears to be saying is that it is grammatically and lexically feasible for any subject to be dealt with in any dialect, and dialectal versions of the Lord's Prayer and the New Testament exist as linguistic curiosities to back his argument.

At this point, therefore, our discussion may well move from a consideration of intelligibility to look at that other will-o'-the-wisp, correctness, for it needs to be stated clearly that because a particular language form is used *somewhere*, it does not follow that it is socially acceptable to use it *anywhere*. There is nothing new in the problem of dialectalism: as far back as 1125, William of Malmesbury – a southerner – was writing (in Latin, and was translated by John de Trevisa in 1350): 'Al the langage of the Northumbres and specialliche at York is so sharp, slitting and frotynge and unshathe, that we southerne men may that language unnethe understonde.'

It was of course largely a geographical accident – the incidence of London, Oxford, and Cambridge – that led to the supremacy of southern English, and it was left to Caxton to wrestle with the problem of turning a flexible and unwieldy group of dialects into a single entity: 'Loo, what sholde a man in thyse dayes now wryte, egges or eyren. Certaynly it is harde to playse every man, by cause of dyversite and chaunge of language' (quoted in Jespersen, 1938).

By the end of the fifteenth century, standard (printed) English of a sort had been established, although even a hundred years later pronunciation was largely unstandardized – as witness Raleigh's unmistakeable West country accent at the Elizabethan court (and we are reminded of Wordsworth, two centuries later, with the strong northern burr which helped to alienate him from his fellow-students). It was the critics of the Renaissance who first turned their attention to the weighty problem of keeping the infant English language 'pure' and free from taints of inkhorn terms and excessive borrowing from other European languages.

From the time of the battle-cry of Mulcaster – the first English teacher – 'I honour the Latin, but I worship the English' – it was clear that the language of the Renaissance was to be English rather than any classical tongue, and for more than fifty years the battle raged between those who considered (with Ascham) that 'everything in English is written in a manner so meanly that no man could do worse', and those who thought that English was 'in itself sufficient and copious enough'.

So English continued on a course of its own, testing, sifting, rejecting, or accepting the flood of foreign (and dialectal) terms that seemed likely to swamp it, and emerging at the close of the sixteenth century as the unrivalled literary language of Europe, the language of Shakespeare and the Bible, the language of 'the multitudinous seas incarnadine' and 'pray you, undo this button'.

During all this time critical emphasis had been upon the detailed elements of the language, especially vocabulary: with the coming of the Restoration and a new critical temper, the apostles of plainness, led by Joseph Sprat and the Fellows of the Royal Society, held the day. English had proved its worth as a literary test: the question now was how was it to be fixed at its peak of perfection for all generations to come? Dryden grumbled, 'We have yet no English prosodia, not so much as a tolerable dictionary or a grammar, so that our language is in a manner barbarous.' Still the emphasis was on repelling foreign lexical invasions: Addison, at the beginning of the eighteenth century, wished that there were 'superintendants of language' for the express purpose of keeping out the French phrases which war correspondents were introducing into their articles. At the back of his fear – 'that it would be impossible for one of our great-grandfathers to know what his posterity have been doing' – lies the persisting doctrine that language should not be allowed to change from its then state of refinement, an obsession which is with us still, as we shall see.

It took the sound common sense of Dr. Johnson to realize that in the end a language must always be subject to change, and to laugh to scorn Swift's hare-brained scheme for an academy 'for ascertaining and fixing our language for ever' as being written 'without much knowledge of the general nature of language, and without any accurate enquiry into the history of other tongues'.

Yet it is precisely this feeling that there can be – and should be – a fixed or final form of English that persisted so strongly into the early years of this century, and underlay the work of the Fowlers, who, ill-intentioned though we now find them to be, did attempt to introduce the concept of *appropriateness*. Today heterodoxy appears to have replaced orthodoxy, and with it the authority of the English teacher, in so far as it ever rested on sound linguistic foundations, has vanished.

Or has it? In their interesting and valuable research project carried out at the University of Newcastle, and now overdue for replication, W.H. Mittins and his associates presented a number of sample 'consumer groups' (teachers, examiners, salesmen, professional writers) with a series of fifty current usages in speech and writing, asking them to evaluate these as 'acceptable' or 'unacceptable' in both formal and informal situations, by applying the test of 'appropriateness' (Mittins et al., 1970). In fact, they were relying on each respondent's intuitive and subjective judgement.

Although the span of acceptability among the different respondents was great (reflecting no doubt their own individual upbringing and formal education), there was a surprisingly wide measure of agreement. For example, the usage 'very unique' was unacceptable to all but 11 percent of the sample; whereas the use of 'contemporary', as a synonym for 'modern' in the phrase 'contemporary furniture', was found acceptable by 70 percent of the respondents.

Not all the items were lexical, and it is disturbing (or is it?) that the prepositional usage in the sentence 'she told Charles and I the whole story' was 'acceptable' to over a quarter of the respondents; and since 1970 this 'ungrammatical' use of the 'incorrect' case appears to be gaining ground steadily. (For those who would take as their standard of reference that emotive yardstick, The Queen's English, there is an irony in noting that one of the first recorded examples of this usage outside 'vulgar' speech comes from her father's letter to Churchill in 1944: 'I have come to the conclusion that it would not be right for either you or I to be where we planned to be on D-Day.')

So far this chapter has been dealing largely with problems of values as expressed through the spoken language: but it is in terms of written language that most teachers judge and most students are judged. Indeed, if asked to declare their primary task as teachers of language, many English teachers, whilst seeing themselves clearly as 'enablers' (those who create conditions under which children may speak and write with freedom and with sensitivity), would also rate highly in a list of priorities their function as 'correcters', those whose professional task it is to 'correct' the language used by their students. The precise ratio between 'enabling' and 'correcting' would vary between one teacher and another, but, certainly as far as the written language is concerned, 'correcting' is a burden that has to be borne.

And a wearisome task it is, too, as witness the young schoolmaster D.H. Lawrence:

> No longer now can I endure the brunt
> Of the books that lie out on the desks; a full three-score
> Of several insults of blotted pages, and scrawl
> Of slovenly work that they have offered me.

And over a generation later, Margaret Langdon, that great 'enabler', in her Wiltshire village school suffered in the same way:

> I mark one, then another, and yet another, scratching through the dumb phrases, the uninspired thoughts, the platitudinous expressions, and end with an unenthusiastic 'Fair', and a private thought, 'What's the use?'. (Langdon, 1961)

Now it must be said that English teachers, as a group, exhibit every indication of an obsession with the externals of written language, its physical appearance in terms of calligraphy and orthography, as witness almost any English teachers' conference, on whatsoever topic, which will rarely get under way for more than a few minutes without the twin topics of spelling and punctuation being raised.

So we return to the distinction made at the beginning of this chapter. Is language the thing said, or the way of saying it? Are we, as teachers, concerned with process, or with product? And how far does our perception of the ideal marriage between content and expression, between means and meaning, influence our day-to-day evaluation of written work?

The practical problems may best be illustrated by a fairly detailed look at one piece of writing, the product of a boy of fourteen-plus in a secondary modern school. Entitled 'The Visit', it was written under examination conditions during a period of an hour and a half:

> It looked like being a good day when I got out of bed on that peaceful Friday morning. The sun was streaming through the window, and I could hear the chirping of a blackbird out in the garden. I pulled back the sheets, and got out of bed on to the cold lino. I went to the bathroom, had a wash, and then got dressed. When I got down to the kitchen my mother said, 'I have a nice surprise for you.'
>
> 'Oh, what's that?' I asked, picking up my coffee.

'Your Aunt Maud is coming to stay with us for the weekend.'

'Aunt Maud? Oh, no!' I was so horrified at the thought of this that before I knew what had happened the cup of coffee slipped through my fingers and smashed on to the floor.

'You are clumsy today,' she said. 'Look at my nice clean floor.' I was rooted to the spot, my mind vividly recalling what had happened last time she had come.

'Why couldn't someone start a Third World War?' I said.

'Now, Stephen, you mustn't talk like that. I know Aunt Maud's a bit of a busybody. . . .'

'Busybody! That's putting it lightly. The silly old cuckoo!' I said under my breath.

The day was spent preparing the house. We had to put up the camp-bed in the dining-room for me to sleep on, while Aunt Maud had my bed. How I hated Aunt Maud! I had to keep on going down to the shops after little dribs and drabs. Out came the best china and cutlery: what all the fuss was for I don't know. When I woke up on Saturday morning it was pouring with rain. I never heard the blackbird sing, but instead I heard the unmistakeable voice of Aunt Maud.

'Where's Stephen?' she said, in a high-pitched witch-like voice. 'Still up in bed most likely. Typical of the youngsters today. Now, when I was young. . . .'

'Oh Christ, it's here! What have I done to deserve this?' I said, pulling the sheets over my head.

When I got downstairs I was still half-asleep. I had hardly slept a wink last night thinking of Aunt Maud, and I walked straight past her.

'Humph. That's a fine thing, walking straight past me without even a "hallo"!' I stopped, turned, and came face to face with her. She was thin and upright, and for a moment I thought I saw fangs coming out of her mouth.

'Oh, 'morning, Aunt Maud. Had a nice trip down?' I said, trying to be civil.

'Yes, thanks,' she said.

'What a shame,' I thought.

'If the rain leaves off, will you run me into Slough on your motor-bike?' she said.

Last time she said that I shouldn't have had a motor-bike and that they were death-traps. Now because the bus fares had gone up she wanted me to take her.

'Yeah, I s'pose.'

I had breakfast, and then I was ready. I put on my leather jacket and my crash-hat, and waited outside my gate revving up my Royal Enfield 250 Olympic. Before she had got on properly I had changed into first and was away. As I turned the corner at the end of our road, I heeled my bike over so that the footrest scraped the road. I went straight across the Crispin Corner. My Aunt was screaming in my ear to stop, and when I stopped, she got off my machine and staggered away. I rode around for about an hour, and when I got home I found my Aunt's cases packed, and she was ready to leave.

My mother and father smiled at me as she walked down the path and out of the gate.

The response of most experienced teachers upon reading this piece – and more still upon hearing it read aloud – is that it exhibits many of the qualities that they hope to find in children's spontaneous and uninhibited writing today. The short-story form is handled with some skill; the characters, including that of the narrator, are shrewdly observed, and quickly and boldly presented; the dialogue is naturalistic and immediate; the pathetic fallacy (the rain and the voice of the blackbird) is handled with confidence; the swing from realism into adolescent fantasy at the close is not without irony; and the climax is economical and witty. True, there is some clumsiness in the opening paragraph – the repetition of 'got' is an example – while the writer is still feeling his way; but the overall impression is of a lively and confident writer who is in control of his medium. On a 10-point scale most experienced teachers will award this story an impression mark of 8. Some are prepared to go even higher.

But when we come to look at what the boy actually wrote on his examination paper (and a printed transcript cannot of course convey the additional prejudicial impression made by slovenly and ill-formed handwriting), we are faced with a very different picture.

Here – reproduced as exactly as possible – is the actual script:

It looked like being a good day when I got out of bed on that picefull friday morning. The sun was striming through the window and I could here the cerping of a blackbird out in the garden. I pulled back the shelts and got out of bed onto the cold lino. I went to the bathroom had a wash and then go dressed. When I got down to the kitchen my mother Said, "I have a nice supprise for you." "Oh whats that", I asked picking up my coffe. "Yor Ant Morde is coming to stay with us for the week end. Ant Morde ow no," I was so horifided at the thought of this that befire I knew what happened the cup of coffe sliped through my fingers and smashed onto the floor. "You are clumse to day", she Said, "Look at my nice clean floor. "I was ruted to the spot my mind vividley recorling what had happened last time she had come. "Why couldent some-one start a third world war," I said. "Now Stephen you musent talk like that. I know Ant Mord's a bit of a biseybody." "Biesbody! thaths putting it lightly. The silly old Cock Coo," I said under my breath. The day was spent preparing the house. We had to put up the camp bed in the dining room for me to sleep on wile Ant Morde had my bed. Hou I hated Ant Morde. I had to keep on going down to the shops after littel dribs and drabs. Out came the best china and cullery, what all the fuss was for I dont know. When I woke up on Saterday morning It was poring rain. I never hered the blackbird sing by insted I herd the unmustackabeld voice of Ant Morde.

"Whers Stephen," she said in a high pitched which like voice, "Still up in bed most likely. typical of the youngster's today. No when I was yong." "Oh Christ its here what have I done to deserve this", I said pulling the shetts overe my head. When I got downstairs I was still half aslep. I had hardly sleped a wink last night thinking of ant Mord and I walk straight past here. "Humph thats a fine thing walking straight passed me with out even a halow." I stoped turned and came face to face with here. She was thin and upright and for a moment I thought I saw fangs coming out of her mouth. "Oh 'morning ant morde had a nice trip down," I said trying to be seviel. "Yes thanks," she Said "What a shame I thought. "If the rane leaves of will you run me into slough on your motor bike," she said Last time she said that I shoudent of had a motor bike and that they were death traps. Now because the bus fairs had goon up she wanted me to take here. "Year I spose" I had breakfast and then I was ready. I put on my leather jacket and my crash hat and wated outside my gate reving up my Royal Enfield 250 olympick. Before she had gotton on prpely I had changed into first and was away. As I turned the corner at the end of our road a heald my bike over so at the footrest scraped the road. I went straight across the Crispin Cornere, My ant was screming in my ear to stop and when I stoped she got of my machine and stagerd away. I road around for about an hour, and when I got home I found my ant's cases packed and she was ready to leave. My mother and father smiled at me as she walked out of the gate and down the path.

To save the reader a deal of laborious work, it can be stated that there are some 125 formal errors, whether of spelling, punctuation, or syntax, in about 600 words. Clearly the writer is far from 'literate'; and many assessors react strongly to the script itself by downgrading their original impression mark to 5 or 6 (in itself an equivocating signal).

Yet if we look in more detail at the form this 'illiteracy' takes, we note that it is impossible to categorize the writer as (to take one criterion only) a 'bad speller': certainly, many simple words are either misspelt or spelt variably – *supprise, coffe, ant, rane* – but many of the spellings can be seen to be straightforward phonetic confusions – *witch/which, fair/fare* – or clearly errors made by a rapid writer who is concentrating on the effort of story-making: such words as *shelts* (for sheets), *here* (for her), *of* (for off). But when we look at some of the words that a fourteen-year-old of average ability might be expected to have difficulty with, we find that *kitchen, typical, breakfast, machine* are all correctly spelt.

More important, however, than this detailed error-analysis – and the same process could be carried out for punctuation and for syntactical errors – is the realization that, with all its blemishes, the piece can still communicate effectively to the reader, and his reading fluency is hardly, if at all, impaired. This impales the evaluator firmly on the horns of the English teacher's eternal dilemma: if he continues to award the piece of writing an overall above-average grade, he appears to be condoning sloppy and inaccurate presentation, and to lay himself wide open to the charge of 'encouraging illiteracy'; if on the other hand he penalizes content in his search for the mirage of total accuracy, he appears to be saying that table manners are more important than the quality of the food.

Nor is there any escape by means of a dual evaluation: 8/10 for content plus 4/10 for accuracy still produces an overall 12/20 – and whatever the virtues or vices of such a piece of writing it is *not* an example of average mediocrity.

In such a situation where can teachers and other professional evaluators look for help? Before the recent arrival on the scene of the Assessment of Performance Unit (Language), whose criteria for language-assessment are as yet not fully and publicly declared, the first time that language is, as it were, held up for public scrutiny and accountability is through the implied value-systems of the various G.C.E. and C.S.E. Examination Boards. It might be assumed, then, that teachers, employers, and students could look to them for a clear statement of aims and objectives in language-evaluation.

In fact, of the eight G.C.E. Boards, only two make any statement of objectives at all, and one of these, the Joint Matriculation Board, hides behind a smokescreen of abstract nouns, asking its candidates to reveal 'the ability to write with facility, clarity, and accuracy, and . . . to use a vocabularly appropriate to an Ordinary Level candidate's age, experience and needs', as though an 'O'-level candidate had some kind of independent existence outside the examination room. The C.S.E. Boards, as might be expected in view of their more recent emergence, are more forthcoming, but even here many questions are begged: 'to develop the candidate's abilities in the basic communication skills of the English language. . . .' (East Midlands Regional Examination's Board) or '. . . to make correct use of written and spoken English' (Associated Lancashire Schools Examining Board).

Against this vagueness and imprecision of aim must be set the complex realities of today's classrooms, full as they are of children of widely different abilities from widely different cultural, linguistic, and ethnic backgrounds. Any discussion of language values and evaluation today must therefore take account not merely of the regional and social class differences mentioned earlier, but of the demanding and often puzzling situation created by the sizeable number of children whom we still confusingly refer to as 'immigrants'. Increasingly they are no longer immigrants, but second-generation English boys and girls, born in Britain, but speaking at home either a totally 'foreign' language, or some extreme form of patois. Many of these children, so far from lacking linguistic ability, are coping daily with three or four working languages, and very complex patterns of bilingualism are developing. One of the most disturbing examples concerns a growing number of second-generation West Indian settlers. Whereas black parents demand of the schools that their children become proficient in standard written and spoken English, for obvious vocational reasons, the black youths themselves are rapidly creating an exclusive 'Rasta' subculture, deliberately using language to isolate themselves from the whole community, and to exclude their teachers.

So, finally, we return to the important question of language and personal identity – language as 'the most prized possession of a human being': at the moment too many of our curricular assumptions are based on the premise that the minority communities do not exist, or are not there except when 'problems' arise that directly affect them. But if schools are to be, and are to continue to be, places for everyone in the community, language policies, not only within the English department but, as the Bullock Report clearly underlines, 'across the curriculum', have to become a reality.

The resulting dialogue, amongst the teachers themselves, between teachers, parents, and employers, between traditionalists and radicals, between 'enablers' and 'correcters', will be a complex and disturbing one, but it has to be. In the course of it, teachers may well have to re-examine very carefully their own attitudes and prejudices towards the language *they* use in the classroom, and to the demands they make of the children with whom they are working.

Let one such child speak for himself in conclusion, a small boy in his first term at secondary school, attempting, however inadequately, to use language to communicate to an adult the sense of isolation and tension he feels in a situation he cannot control. He was meant to be writing a 'story': instead he has put something of himself on paper, with the implied demand that must always be there every time we use language to communicate with others: 'evaluate *me*'.

When i am at school i am in a dream world i don't like going into the class if I
am the last one every one stairs at you and I feal a right twit and the teacher
asked what are you late for I often say i was late coming from the other lesson

or other wise they give you lines to do saying i must not be late for lessons. This is about a boy who always gets into trouble. One day he went into the class and he told a lie so he got the cane on his hands. he always stole things off other people. One day he got into a fight he starrted it and got the cane he was allways getting the cane allways. he allways wanted to be a footballer.

References

Capey, A.C. (1978) *Fair Attitude(s)?*, in *The Use of English*, Vol. 29, No. 2.

Gardner, B.T. and Gardner, R.A. (1969) 'Teaching sign language to a chimpanzee', *Science*, p. 165.

Jespersen, O. (1938) *Growth and Structure of the English Language*, Oxford: Basil Blackwell.

Langdon, M. (1961) *Let the Children Write*, London: Longmans.

Mittins, W.H. et al. (1970) *Attitudes to English Usage*, London: Oxford University Press.

Sissons, M. (1971) *The Psychology of Social Class* (Open University Course D100 Unit 18), Milton Keynes: Open University.

Trudgill, P. (1975) *Accent, Dialect and the School*, London: Edward Arnold.

Warburg, J. (1961) *The Best-Chosen English*, London: University College.

CHAPTER 9

LITERATURE
Raymond Wilson

'. . . such as accustome themselves, and are familiar with the best Authors, shall ever and anon find somewhat of them in themselves . . .'

Ben Jonson

'. . . a man who is *emotionally* educated is rare as a phoenix . . .'

D.H. Lawrence

In recent years there has been an unhappy tendency for travel agencies to refer to their brochures and handouts collectively as 'literature'. As the word becomes more and more appropriated by advertisers and bureaucrats, it will predictably follow the word 'culture' in becoming intractably ambiguous and we shall have to ask ourselves, when we meet with it, whether 'literature' any longer relates to literary achievement or is merely used to designate any kind of printed matter, without regard to quality. But for the present and in the context of education, the word 'literature' retains its traditional sense and is, in itself, affirmative of achieved value. Literature is (as examination papers from 'O' level to degree level confirm) the published work of such literary geniuses as Shakespeare or Wordsworth or William Golding, not the hack journalism of Grub Street nor the thousands of blessedly forgotten three-decker Victorian novels nor the pulp romances and cretinous best-sellers displayed by newsagents. Merely to *use* the word literature of a piece of writing is to confer a kind of accolade on it and affirm that it has value.

A sceptic might at this point inquire who exactly determines whether a book is in fact a work of literature or something of lesser worth, like a piece of journalism or pornography. The only answer possible is, surely, that the matter is decided not at all democratically, by an appeal to public opinion, but by a minority within the public who claim competence in the passing of literary judgement: publishers, literary agents, librarians, critics, teachers of English, examiners, and 'informed' readers dispersed throughout society. Following Coleridge, we might call this educated minority a 'clerisy'. But, it may be asked, isn't it desirable that decisions about what constitutes or what does not constitute literature should be taken out of the hands of a clerisy which, given the egalitarianism of the times, is bound to be branded as élitist? Should not *all* those whose mother tongue is English make the decision, rather than a minority? If we all speak English, shouldn't it follow that we can all judge the merit of a book written in English?

The answer to every such question can only be no. Confusion arises because English, in its literary use, is by and large 'language such as men do use'. It is, characteristically, everyday language; but it is everyday language that is sufficiently heightened to be often beyond the reach of many or even most of those who speak it. This is not generally understood and is, indeed, often resented. The curious fact is that people who sheepishly confess to their own linguistic inadequacy when confronted with the rather specialized English of their income tax forms are often strongly resistant to recognizing their inadequacy when they are brought face to face with the far more subtly specialized language of a poem or play or novel. Public prejudice has it that poetry is typically a woolly and verbose way of saying something simple. Only the clerisy are aware that it is typically the most exact and condensed shorthand for expressing what is complex, and it is *they* who determine what counts as literature in education, just as certainly as other minorities within the population – mathematicians, historians, and chemists – determine what mathematics or history or chemistry will be in education.

In general it is true that most art, including literature, is at some level, though it may be an extremely naïve level, more accessible to the layman than the huge bulk of mathematics or science. However untutored in fine art someone may be, if he is shown the *Mona Lisa* he can confidently volunteer that it is a portrait of a lady – a judgement which, so far as it goes, is impeccable. Given a bare literacy, anyone can read:

> The flowers appear on the earth;
> the time for the singing of birds is come,
> and the voice of the turtle is heard in the land

and firmly assert that nature is the subject. But brought up against:

$$\cos(n\theta) + i\sin(n\theta) = e^{in\theta}$$
$$\text{or} \quad {}^{37}_{17}\text{Cl} + \upsilon \rightarrow {}^{37}_{18}\text{A} + \beta^-$$

the layman without an 'A' level in mathematics or physics admits to instant defeat. He knows he is unable to make any sort of showing in decoding what he acknowledges to be a 'language' so specialized that he would never for a moment claim to be in a position so much as to begin passing judgement about it.

This is not the case with the picture or the words quoted. Since both are *in some measure* available to him the layman may not be at all prepared to concede that his judgement of their merit is less valid than that of an art critic or literary critic; indeed, his reluctance to do so may not be uninfluenced by his knowledge that critics notoriously squabble among themselves. And up to a point, his attitude is right. It is in fact reasonable for the layman to accept that he is simply *not in a position* to challenge a theorem the symbols of which he cannot understand, but about which mathematicians are entirely agreed. And it is reasonable that he should exercise his own judgement on the worth of the lines quoted above and not weakly defer to a clerisy who are rarely in entire accord in their evaluation of literary merit, *provided he genuinely is in a position to exercise judgement*. But before literary judgement can so much as be essayed, some scholarship is necessary and the fact is that there is substantial agreement among the clerisy about what, at a basic level, this should be in respect of any given text. It is not difficult to demonstrate that *without* such basic scholarship, anyone attempting to judge literary merit is trying to run before he can walk and is simply *not in a position* to do so, whatever he may believe to the contrary. For example, to the majority of readers the line 'and the voice of the turtle is heard in the land' will suggest the scrawny-necked vocalization of a marine tortoise, but however great the majority may be they will be wrong – demonstrably and certainly wrong.

Literature examinations at virtually all levels seek to ensure that the candidate is in possession of such basic information or scholarship as may be necessary to forming critical judgements. In respect of the three lines quoted, a candidate could, for instance, be asked a variety of 'context' and factual questions of the kind:

1 Who is the supposed speaker of these words?

2 To whom are the words supposed to be addressed?

3 What season of the year is the passage about?

4 What do you understand by 'the voice of the turtle'?

5 What *genre* does the *Song of Solomon* belong to?

Questions of this kind, which admit of precise and straightforward answers that may be marked right or wrong, serve to sort out those who are minimally qualified to embark on literary judgement from those who are not; but correct answers to them do not and cannot give any guarantee of the candidate's specifically *literary* understanding or aptitude. If I have so far dwelt on what is either fully factual or philological in literary study, I have done so to establish that, so far from being merely opinionative or 'a matter of taste', the reading of a text frequently requires of the candidate a specialized or unusual knowledge about the text's range of reference, historical background, language, and so on. While anyone who speaks English can get *something* out of, say, an Elizabethan text, it is certain that if he knows nothing about 'the Elizabethan world picture' his response to the text will be not only deficient, but deluded: not only will he substitute marine tortoises for cooing doves – he will commit howler upon howler, to go no further than the body, over coral lips, high stomachs, stuffed bosoms, and divers complexions and humours; and for good measure he will attribute to a variety of words – 'let', 'prevent', 'awful', 'ecstasy' – a sense that is directly opposite to their modern meanings.

To draw together what has been said so far: knowledge is demonstrably necessary for a relevant reading of literature, but this should not mislead anyone into the error of supposing that because this is so, knowledge is valued in literary experience *for its own sake*. Still less should it be supposed that the literary merit of a text is in any way commensurate with the scholarly or linguistic demands it makes upon the reader. All that is being argued here is that knowledge is a necessary, but not a sufficient, condition for literary appreciation and that while most other subjects in the curriculum (music and art excepted) are primarily and formally concerned with knowledge and its organization, literature is *not*. Far from valuing knowledge *per se*, literature uses it only instrumentally in seeking to achieve ends that teachers of literature satisfy themselves are altogether worthier and more important.

To say this powerfully suggests that teachers of literature are not altogether shy in declaring their concern about values. Notoriously, they see themselves and write of themselves as missionaries and apostles and preachers of culture in a society given over to a philistine materialism. But why should teachers of literature be persuaded that they, more than teachers of all other subjects, especially science subjects, are peculiarly well fitted and entitled to deal with issues of morality and value? The answer to this lies primarily in the very nature of imaginative literature.

The claim that literature is preeminent among subjects in promoting a sense of values – the claim that it, above all other subjects, is truly educative – involves our looking briefly at other areas of the curriculum in the light of what we mean by 'values'. Briefly then, 'values' are taken here to be those *never* strictly or merely rational beliefs, convictions, and intuitive insights by which we seek to achieve purpose and order in our lives and by which we are enabled to exercise moral choice. Our judgements of other people and their actions, our judgements of ourselves in relation to other people, or to all living things, or to God, if he exists for us, are characteristically value-judgements and involve us in very much more than an application of our mathematical intelligence. Values are qualitative, not quantitative, and the more quantitative any subject is, the more it will have ceased to have any truck with values.

This is at once evident when we examine mathematical and scientific discourses, where the symbols used are usually and ideally invested with a single, unambiguous, and exclusively rational sense. The symbols do not *in themselves* matter and the clear and arbitrary sense they have can in principle and without detriment to the logic or facts involved be 'translated' into a wholly different symbolism. Indeed, we are all familiar with this. We know that there is not an atom of difference between $\frac{1}{2}$ and .5 and 50% and that we shall be not a whit the warmer or colder if a Fahrenheit temperature is converted into Centigrade. When in 1664 the Royal Society appointed a committee 'for improving the English tongue', its members were most solicitous about 'the manner of their *Discourse*', which they wanted to be: 'a close, naked, natural way of speaking, positive expressions, clear senses, a native easiness, bringing all things as near the Mathematical plainness as they can. . . .' The endeavour to cast out of the language its ambiguous, subjective, and poetic elements so as to make English into an exact and logical instrument inevitably failed. It soon became obvious that no amount of paring language or narrowing it for scientific purposes could achieve the desired 'mathematical plainness'. For this, a wholly artificial and arbitrary 'vocabulary' was needed – a scientific symbolism such as physics and chemistry devised for their own evolution, a symbolism that is impersonal, cognitive, and scoured, as far as may be, of all affective and moral considerations.

Mathematics and the sciences are prized in so-called advanced societies and their educational systems for the purity and certainty or near-certainty of their knowledge. They furnish the approved paradigms of knowledge and its organization not only for mathematicians and scientists, but for the overwhelming majority of formally educated people in five continents. Some of our educational philosophers are so preoccupied with this knowledge that they apparently feel they are doing literature a favour when they stretch a point to allow that it may be 'a form of knowledge': less pure and certain than these great paradigms, of course, and less pure and certain than even history, geography, and the social sciences; but even so, and however dilutedly, knowledge still. This is itself an inversion of any scale of values the teacher of literature understands. It is grotesque in supposing that the arts, which speak so much more comprehensively (and *therefore* uncertainly) to our human condition, are inferior to the sciences which achieve their success reductively and by the expulsion of the very vocabularies of feeling and morality that alone guarantee our human identity.

We shall presently examine how the discourse of the arts lies at an opposite extreme from that of mathematics or the sciences, but before doing so we should pause briefly at those subjects which, in varying degrees, share something of the nature of scientific discourse while having, at the same time, a concern for values. History, geography, the social sciences, theology, moral education, and literary criticism are such subjects. Like mathematical and scientific discourses, their discourses are primarily designed to systematize knowledge and are, ideally, rational, even if the relatively unspecialized language they employ is often recalcitrant to strict rationality. As subjects they have neither the formal certainty of mathematics nor the near-certainty and predictive capacity of most science, since the knowledge they encompass is not only incalculably broader in scope than that afforded by mathematics and the sciences, but it is at the same time lifted into a whole new dimension of values from which mathematical and scientific discourses are purged. This is very properly acknowledged when we designate these subjects 'humane studies' or 'the humanities'.

What characterizes the social sciences and the humanities (excluding the arts) is their yoking of knowledge with values; but, as discourses, they *reckon with* values – to use a term that suggests rational calculation – and do not seek deliberately to *embody* and *enact* values as the arts characteristically do. They handle values disinterestedly and dispassionately and, at least in principle, they are translatable into other terms as the arts are *not*. Even so, the discourse of the humanities may occasionally be heightened to approximate to that of literature: an historian like Gibbon is read more for his style than the accuracy of his matter. Typically, however, the humanities and social sciences use a discourse that requires the learner to stand back from whatever is under discussion and view it critically and evaluatively from the outside.

It is exactly opposite with literature and the arts (the category embraces religion, too) which simply *as discourses* require the learner to surrender disbelief and to seek an empathetic involvement in the *un*translatable experience they embody, enact, and afford. Here form and content coalesce and are in principle identical. All other discourses, whether tight and narrow, like mathematics and the sciences, or broader and commensurately slacker, like the social sciences and the humanities, are descriptive and markedly abstract. The arts, on the contrary, achieve an actual embodiment of experience in and through a discourse that, far from requiring the learner to stand detachedly back, engages and involves him in a sensuousness of response that lies below the threshold of consciousness, let alone rationality; characteristically, they have as their object not the systematization of knowledge, but the disciplined shaping and ordering of feeling into insight and illumination.

From the very beginning of education, literature has been acknowledged to be grounded in values: it has been held, by advocate and critic alike, *necessarily* to embody values and to work within a moral perspective; and it has been traditionally taken for granted that it *cannot but* influence the beliefs, values, and ultimately the conduct of the learner. Just as certainly as mathematics and the sciences achieve their spectacular successes by reductively excluding from their discourses all considerations of morality, emotion, and value, so literature achieves its success by virtue of its having a discourse that is *inclusive* of precisely these considerations. Literature, so far from being confined to exercising the intellect in respect of positive knowledge, seeks, as Yeats says, to make the blood, the intellect, and the imagination run together in an understanding that engages not an isolated faculty, but the whole man; and to accomplish this it has, as a discourse, to engage the learner in responses that, so far from being ideally abstract and morally and emotionally detached, are on the contrary ideally concrete, sensuous, and morally and emotionally committed.

It is of course true that the claims advanced here for literature extend to other arts, too: to music and fine art, for example; and it is no part of my argument to deny that, for any given individual, any one of these may communicate an illumination beyond the reach of words by offering its own unique and untranslatable insight into human emotion and experience. But admitting all this, it is none the less true that, very much as language, rather than pure sound or visual image, has, as an evolutionary fact, established itself as mankind's pre-eminent mode of communication, so literature has proved itself mankind's greatest, most flexible, and most generally useful art form. If literature has throughout history been regarded as much more central to education than the other arts, this is not because its manner of working upon the learner differs from theirs in kind or in essentials; rather, it stems from literature's being more directly and obviously, and above all more *comprehensively*, related to the whole range of human experience. It is significant that when on occasion, as in the latter part of the nineteenth century, literature has limited its commerce with everyday life by seeking refuge in aestheticism or by 'aspiring to the condition of music', its achievement has become anaemic and never more than second rate.

The claims made by the clerisy for what they honour with the name literature are literally as old as education. This is so because 'poetry is the mother tongue of all languages' and the earliest schools were bardic schools, like those of preliterate Greece. In nonliterate societies, the transmission of tribal lore or culture is primarily achieved through poetry, which is originally a functional technology employing an array of mnemonic devices (figures of speech, repetition, rhythmic patterning, etc.) usually reinforced with musical accompaniment and dance or bodily movement. The whole object of poetry was originally to ensure an exact imprint on the learner's mind of what was regarded as a divinely inspired and encyclopaedic wisdom. In Xenophon's *Symposium*, when called upon to say on what score he most values himself, Niceratus replies: 'It is that my father, designing to make a virtuous man of me, ordered me to get by heart every verse of Homer; and I believe that I can repeat you at this minute the whole *Iliad* and *Odyssey*.'

An oral poetic tradition provides at one and the same time both the content and the medium of instruction. In the poetic *paideia* of Greece, *what* was said and *how* it was said could not be separated: the technique of Homer was believed to have *in itself* the power to mould the listener to the same kind of virtue or excellence that characterized the epic heroes. Boys in school were taught to receive the imprint of a lofty literature because most Greeks believed, like Niceratus' father, that it ennobled character. To qualify to be a Greek was to know something of Homer, and this meant, as Professor John H. Finley says, that no Greek was altogether uneducated:

. . . in everyone's mind, singer and listener alike, lay the words of the poetic tradition that he had known since childhood and that alone lifted above the small present its arc of completer relevance and meaning . . . everyone in a part of his being thought in this greater language. . . .' (1966)

Even earlier, Brahmanic education was built on an identical supposition. Without the twelve-year task of memorizing every hallowed accent, letter, syllable, and word of a *Veda*, a Brahman could not be regarded as truly enlightened or (it meant much the same) educated. But we are concerned with more than remote history and should reflect that Matthew Arnold advocated the learning by heart of the best models of English poetry by our elementary school children, since he was convinced this afforded them access to a 'sweetness and light' unavailable in non-literary subjects; and to this day, no Brahman who has failed to memorize at least one *Veda* can be considered a Brahman by anything but birth, whatever other accomplishments he might have.

We shall take up the claims made for the educative value of literature presently. What matters first is that we should fully grasp what literature is, as a medium, and how, as a medium, it operates on the learner. Understanding the original function of poetry, which is literature distilled to its most characteristic and quintessential expression, helps us to grasp what the nature of literary experience still is and how it is accomplished. From classical antiquity on, poetry has been traditionally considered to instruct by means of pleasure, to teach by delighting the learner, so absorbing him within the brilliant imaginative world of the poet's invention. When we look back to a time when poetry was still undifferentiated from religion and myth and education, we see it more clearly as a kind of psychoneural conditioning. Professor E.A. Havelock, writing of education in preclassical Greece, offers us what looks very like a behaviouristic account of learning and the transmission of a value-system:

> The learning process . . . was not learning in our sense but a continual act of memorisation, repetition and recall. This was made effective by practising a drastic economy of possible linguistic statements, an economy enforced by rhythmic patterns both verbal and musical. In performance the co-operation of a whole series of motor reflexes throughout the entire body was enlisted to make memorisation and future recall and repetition more effective. These reflexes in turn provided an emotional release for the unconscious layers of personality which could then take over and supply to the conscious mind a great deal of relief from tension and anxiety, fear and the like. This last constituted the hypnotic pleasure of the performance, which placed the

audience under the minstrel's control, but was itself the ready servant of the paideutic process. Pleasure in the final analysis was exploited as the instrument of cultural control through poetry. (1963)

Once language could be given a written form, the cultural need for exact memorization lapsed and the psychoneural conditioning that poetry originally was gave way to prose, the instrument through which differentiation and rationality could gradually emerge. But the nonrational devices and techniques that characterized the epics of antiquity lived on in all subsequent poetry and, to some extent, in all imaginative literature up to this day. What all genuine poetry offers us, whether we are speaking of Homer or Ted Hughes, is a verbal vividness that, reinforced by rhythm, affectively involves the listener in the brilliant world of its own creation, and the very means it employs to achieve this precludes the possibility of the listener's assessing this world in an 'objective' manner from the outside. Even so sophisticated and intellectual a critic as F.R. Leavis insists that 'the reading demanded by poetry is of a different kind from that demanded by philosophy'. He goes on to say:

Words in poetry invite us, not to 'think about' and judge but to 'feel into' or 'become' – to realize a complex experience given in the words. (1952)

Though it would be a simple matter to fill a whole chapter with instances, I have space only to indicate a few of the ways in which poetry brings its subliminal manipulations to bear on the listener or reader. That these manipulations can penetrate not simply the unconscious mind, but also our physical sensations, is a fact well attested in the experience of many, if not all, of us. Lines like: 'O! She doth teach the torches to burn bright', or 'Cover her face: mine eyes dazzle: she died young' can, in their dramatic context, produce an actual *frisson* or move us to tears. A.E. Houseman had to take special care, when shaving, to shut poetry out of his mind, since his whiskers stiffened to stubble at its recollection, causing him to cut himself. Keats' whole countenance would light up at 'the force and felicity of an epithet': more specifically, his shoulder would hunch at Spenser's 'sea-shouldering whale', as if to take the weight and volume of water. But can anyone read aloud Gerard Manley Hopkins's:

like each tucked string tells, each hung bell's
Bow swung finds tongue to fling out broad its name . . .

without onomatopoeically re-creating and in a sense *becoming* the clamour of the pealed bell? And when Hopkins writes:

> I walk, I lift up, I lift up heart, eyes,
> Down all that glory in the heavens to glean our Saviour . . .

the faltering and mounting excitement of the first line is as dramatically unmistakable and apposite as the sweep of rhythm that in the following line carries the eyes triumphantly down the wide reach and expanse of sky in adoration. These are not words *about* an experience: they *are* the experience. The meaning of what is being said is uniquely realized in these words, in the colour and texture of vowel and consonant, in the weight and movement and variation of rhythms that in themselves constitute an essential and unsubstitutable part of the total meaning.

When D.H. Lawrence writes in 'Snake':

> He trailed his yellow-brown slackness soft-bellied down, over the edge of the stone trough . . .

even the length of the line on the page contributes to what is being said; but the repeated dragging sibilants and liquid 'l' sounds of the first half of the line are functional in reenacting the snake's slow movements – movements that 'soft-bellied' invites us to feel from *within*. Try examining what, physically, is happening in your mouth when you recite the lines above; then repeat the experiment with:

> He sipped with his straight mouth,
> Softly drank through his straight gums . . .

and ask yourself whether your own mouth has not performed precisely the actions attributed to the drinking snake.

What is being argued here is that, aside from whatever conscious surface meaning it may have, poetry exploits the iconic properties of words, imagery, metrical structure, and so on in a complex verbal interplay that involves the reader's response at levels that are demonstrably nonmental and even physiological. And all this before we have so much as mentioned, what is common to all art, the use of symbolism. But the success Lawrence's 'Snake' has with virtually all secondary school children can hardly be owing to its slight narrative content. The poet watches the snake drink, realizes it is potentially dangerous, is tempted by his 'human education' to kill it, but cannot do so because he feels honoured by its regal presence; and it is only when the snake begins retreating into the 'dreadful hole', accepting its own exile in the underworld, that the poet hurls a log at it in protest – then thinks guiltily of Coleridge's albatross and a chance missed with 'one of the lords/Of life'. Though brilliantly realized in Lawrence's description, the snake is much more than a zoological specimen, and this is sensed by even unsophisticated readers. It is, among other things and simultaneously, a positive life-force, instinctual and spontaneous feeling, sexual drive and Freudian 'id'; and it is beset by the deathliness of intellect, by the taboos of miseducation, by repression and denial and the censorship of the 'super-ego'. Or the poem can be regarded as a plea for the poetic imagination itself, in a world of rational conformity that fears and suppresses it.

We could go on extending the list of the poem's simultaneous meanings, but no symbol can ever be exhausted by what can be rationally asserted about it. In an interesting chapter on 'The Hinterland of Thought', the psychologist Professor D.W. Harding quotes L.L. Thurston's view that:

> Genius is essentially the capacity to deal effectively with impulses at the stage of formation when they are still only roughly affective states, before they have absorbed enough attributes to become the cognitive terms with which most of us are limited in our field of rational control. (1963)

It is a convenience to cite brief, poetic examples to indicate a few of the devices by means of which we are drawn into an experience that is realized in and through language, but plays and novels work on audiences and readers by identical or similar means. Plays, of course, require actors, stage, lighting, and often costume, scenery, sound effects, and music for their full realization; even setting aside linguistic features they share with poetry, they very obviously manipulate us into suspended disbelief by subliminal means. Watching *Macbeth*, the sense we have of evil comes not simply from the plot, but from the shadowy darknesses of vocabulary and stage lighting. Novels, like poetry, demand an individual response and are brought to realization in the creative act of reading: words are their whole substance and are all they have to offer. Though in general novels use a language that is less dense, imagistic, symbolic, and elliptical than that of poetry, their language differs from poetry not in kind, but in concentration; it is more diluted and diffuse, but its object is the same – to engage the reader in an imaginative world that is inaccessible to rationality alone and that we have to feel our way into and become. Moreover, the language of the novel can achieve its subliminal hold on the reader in ways not always or not often present in poetry: for example, by character creation and the empathy this demands of the reader, by the gradual building up of suspense through plot or by an accumulative and far-ranging deployment of image and symbol. As with poetic response, the reader's response to a novel can take shape in the unconscious layers of the mind; and it, too, can manifest itself physically.

When Dickens's *The Old Curiosity Shop* was originally published as a serial, strong men grew pale and wept in the streets of New York and Chicago at the news of the death of Little Nell. Only a deficient reader could read the opening of *Bleak House* without feeling the fog in his nostrils and throat – or read on without sensing its affinity with the miasma of corruption pervading the law courts.

There are several reasons why I have so insistently dwelt on the affective and subliminal nature of literary discourse. If we except music and art, which are peripheral and often no more than optional school subjects, the affective involvement that characterizes literature sets it apart from *all* other areas of the curriculum. I have tried, moreover, to show that this kind of involvement, while making cognitive demands, is far from being confined to 'the cognitive terms with which most of us are limited in our field of rational control', and that *therefore* it has a distinctive and for many pupils a unique function to perform within education. This function, I hope to show, makes literature supremely important among subjects (*pace* so many philosophers) and I would argue that, in alliance with other art subjects, it should take over much more of the curriculum than it does by displacing some of the cognitive discourses that are so heavily predominant. But this is to run ahead. First we should look at what has been said for and against the educative value of literature.

Let us now look more closely at Xenophon's Niceratus, whose father, designing to make 'a virtuous man' of him ordered him 'to get by heart every verse of Homer'. The assumption is explicit: virtue and the memorization of verse are intimately, even causally, linked. The Greeks were very far from modern notions about 'art for art's sake' and poetic 'purity' – notions which significantly came into prominence during the last century when the arts were put on the defensive by the challenge science and technology presented; rather, they believed in both the divine source of poetry and in its complete potency to shape the character and conduct of the learner. So far from affording merely aesthetic experience, poetry for the Greeks, as for the Romans later, was essentially a craft (*techne*) prized for the moral, social, and even utilitarian ends it achieved, or was supposed to achieve, and the delight it gave was not for them differentiated from its profitable instruction.

If the question is now raised as to *how* poetry comes to shape and mould the character and conduct of the learner, the answer lies, I would argue, in all that I have tried to say about the nature of poetry and the response it demands of the learner. In Havelock's words, its 'hypnotic pleasure' makes it 'the ready servant of the paideutic process'. It works on the learner manipulatively and at various levels, involving him in a 'greater language' that saturates his thinking and feeling and lifts above his humdrum existence its 'arc of completer relevance and meaning'. Memorization ensures that this greater language enters not simply into the narrowly intellectual awareness of the learner, but into those areas of self where impulses are 'at the stage of formation when they are still roughly affective states'; it even penetrates the materiality of the body and its senses. Poetry absorbs the learner into the imaginative world of its own creation by enabling him to 'feel into' that world and make it an *organic* part of himself. It works by assimilating the learner to its own nature.

The belief that by the study of literature the learner's moral being will, like the dyer's hand, become subdued to what it works in has been taken for granted throughout the history of education by advocate and critic alike. Plato, who in principle though not in practice deplores poetry, gives us this cameo of its place in traditional Greek education:

> And when the boy has learned his letters and is beginning to understand what is written . . . they put on his desk the works of great poets for him to read; in these are contained many admonitions, and many tales and praises and encomia of famous men of old, which he is required to learn by heart, in order that he may imitate or emulate them and desire to become like them. Then, again the teachers of the lyre take similar care that their young disciple is temperate and gets into no mischief; and when they have taught him the use of the lyre, they introduce him to the poems of other excellent poets, who are the lyric poets; and these they set to music, and make their harmonies and rhythms quite familiar to the children's souls, in order that they may learn to be more gentle and harmonious, and rhythmical, and so more fitted for speech and action; for the life of man in every part has need of harmony and rhythm.

The poetic *paideia* clearly sought to inculcate morality; it set forth a gallery of heroes for emulation and its aim was to fit the pupil 'for speech and action'.

Despite Plato's objections, education became more, rather than less, literary and, as Marrou says, 'the higher Hellenistic culture remained faithful to the archaic tradition and based itself on poetry, not science' (1956). Literature, right through to the fall of the Roman empire, became the primary and most important content of education and the bulk of Greek literature we possess today has come down to us from selections and anthologies used as classroom texts. Rhetoric, the highest systematic education of antiquity, set itself to influence the total actions of men in their everyday living: it was indissolubly linked with ethics and was grounded in literary studies – too often, deadeningly so – and in Isocrates' conviction that great literature quickened in the pupil a love of the beautiful-and-good, and so guaranteed a moral integrity without which no true eloquence was possible.

During the Renaissance, educators like Vergerio sought by immersing the pupil in classical literature to transform his mind so as to make it resemble in its contents and operations the mind of a fifth-century Greek. Nobility of conduct was their explicit aim. Vittorino da Feltre typically believed that the ideal of 'the complete man' fulfilled in living 'the good life' was to be accomplished through the agency of literature. The high claims advanced for poetry were essentially restatements of claims made in anti- quity: in *Timber; or Discoveries*, Ben Jonson, for example, concurs with 'the wisest and best learned' in his belief that poetry, which is the 'absolute Mistress of Manners and nearest kin to Vertue . . . leads on, and guides by the hand to Action'.

For the Romantics, the ennobling function of literature was an article of something like religious faith. They recognized in the imagination an agency of divine origin and power; through it, the poet, ideally, 'brings the whole soul of man into activity'. Shelley, in his *Defence of Poetry*, makes the interrelatedness of imagination, morality, and poetry wholly explicit:

> A man to be greatly good, must imagine intensely and comprehensively; he must put himself in the place of another and of many others; the pains and pleasures of his species must become his own. The great instrument of moral good is the imagination. . . . Poetry strengthens the faculty which is the organ of the moral nature of man, in the same manner as exercise strengthens a limb. . . .'

As poet, man of letters, and inspector of schools, Matthew Arnold similarly affirmed, in the teeth of those clamouring for a curriculum grounded in useful knowledge, that literature affords a 'criticism of life' unequalled by other disciplines: 'good poetry,' he asserts, 'does undoubt- edly tend to form the soul and character; it tends to beget a love of beauty and truth in alliance together', and in an age threatened by materialism, vulgarization, and a dissolution of all values, including those of religion, it remains 'the greatest power available in education'. In our own day, F.R. Leavis has relentlessly insisted not only upon the value, above all the moral value, of great literature, but upon the central, integrative, and civilizing discipline of literary criticism itself, which, he claims, by training the

sensibility, equips us to help stem the same swelling tide of shoddy materialism and shoddy feeling that Arnold saw engulfing industrialized society.

Briefly then, the paramount value of literature in education (only religion
competing with it in importance) is attested throughout European history.
Its traditional justification is moral and social and supposes that the learner,
submitted to its inherently noble influence, will himself acquire nobility in
thought, word, and deed.

When we turn to the long tradition of opposition and hostility to literature's preeminent place in education, it is of the utmost importance to grasp
that the objections traditionally brought against it in no way deny that
literature is rooted in values: on the contrary, this is freely admitted. What *is*
urged is either that the nature of literature *as a medium* makes it educationally bad and stultifying or that literature, *in terms of its content*, is erroneous,
or both.

Plato's attack on poetry will serve to demonstrate both types of objection.
He was the beneficiary of a recently evolved rational discourse and its
related body of mathematical and scientific fact. This enabled him to stand
critically back from Homer and the poetic *paideia*. He saw poetry as a
technique that blinded men's minds to the values it induced, since it used
means similar to hypnotic suggestion. Certainly the 'honeyed muse' was
pleasurable, but the learner who surrendered to its pleasure was no better
than a dreamer or sleep-walker. So far from denying the delights of poetry,
Plato allows these, but points to the shameful price at which they are
purchased. It is precisely because poetry is enthralling that it must be
resisted, for emotional thraldom stultifies the learner's development by
blinding him to truth, which is available to the mathematical intelligence
alone. Plato opposes a real world of Forms, illuminated by reason, to the
shadow-world of everyday existence. Among the shadows, and attuned to
them, are the physical senses, which the mind transcends in its contempla-
tion of the Forms; and just as the language corresponding to positive
knowledge is, for Plato, typified in geometry, so the language corresponding to the distorted 'knowledge' supplied by the senses is typified for him in
poetry, which because of its very nature leads the learner into error and
confusion. Homer, for example, stands condemned for telling lies about the
gods, whom he portrays as acting in ways that would be morally disgraceful
even among men.

Plato heads a formidable list of depreciators of literature: logic-chopping
schoolmen and educational thinkers as diverse as Locke, Rousseau, and

Spencer. Across the centuries, positivists, rationalists, narrow-gutted theologians, and pleasure-denouncing puritans have deplored what they regarded as the seductive delights of literary style, on the one hand, and, on the other, the squalidly subjective errors and fanciful fictions that they consider to be the only 'substance' literature has to offer.

So far from denying that literature is not wholly rational, I have positively affirmed this and tried to demonstrate it by giving examples of the kind of subliminal manipulation literature exercises on the learner: I have, moreover, acknowledged that literature operates on the learner very much as a *conditioning* agent, and virtually all educational philosophers are at pains not simply to deplore conditioning, but to regard it as irremediably *anti*educational. On the contrary, I believe that the kind of conditioning effected by great literature is supremely educative, being grounded in values, and that subjects primarily concerned with knowledge and its organization come nowhere near it in importance, being scoured of all that determines our individual identity and all that is deepest in our humanity. And of course it follows that, just as the best literature habituates the learner to the virtue and nobility it portrays, so books that are bad or corrupt habituate the learner to what is evil and ignoble, as no merely cognitive subject can do. Homer and Hemingway, the lavatory artist or graffitist, and the punk-rock singer whose atrocious success makes him a multinational corporation, all lie within one universe of discourse. To be educated is not merely to *know* that Homer is superior to the punk-rock singer, but so to have *responded* to poetic discourse as to be organically resistant to its trivialization and debasement. What is slightingly called 'taste' is, in fact, profoundly moral. Style, as A.N. Whitehead says, is the ultimate morality of mind (1929); and so is its appreciation.

It is for this reason that the untranslatableness of literature has been emphasized. Style is not, as is often naïvely supposed, a detachable element in literature; rather, as Matthew Arnold says:

> The superior character of truth and seriousness in the matter and substance of the best poetry, is inseparable from the superiority of diction and movement marking its style and manner. The two superiorities are closely related and are in steadfast proportion one to the other.

Briefly, the identity of what for analytic purposes is called 'form' and 'content' in literature means that, for example, nobility of thought or action can only be realized in nobility of language (language is all the author has to work with), and any failure or unsureness in 'form' is exactly reflected in a

failure or unsureness in the realization of the nobility aimed at. The taut-
ology is inescapable. Literature that successfully and maturely integrates
thought and feeling at a serious level cannot but be moral in its effects.

But it can, of course, be wrong in its facts or logic. Shakespeare was
liberal with such anachronisms as striking clocks in ancient Rome; Kipling's 'Road to Mandalay' and Masefield's 'Cargoes' are geographically
grotesque; Keats's Cortez, staring from a peak in Darien, is historically
wrong (it was Balboa) and the logic that leads him to call the nightingale an
'immortal bird' is wholly spurious. In general what one must say is that *none
of this matters much*; it is mostly, if not entirely, beside the point, and if
Kipling's verse is manifestly inferior to Keats's poems, what makes it so has
nothing to do with errors of fact. As Dr. Johnson remarked, Shakespeare's
anachronisms are an offence against history, not against poetry. A work of
literature may contain local instances of falsifiable statement without its
merit being significantly impaired for the excellent reason that its real life
lies elsewhere: not in propositional statement, but in realization and insight.
When Arnold refers to literature's 'truth', he is not speaking of its rational
or pragmatic truth, but of its truth to our total (not merely mental) experience, including our subliminal response.

It is obvious that literature's insights, as I prefer to call them, do not
depend upon truth as the positivist sees it: Homer's licentious gods may be
wholly fictional to our intellect, but they still hold sway over our imagina-
tions and perhaps retain their psychological validity for us as archetypes.
Balzac used to refer to his novels as being 'more real' for him than everyday
life, and a reader 'lost' in reading them might agree that their characters and
happenings have more 'reality' for and influence over him than the actual
people and events in his own life. Aristotle argued that great literature
completes and consummates nature's purposes more representatively and
perfectly than unaided nature itself can do. But however much words like
'true' or 'real' are applied to it, literature is too large in scope and importance ever to be falsifiable. Its fictions are, in fact, insights, and insights can
and do transcend all rules of logic by having validity, even when they stand
in open contradiction of one another. *Genesis* and Marlowe's *Dr. Faustus* do
not invalidate the Prometheus poems of Aeschylus and Shelley, nor vice
versa. Even Goethe, the all-round genius of an age of rational enlighten-
ment, rejected with horror the supposition that the literary works into
which he had thrown his whole life could be limited 'to so merely logical, so
merely rational, so merely intellectual a concept as *an idea*'.

Let us look now at the evaluation of literature. From everything that has been said, it should be obvious that what matters most in literature cannot be circumscribed or encompassed by merely rational means and, therefore, cannot be satisfactorily measured. What literature has to offer the pupil is one thing. What is offered in its name in our schools and colleges is often another, radically different and distorted thing, determined by examination requirements. As we have seen, at least some textual knowledge – some hard fact – is a necessary condition for a relevant reading of literature; moreover, it is examinable – a fact which cannot but recommend it to examiners. In the ancient world, it was the practice of teachers to bury the challenge afforded by literature as imaginative experience under slag-heaps of excessive and easily taught erudition. The living text was done to death by piecemeal dissection of its factual content and formal properties, so that all archaisms, etymologies, mythological genealogies, geographic place-names, grammatical and prosodic oddities, together with any and every figure of speech, were required to be analysed and memorized by the pupil. Anyone who has studied even an 'O'-level Shakespeare text will know that rather more than the vestiges of this tradition survive still because they are honoured in examinations; and it is always so much easier to teach the examinable features of literature, which make it respectably like any other subject, than to initiate the pupil into what distinctively *matters* about literature and lifts it in importance above all other subjects.

Undue concentration on the merely factual and cognitive features of literature is common among insecure untrained English teachers, who are responsible for one-third of all English teaching. (English does not, curiously, count as a shortage subject with the DES.) As one would expect, specialist teachers of English do better. They are, it is to be hoped, aware at first hand of the value of literature in their own lives and often of the centrality it certainly is not given, but that it *could* be given, in the lives of their pupils. However, they tend to a generally abstract and cognitive approach in their teaching and examining of literature: not at all surprisingly, given the almost exclusively historical and critical bias of English studies in their own higher education. As Professor Graham Hough has sensibly observed, undergraduate English leads to one of two vices:

> a conventional hack through a series of names and dates and received opinions, which was the vice of an earlier generation; or a perpetual demand for literary analyses that the generality of students are not really capable of making, for critical judgements that they have not really felt. This is the vice of our own time. (1964)

Both vices, but especially the latter, requiring from pupils abstractly stated critical judgements that may never have been proved on their own pulses, are commonly found in G.C.E. and even C.S.E. literature examinations. All too often, the teacher's well-rehearsed views (themselves often derived from works of criticism) determine what gets said in his pupils' examination answers to prescribed texts. Experienced examiners know this perfectly well, just as experienced teachers know perfectly well the marking schemes of examining boards and drill their pupils in whatever are the appropriate strategies for maximizing marks. Not long ago it was useful to know, for example, that one 'O'-level examining board, when setting a character study question, allowed eight marks for any eight appropriate adjectives (kind, humorous, brave, etc.) and a further eight marks for references adduced in support of the adjectives. A candidate who selected, say, four crucial qualities of character and analysed these in depth could achieve no more than half marks on the question, while another candidate, taught to toss up as many adjectives and single references as he could remember, would get full marks. Even if this is a particularly mechanical instance of examining procedures, there is savage irony in its being brought to bear on literature, which is prescribed with the object of enhancing the candidate's understanding and sensitiveness.

There can be little doubt that practical criticism achieves highest validity in what passes for the examination of literature. At its very best it has been held to approximate to literary creation. But, of course, it is still open to objections. Short unseen passages fail to test the candidate's response to long works, which depend crucially on their architectonic qualities; they may even encourage a snippet mentality. None the less, the setting of unseen prose and poetry for analysis, critical comment, evaluation, and dating, if it does not wholly eliminate stock response and the insincere prepared answer, comes a long way towards doing so. As things are, it is probably the best that can be made of the intractable problem of examining literature. But Hough's objection still stands: most pupils and most university students have neither the maturity nor the finely discriminative intelligence and sensibility it demands of them.

But of course, the most radical and usual charge levelled at literature is that it cannot be objectively evaluated. This is, for reasons already stated, both undeniable and misguided in its assumption that what is not quantifiable is of lesser worth than what is. While it may be true that the greater a work of literature, the wider its appeal will be across barriers of time and place, it is still more certainly true that cultural differences very much determine our response to even the best literature and may cut us off from it altogether. For more than a millenium Homer was downgraded in favour of (as we judge it) his inferior imitator, Virgil, on the spurious grounds that Virgil was, in effect, an honorary Christian. It is significant that the whole revaluation of English literature in our own century of dissolving values has brought into prominence writers who were tormentedly preoccupied with the dissolution of values in their own period: notably Donne and the Jacobean dramatists, who had no appeal for either the intellectually complacent eighteenth century or the materially self-satisfied and progressive nineteenth century. Not even Shakespeare can sustain the extravagant claim for the universality of great literature. In the many cultures where romantic love is unknown, *Romeo and Juliet* and *Othello* are incomprehensible, and however fine we may think *King Lear*, it would cease to have meaning for our descendants if, as in Huxley's *Brave New World*, the family were to disappear from society and key words like 'father' and 'daughter' were to become part of smutty vocabulary.

Though the subjectivity of literary evaluation is more apparent when we cut across cultures and history, it is never avoidable. Differences must and do occur among the clerisy concerning the value to be placed upon the most widely acclaimed traditional authors, let alone the often ephemeral work of living writers. Critics of approximately equal learning, sensibility, and intelligence may defend or deplore Shakespeare's rejection of Falstaff, Milton's poetic diction, or Dickens's characterization. Very unsurprisingly, they will disagree more over the merits of present-day literature, a good deal of which is now prescribed by examiners.

In glancing at Lawrence's 'Snake' we saw how the richness of its symbolism admitted a whole range of possible interpretations, and disagreement as to which of these are most vital and central is only to be expected, since different readers will judge the poem differently and in accordance with their own experience and values and psychological dispositions. This, of course, does *not* mean that there is nothing to choose between evaluations. As W.H. Auden remarked, a real book reads *us*. Debate among the clerisy takes for granted extensive reading and scholarship and analytic skills, and it has interest and point precisely because some evaluations can be *demonstrated* to be preferable to others – by, for example, appeals made to the text itself, or to other works of the author, or perhaps to works that influenced the writing of the text. But when all has been said about the level of debate and scrupulous appeals to evidence, it remains true that critics can reach a high degree of unity in their views about the formal features of a work of literature – its language, structure, symbolism, characterization, 'commitment', etc. – yet still diverge conspicuously in their appraisal of its merit, since they will differ, sometimes sharply, in the rank-order they accord such formal features. And at this point we have to accept that, short of the Almighty, there *is* no court of appeal. We are back to where we began and must acknowledge that literature cannot be encompassed by rationality and cannot, therefore, be reliably assessed.

What, then, might be done? Should we follow the 1941 Norwood committee's advice and stop examining literature altogether? Ideally, yes; but as long ago as 1921 the report on *The Teaching of English in England* was alert to the practical consequence: 'For good or ill, the examination system is with us. To exempt literature alone from its scope would simply exclude the teaching of literature from a number of schools.' Or, perhaps, reduce it to the peripheral status of music or art or dance – subjects that are shamefully slighted in an educational system which all too faithfully reflects the philistine positivism of our society. For it is a fact that *cognitive* discourses occupy almost the entire secondary school curriculum. Affective discourses (the arts) get scant or no recognition on the timetable. The imbalance is both huge and frightening. It is, therefore, a tragic irony that literature, which has as its object the education of the emotions, should be perverted by examination requirements into a predominantly cognitive mode.

To stop examining literature would be to remove from huge numbers of pupils the *only* affective discourse they are exposed to at school. To examine it by present methods is to subordinate what really matters, the *experience* of literature, to abstract, critical talk *about* literature. If a way is to be found out of this dilemma, it must be by means of new kinds of examinations which will have a less detrimental, or even a benign, effect on teaching. To begin with, assessment should be by course work, since it is absurd to suppose that responsiveness lies within the candidate's volition and can have its measure taken between, say, two and four o'clock of a June afternoon. Moreover, we ought to be examining less for rapidity of response than for depth and relevance of response, and less for the explicit assertion of response (which comes all too easily) than for its implicit embodiment.

I can do no more here than hint at an alternative kind of assessment. To begin with, it would encourage pupils to write in imitation of authors they admire. This is how all writers learn their craft, anyhow, and I can see no good reason for supposing that a pupil able to embody in pastiche a heightened everyday speech, heterogeneous ideas, dialectical progression, conceits, puns, etc. is offering less valid evidence of his understanding of Donne than the pupil who writes an essay asserting, with customary quotations, that these features are to be found in Donne. Or again, a pupil studying *Macbeth* might offer a conversation piece between the doctor, home from attending Lady Macbeth at Dunsinane castle, and his determinedly inquisitive wife. Another, studying *Pride and Prejudice*, might invent the diary entry made by Mr. Collins on his hearing that Elizabeth Bennett is to marry D'Arcy. Such possibilities are endless and they challenge the pupil imaginatively to extend an understanding derived from a careful reading of the texts.

Confronted with a play, the obvious thing to do is to act it. From original casting to actual performance, drama production is a profoundly educative experience and, difficult as assessment is, it still should not be beyond the wit of a teacher to gauge the contributions of individual pupils. Nor do pupils lose anything in their understanding of short stories or parts of novels when they try adapting and rewriting them for the stage. On the contrary, their understanding and appreciation are quickened in their own struggle with recalcitrant problems of form and technique. Similarly, a great deal is to be learned from making and comparing tape-recordings of poetry readings or from producing materials for a radio programme on a literary theme. Finally and importantly, the teacher should throughout the year discuss the pupil's original writing with him and thus be in a position to assess its range and worth. As the Schools Council Project English 16–19 indicates, such alternative procedures are at least being experimentally tried out by some lively groups of teachers of English, together with open book examinations, workshop approaches, and personalized courses.

What matters is that literature should be carried alive into the sensibility and understanding of the pupil. We will predictably never be able to assess with exactness how far so imponderable an aim is achieved. Even so, it is better that we should devise new forms of assessment, accepting their imprecision, but knowing them to be conducive to the enlightened teaching of literature, than that we should kill literature in the classroom by having it taught in conformity with more precise, but badly misconceived, examination requirements that afford no opportunity for *operative* critical insight.

The alternative type of assessment I have indicated is intended to get priorities right by, first, placing an emphasis on the pupil's total experience of literature, rather than on what he abstractly knows about it, and by, second, testing the nature and quality of that experience through the broadly creative, rather than the narrowly cognitive, expression the pupil is able to give it. Objections are inevitable. Many teachers of English will feel that it is not possible to assess creative work, though just why the authoritative critical intelligence they exercise in marking essays on Dryden or Dickens should fall into sudden abeyance when called upon to discriminate good from bad in their pupils' creative writing is very unclear. It may be relevant to note that, *unlike* courses in art and music, their own undergraduate courses, so far from requiring creative effort of them, make virtually no allowance for it; and, regrettably, teachers of English are more apt to look to the bad example of English dons, who offer their students the scholarly critic for a model, than to primary school teachers, who more sensibly offer pupils the poet for a model and make no fuss about assessing the creative work they positively promote.

In passing, it should also be noted that literature has to struggle for survival not only against the reductionism of imposed examinations, but against the reductionism of ideologues, linguists, and sociologists, who seek its degradation by using it for propaganda purposes, or by feeding it piecemeal to children as part of 'social competence' or by incorporating it into humanities programmes *subordinately* to mere discussion and argumentation. All such endeavours to reduce literature to instrumentality and subservience to political, social, and rational ends are both a violation and an inversion of acceptable values.

Literature, I have argued, is not just one subject among many. Along with art and music, it differs from other subjects in being primarily affective, and it differs from art and music both in the comprehensiveness of its concern for values and in its having, for the present at least, much more recognition than they do on the timetable of a majority of pupils. By its very nature, literature is, when properly taught, the major civilizing force in an educational system that is alarmingly positivistic and utilitarian. This, of course, goes unperceived by the majority of teachers, curriculum planners, and educationists, who are bedevilled with the notion that education is a matter of initiating pupils into 'forms of knowledge' – more especially into those paradigm forms that are instrumental in promoting material and economic progress, along with the total capacity to bring about our species' annihilation, whether environmentally, genetically, militarily, or psychologically.

When I listen to all the fuss and pother educationalists make about 'cognitive development', I quietly reflect on Coleridge, with his mind 'habituated *to the Vast*' at eight years of age from his reading 'of fairy tales and genii'.

'I have known some,' Coleridge tells us, in a letter to Poole, 1797, 'who have been rationally educated, as it is styled. They were marked by a microscopic acuteness, but when they looked at great things, all became a blank and they saw nothing, and denied (very illogically) that anything could be seen, and uniformly put the negation of a power for the possession of a power, and called the want of imagination judgement and the never being moved to rapture philosophy!'

It is a similar raptureless philosophy that now sets such store by cognitive development and fraudulently sets rationality above 'a love of the Great and the Whole' which Coleridge believed it lay uniquely in the power of literature to confer. Given our society's overvaluation of rationality and its Faustian preoccupation with knowledge unrelated to value, there never was a time when education stood more in need of the arts and literature than it does now. Yet their place in education is marginal and they stand the risk either of being dropped and disregarded or of being absurdly brought into compliance with the positivism of more acceptable and examinable 'forms of knowledge'.

'*Cette belle raison corrompue a tout corrompu*,' Pascal warned. And who better fitted than a mathematical genius to perceive the contamination of a reductive reason that, denuded of human concern, seeks to assimilate all things to itself!

References

Finley, J.H. Jr. (1966) *Four Stages of Greek Thought*, Stanford: Stanford University Press.
Harding, D.W. (1963) *Experience into Words: Essays on Poetry*, London: Chatto & Windus.
Havelock, I.E.A. (1963) *Preface to Plato*, Oxford: Blackwell.
Hough, G. (1964) 'Crisis in literary education', in Plumb (ed) *Crisis in the Humanities*, Harmondsworth: Penguin.
Leavis, F.R. (1952) *The Common Pursuit*, London: Chatto & Windus.
Marrou, A.I., translated by G. Lamb (1956) *A History of Education in Antiquity*, London: Steed & Ward.

Whitehead, A.N. (1929) *The Aims of Education and Other Essays*, New York: Macmillan.

CHAPTER 10

ART
Fraser Smith

This is a paragraph from an article in a national daily newspaper advising parents on ways of assessing a school:

> If you can find out who is responsible for the school's curriculum, then try to get an explanation as to why teachers teach what they do that goes back beyond the surface assertions of intellectual fashion to a thought – a philosophy. As a test case, the art teacher might be a good start. You would be exceptionally lucky to get a coherent explanation.
>
> John Fairhall, *The Guardian*, 11 May, 1976.

These are immediate off-the-cuff reactions to the piece from some art teachers to whom I spoke the following day.

'It seems a reasonable thing to say.'
'A bloody lie.'
'Not many of our parents read *The Guardian* – thank God!'
'I agree – but it's not that simple.'
'Of course you wouldn't – we are experimental.'
'After all the work I've done on the curriculum this term.'
'We are interested in creativity and imagination.'

They may be seen to range from indignant through open or implied assertions of irrelevance and lack of sympathy or understanding on Fairhall's part, to reserved approval. 'It's not that simple' is what this chapter is about. Why is it that many teachers of art encounter difficulty in evaluating what they do in schools to the point where this kind of criticism is not altogether unjustified or uncommon?

In the first section of this chapter I suggest that art teachers may be seen in terms of types, each of which exhibit, in their writing or performance, clusters of values, which may simultaneously explain observed differences within the group as a whole and highlight problems of value in art teaching.

It will be useful to bear in mind the following concept of value throughout the chapter:

> To say that a person has a value is to say that he has an enduring prescriptive or proscriptive belief that a specific mode of behaviour or end-state of existence is preferred to an opposite mode of behaviour or end-state. This belief transcends attitudes towards objects and towards situations; it is a standard that guides and determines action, attitudes towards objects and situations, ideology, presentations of self to others, evaluations, judgements, justifications, comparisons of self with others and attempts to influence others. Values serve adjustive, ego-defensive, knowledge and self-actualising functions. (Rokeach, 1973, p. 25)

The second section is concerned with some brief discussion of these types in terms of what it might mean to be an authoritative art teacher with the obvious implications for evaluation that this raises.

Teachers of art and their values

To tease out and examine types of art teacher in an attempt to isolate and account for the values and beliefs they hold, I intend to develop a series of models or stereotypes. There is a danger in doing so especially perhaps in a field where individual differences are often proposed as having overriding importance; nevertheless, this offers an opportunity to clarify problems of value. Thus, as in the 1960s it would have been possible to identify groups of art teachers as 'Free Expressives' or perhaps, 'Basic Designers', it is possible to identify contemporary groups, many of which are of a less temporary nature than these two. In art, as in any other field where a gulf in expertise, knowledge, or ritual has grown up between those thought to be at the forefront of development and those anxious or compelled to share in the delights or benefits those developments might bring, a priestly mediating caste has evolved. There are a number of classes of High Priest in art education of whom the art historian or Connoisseur is often seen from outside as the most 'respectable' by virtue of most universities' refusal to acknowledge an 'O' or 'A' level in art as sufficient for admission without a written or 'academic' component. Despite the recent flood of art historians from universities and polytechnics, few are employed full time in schools where other types of teacher become Connoisseur for two periods a week with the sixth form.

But by far the most common High Priests to be found as art teachers are

Magicians. Indeed the 'father' of present-day art education, Sir Herbert Read, was perhaps the most well-known Magician of all:

> Independence, freedom, law and art – these are all implicit in esthetic education, and it is only in so far as we oppose esthetic education to scientific education, and to intellectual education in the tradition of the Renaissance, oppose it as a complete and adequate substitute for these bankrupt traditions, that any hope can be entertained for the future of our European culture. . . . The only habit that is enobling, penetrating to the frame and physique as well as the soul of man, is the creative activity in all its rituals, exercises, festivities and practical services. (Read, 1948, p. 14)

The Magician occupies a position in art education which attracts many adherents. As Lanier (1977) suggests:

> What is particularly appealing about the Magician's posture – one is led to suspect – is the delightful mindlessness which is all it requires as a scholarly position. After all, if the essential quality of art and art teaching is magic and mystery, why struggle to understand it?

Indeed the basis of 'magicianism' is that very religious fervour that leads me to use High Priesthood as a category.

> Until we can halt these processes of destruction and standardisation, of materialism and mass communication, art will always be subject to the threat of disintegration. The genuine arts of today are engaged in a heroic struggle against mediocrity and mass values, and if they lose, then art, in any meaningful sense, is dead. If art dies, then the spirit of man becomes impotent and the world relapses into barbarism. (Read, 1965, p. 187)

A much smaller sect of High Priests is formed by the Mystics. Mystics are subjective to an anarchical extreme and the making of art for the Mystic is so intensely personal, so totally subjective and mysterious an activity that it is inexplicable, and of course unteachable. Both Magicians and Mystics, like all High Priests, are of course élitist but not, generally speaking, violently so, feeling genuine sorrow for those who, unlike themselves, do not share in the ritual or its products. This is a position akin to the archaic one of the clerisy in literature or, reaching even further back in time, the literati in Chinese painting and poetry. Concepts of 'talent' or 'giftedness', at least as popularly held, lend themselves wonderfully to the propagation of the Priesthood in whatever form.

Not surprisingly, most High Priests, certainly the vast majority of Magicians and Mystics, have received a training in fine art for it is the departments of fine art in higher educational institutions which are the seminaries through which novices are initiated. There is not sufficient space here to contain a detailed account of how this process unfolds although it will be useful to summarize the emphases of value to which students are expected to conform. Ironically, fine art students are rigidly conformist in a number of respects.

The pre-eminent value is laid on personality and personal development. In Madge and Weinbergers' sample, 92 percent of students agree that 'The value of an art education lies in furthering personal development in whatever direction this may lead' (1973, p. 70). It becomes clear, however, from tutors' reports included in this same study that some directions are not allowed, some modes of working are not approved, and that students who choose these directions or modes are, sometimes brutally, rerouted into tutor-approved ways of behaving. This, for example, from the participant observer's notes:

> November 25th, 1968. Talked to Diana [student] who said Gibson [tutor] had slated her work – and had called it amateurish, art-schoolish, Graham Sutherlandish, etc. She said it had upset her a great deal and that was the reason she had got drunk. (1973, p. 153)

Perhaps nowhere in the educational system is the game of 'Guess what the teacher wants – and stand the consequences if you are wrong' played with such bitter gusto than in the departments of fine art. In the training of High Priests there need be no appeal to reason. In the sample quoted here 63 percent of students and 50 percent of tutors agreed that art cannot be taught. (There is no evidence to show that 50 percent of tutors were unpaid.)

Values with regard to teaching are imbued during the noviciate as this study shows. For example:

> *Statement 6*. The professional artist who also teaches is of greater value at art college than the professional art teacher.
> *Staff Norm*. Art teaching as a career is talked about in derogatory terms or not discussed. Students are told they are learning to become professional artists and are being taught by professionals. Several tutors do their own work in the college and discuss their work with students.
> *Student Response*. Agreed. This leads to a sense of let-down in the final year when students realise, seemingly for the first time at college, that little other than teaching is open to them. Several refuse to consider teaching preferring to take casual jobs which leave them free as artistic personalities (even if they do not continue to produce any art work).

Despite this, fine artists form far and away the biggest single group by subject division to apply for postgraduate art and design teacher training

(445 from a total of 863 nationally in 1977-1978) and High Priests are, quite possibly for the reasons Lanier suggests, to be found throughout art education. Consider this verse from a poem by a senior art inspector.

Above all else
The trust we seek
Was there at the beginning.
Believing that there is an inner life of images,
Rooted in sensations that we only later know,
Striving for persistence in material form,
Its times and rhythms beyond our knowing.
But yet a task more real to see
Because it's there in you and me. (Gentle, 1977)

Not sufficient to establish Gentle as a poet but his Magician's credentials are well to the fore.

The next identifiable group I shall call the Technocrats. They are, as their title suggests, in diametric opposition to the High Priests and, because they are nothing if not plausible, have experienced an upturn in their fortunes with the advent of 'accountability'. Technocrats divide into two unequally sized groups, Engineers and Designers. The title of the smaller group, Engineers, refers neither to their training, for, indeed, Engineers may be High Priests, defrocked for excessive rationality, nor to their practices in the classroom, for Engineers are not usually too clear about what the content of art education might be, but to their endless tinkering with the structures of education: curriculum, syllabus, and timetable. The Engineer's essential equipment is the blueprint and the computer, or, failing that, 'statistics', which are to him what the magic act of creation is to the Magician. In so far as empiricists may be found in British art education, it is in this group:

. . . consideration of means leads to *instructional* questions in which efficacy can be empirically determined – which (sic)n for instance, of a variety of methods can two point perspective be taught to a specific group? (Allison, 1978)

Indeed the article by Allison from which this piece is taken contains many of the hallmarks of an Engineer's contribution. There is the standard attack on Magicians:

A school I visited recently had the name 'Studio' in large bold letters painted on the art room door. Apart from cultivating what appears to be an appropriate 'atmosphere', the material provisions had done much to satisfy the teachers' self-concept of fundamentally being artists, who in some cases regrettably, have to teach. (1978, p. 9)

There are five blueprints ranging from a diagram entitled 'Tyler's curricular rationale', through three entitled respectively, 'The Spiral Model', 'The Lattice Model', and 'An Empirical Instructional Model', to a chart labelled 'Example of Response Situations Relating to Art Forms of Differing Cultures'.

It is perhaps symptomatic of the Engineer's stance that the *last* seventeen words of this lengthy piece are: '. . . and it is to clearer definitions of the content of art education that we must now turn' (1978, p. 14).

Engineers are found most often as heads of faculty or advisers or in departments of art education where their Engineering zeal and positions of presumptive authority offer considerable scope for influencing the beliefs and values of art teachers and student teachers, many of whom take up the calculators and blueprints with a will, writing 'behavioural objectives in the affective domain' and weeding out Magicianship everywhere.

The second and larger group of Technocrats, the Designers, is one of the most problematic under review here. This is partly because Designers, although quick to close ranks when challenged, usually by Magicians, upon whose territory in the schools they seem to have encroached, are themselves not quite sure what 'Design Education' is. Indeed it is said to manifest itself in many forms from the highly professional courses leading to the Oxford Board 'A' level in Design, to a thin but often showy veneer on what was usually called woodwork in most schools, via something called the 'materials circus' or 'crafts cycle' which appears to be the name given to a method of timetabling first- and second-year children to 'experience, use and enjoy' wood, metal, plaster, plastics, clay, fabric, etc. in as short a time as possible. (There is a clear need for evaluation studies here!) Designers are also problematic in that their position is a comparatively new one and, as with any 'subject' or subject division fighting for status, it is often difficult to sort the beliefs of its proponents from the dross of propaganda produced by them. Some Designers are of course excellent propagandists, having been trained for positions in marketing and publicity, and this makes the sorting process more difficult.

There are however a number of sources to which we might turn to obtain a reliable, if theoretical, account of the Designer's stance and ambience. On the growth of design education Baynes (1969) suggests:

> There are probably two main reasons why these events [developments in design education] are taking place in Britain at this particular moment. One is the complex change which is associated with the final destruction of aristocra-

tic society and the dismantling of world responsibilities. It involves coming to terms with certain facts: that most people live in suburbia or in large industrial cities, that patronage is dispersed throughout the mass market, that traditional social and moral codes are increasingly unworkable under contemporary conditions. An aspect of this is a tremendous desire to understand the mechanisms and possibilities of mass industrial culture. Young people are less and less seduced by a vision of a lost rural or imperial past, more and more concerned to build out of the resources of the present . . . the interest in the practical possibilities offered by design education is based on its obvious relevance to the kind of society which is emerging. . . .

Clearly this has implications not merely for the reshaping or modification of the 'old' art, crafts, woodwork, and metalwork, but for wider curriculum change. This is reflected by Archer (1975):

Design is that area of human experience, skill and knowledge which is concerned with man's ability to mould his environment to suit his material and spiritual needs. There is sufficient body of knowledge for this area called 'design' to be developed to a level which will merit scholarly regard for the future.

Eggleston (1976), with reference to Jones (1970), gives the clearest practical view of what is central to the beliefs of the Designer.

The design process above all else is one of rational, logical analysis. Jones (1970) emphasises this strongly, commenting that the picture of the designer is 'very much that of a human computer, a person who operates only on the information that is fed to him and who follows through a planned sequence of analytical, synthetic and evaluative steps and cycles until he recognises the best of all possible solutions'.

Although it may yet be a little early in the development of design education clearly to bring them into focus, Designers have in prospect what seem to be some very difficult value-choices to make. For example, in Baynes (1969) there is a diagram of the design process seen by a London schoolboy which follows that process to a conclusion which he describes, not illogically, as 'much profit'; 'keep on making and selling them'. This illustrates the value-dilemma rather neatly. Are the aims of design education overlaid or imbued with an implicit acceptance of a capitalistic, consumer-based view of society or are alternative views or models of the social role of the designer available and if so what kind of political implications do they have in turn? Should ideological balance be an aim in design education? Some Designers seem aware of this potential difficulty and any analysis of accounts of examples of design projects in schools tends to show this. Whether we shall see a ranging of Designers to the left and right of an overtly political spectrum may be one of the more interesting developments in art and design education. Certainly the influence of Schumacher (1973) and Papanek (1972) and renewed interest in the ideas of William Morris is increasingly apparent in some student groups.

Designers, therefore, like Engineers, relish and revere a technological approach. The blueprints in their case attend to process rather than to structure but have a similarly ubiquitous relationship to practice in the classroom. They do indicate however, in interpretation, something of the Designers' values and beliefs and those they attribute, or wish to make attributable, to others (see Figures 10.1, 10.2, 10.3).

If, for the High Priest, the world appears to be a place of secrets and mysteries giving up its meaning, and only to a chosen few, through a process of ritual and supplication, for the Technocrat it appears a very much more cut-and-dried affair needing only the application of 'rational logical analysis', a blueprint and some data, not merely to be understood but to be changed.

My third group of art teachers are those that I shall call Social Workers. Their name is not a reference to the remarkable willingness and capacity of most teachers to become involved willy-nilly with the pastoral care or tutor-group paraphernalia of most secondary schools, but rather to their willingness to be seen as Social Workers by virtue of what they come to see as the special nature of their subject – art and design. It is, not surprisingly, difficult to find, certainly from published sources, statements by or about this sizeable group which makes for difficulties in any assessment of beliefs or values they may hold. Many Social Workers see themselves as the true inheritors of the Read position and it is easy to see at a superficial level, if not perhaps fully to understand, why this is so. Put colloquially, if an influential and seemingly authoritative figure such as Read suggests that aesthetic education is the necessary corrective to the forces of mediocrity, darkness, and barbarism, what better place to start than with difficult children in the lowest streams of the secondary school? It is indeed these children with whom the Social Worker often forms a mutually satisfying and beneficial relationship. Whether it is satisfactory or beneficial to the subject in that it is the 'genuine arts of today' (Read, 1965) which are involved in this encounter is of course a matter, like so much in Read, of interpretation and argument.

In so far as the Ministry of Education, now the DES, has accepted the recommendations of certain official reports the Social Worker has received something of an imprimatur. Consider, for example, paragraph 377 of the Newsom Report (1963):

> 377. Some pupils will respond best to a precise and craftsmanlike approach. Others, including some of the most difficult of those with whom this report is concerned, may need a more freely emotional outlet, and find, especially through painting and modelling and carving, some means of exploring feelings which have to be inhibited in everyday life, or of vividly living out again past experiences. Here they can deal imaginatively with the real, and realistically with what is imagined. There are analogies in this with some forms of dance and drama and imaginative writing. A teacher need not venture into the dangerous realms of psychiatry to recognise that for some pupils these experiences may have a therapeutic value, and for most, a strong emotional satisfaction.

Needless to say this concept of the art teacher as therapeutic social worker lives on in the collective consciousness of heads and school staffs. This may be seen for example in the openly discriminatory way in which subject options are organized in the typical upper school curriculum and in the emphasis on 'art' in the 'sin-bins', 'refuges', or 'sanctuaries' which, in some of our large urban schools, receive many of the more 'difficult' children for

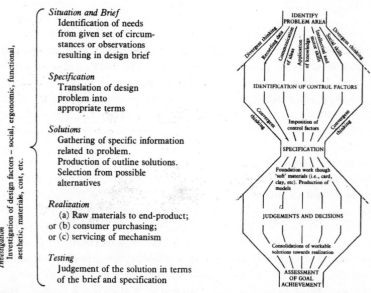

Figure 10.1   Design process – design and craft education project (From Eggleston, 1976.)

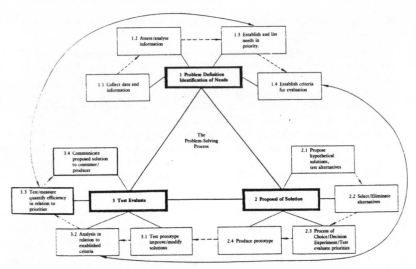

Figure 10.2   The problem-solving process. It is important to stress the necessary reference back from Stage 3 to the initial criteria and priorities in Stage 1. (From Green, 1974.)

large portions of their day. One important way in which Social Workers differ from other types presented here lies with the fact that their role and its concomitant values are almost totally given them by heads, colleagues, and, most of all, children. This is in itself a form of accreditation or authorization, although technically as illegitimate as the charismatic authority which accrues to some Magicians. In order to accept this role the Social Worker tends to see himself as a sympathetic and approachable person, a true friend and confidant with a cosy deskside manner, high on freedom, trust, and tolerant love for others but low on rules, constraints, and what he would call 'authoritarians'. The inability to detect the impossibility of this position is also an indicator of the Social Worker and one which often lands him in trouble, most often with the deputy head (discipline), who may not share his beliefs about their clients. But, if the Social Worker is the sort of art teacher who murmurs, 'Now doesn't that make you feel better?' at the end of a session in which it would appear to an observer that assorted young thugs of both sexes had spent eighty obscenity-laden minutes drawing or painting scenes of appalling violence in which swastika-bedecked Hells Angels or blood-dripping vampires go about their all too well-imagined

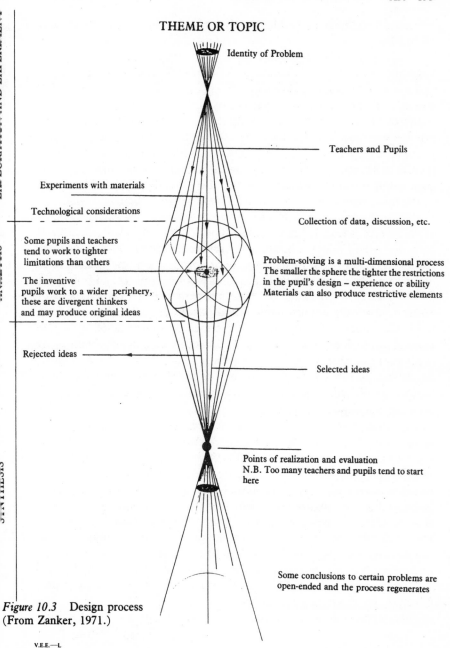

THEME OR TOPIC

Identity of Problem

Teachers and Pupils

Experiments with materials

Technological considerations

Collection of data, discussion, etc.

Some pupils and teachers
tend to work to tighter
limitations than others

The inventive
pupils work to a wider periphery,
these are divergent thinkers
and may produce original ideas

Problem-solving is a multi-dimensional process
The smaller the sphere the tighter the restrictions
in the pupil's design – experience or ability
Materials can also produce restrictive elements

Rejected ideas

Selected ideas

Points of realization and evaluation
N.B. Too many teachers and pupils tend to start
here

Some conclusions to certain problems are
open-ended and the process regenerates

Figure 10.3 Design process
(From Zanker, 1971.)

V.E.E.—L

business, then this is not for him merely a solicitous inquiry but a statement of faith.

It is not possible for a person completely to lack values or beliefs. It is of course quite possible for us to hold unshakeable beliefs which are unrealistic and the indoctrinated would exemplify a group of people of this kind. It is also clear that the holding of beliefs may be and usually is subconscious. Many of us are quite happy to function reasonably satisfactorily whilst holding some, usually peripheral, beliefs which, if we were ever stimulated to examine them closely, would be revealed as mutually exclusive. The key consideration about whether or not our beliefs allow or facilitate our social functioning is that they be coherent, that there should be a lack of confusion in the inner region of what Rokeach (1968) called 'primitive' belief.

My fourth group of art teacher-types seem to lack any coherence of belief or value with respect, if not to their inner regions of beliefs, then most certainly to their values or beliefs about art and education. In extreme cases these art teachers exist in such a state of normlessness and anxiety as to occupy a position in which their alienation from the subject and from most others in the field is almost total. For these reasons I have chosen, perhaps rather dramatically but justifiably I think, to call this group Anomics from the Durkheimian notion of 'anomie' described by Merton (1968) as 'a state of mind in which the individual's sense of social cohesion – the mainspring of his morale – is broken or fatally weakened'. The art teacher as Anomic is, for obvious reasons, difficult to discuss, as his values, in his search for a touchstone of belief, may be seen to swing and veer from extreme to extreme. Nevertheless, from within this limbo some values do emerge which although ambiguous in their nature seem simultaneously to describe and go some way to accounting for the Anomic's position. The Anomic's main value is hostility but not at all like the hostility between the Magician and the Engineer, for this is essentially the product of holders of strong values posturing across an ideological divide. The Anomics hostility is of a blanket, all-embracing variety which stems from the internal turmoil which an incoherence of belief produces. Clearly and understandably the best strategy for some form of tenuous survival for the Anomic is attack, all out and undifferentiating. But linked to hostility is conservatism and here lies the ambiguity to which I refer. Is the Anomic really deeply conservative and his hostility the reflection of his underlying conservatism or is conservatism merely a convenient peg for his hostility?

There appears to be a two-stage developmental process for Anomics;

there are new Anomics and faded Anomics. New Anomics are those art teachers usually at the beginning of their careers whereas faded Anomics are those whose hostility, although still markedly present in many respects, appears to have faded into a conservative attitude toward art and education. For example, new Anomics display, in the work they ask children to undertake, exactly that incoherent veering to which I drew attention. For a term they may be a version of High Priest encouraging self-expression and personal development. The next term or even half-term they may become some kind of Technocrat, insisting on 'careful' thinking, measuring, some kind of objective approach, only to veer once again in the third session. Conversations with new Anomics are difficult, for the justification of present work is usually couched in terms of hostility towards past work and, often, in terms of the brighter future of the next session. Faded Anomics display their conservatism in their concept of what it is that constitutes art. 'Art' for the faded Anomic is capable of a perfectly clear definition which is exemplified by a great painter of the past. For the children in the control of this type of teacher art lessons consist of work which leads up to emulation of the approved model. Some children become very good at it indeed, but many more fail very early.

There might seem, therefore, to be a theory of value-progression and recognition for Anomics. Upon entering teaching new Anomics find difficulty in overcoming their central conservatism and this unease is reflected in manifestations of incoherence of values. Later, as anxiety lessens, those new Anomics who survive fade into positions in which they may come to terms with this conservatism to the extent that it becomes not only possible for them to acknowledge it but also to use it as the basis of their teaching. In which case the faded Anomic is not a case of true 'art-anomie' at all but he remains similarly alienated by virtue of his conservatism and hostility. One might argue, of course, that the faded Anomic has evolved a value-position in which the twin components of hostility and conservatism are so organized as to enable him to forget all about art and art teaching to concentrate on other areas of his life, and to present the faded Anomic as someone capable of turning his conservatism to some positive use in the school may be a very generous view of him indeed.

The size of this Anomic group is difficult to estimate; indeed, this is so to some extent with all the groups I review here. I have teased out types to what may seem to some observers the point of caricature in the interest of isolating their value-stances. I would suggest, however, that one factor which enables the faded Anomic to survive unrecognized is the extremely conservative nature of the work thought to be most acceptable to G.C.E. 'O'- and 'A'-level examiners. If change is initiated within this area, and there are signs that this is likely, then the faded Anomic's cover may be blown and we might see the size of this group more clearly.

Before moving on to my last group, the Pedagogues, it is worth noting that there are groups smaller and even more newly emerged than the Designers, who, by comparison, are establishment figures. There is little doubt that the Schools Council Art and the Built Environment project, coincident as it is with a rising tide of interest throughout the general population in architecture, planning, 'heritage', and quality of environment is attracting a great deal of interest among the many art teachers not already involved in some form of this activity. That this interest will transform into work of some kind in many more schools seems highly likely. The propagandizing of at least one member of the project team (Adams, 1978) suggests that members of this group may become as stridently partisan as the most committed of those mentioned here.

Quality of environment in combination with declining resources and the growth of alternative technology may not lead many to claim, as a student suggested to me recently, that the ecological protest movement is the true art form of the late 1900s, but it would be reasonable to suggest that the art teacher as Ecoman will be a potent force in the schools before long. Some Designers, as I have suggested, seem to be moving quite quickly in this direction.

Certainly one further group will emerge, although because of the intellectual, even esoteric nature of their concern it seems unlikely to be large, and these are the Semiologists. Quite how the Semiologists, following, amongst others, Barthes (1977) and deriving their method from film studies, information-processing, kinetics, and paralinguistic systems, will develop as art teachers is as yet unknown. One teacher I have worked with, Bennett (1978), has consolidated his interest in this area by introducing a very ambitious and successful environmentally based project which was carried out within his school.

We may also see some expansion and realignment of that small group, the Mystics, into a new group which could be called Visionary Anarchists. If one can imagine a loose assembly of values and beliefs derived on the one hand from Laing (1967) and other 'alternative' figures in the 'social' sphere and, on the other, from artists such as Klee ('Genius is the flaw in the system, not the system itself,' 1928), and more centrally, Dubuffet ('Art does not lie down on the bed that is made for it; it runs away as soon as one says its name; it loves to be incognito. Its best moments are when it forgets what it is called,' 1979), with ideas from Prinzhorn (1978) and Cardinal (1972) about the art of the mentally ill and the social outsider, one might glimpse a platform for this group. Further planks in the platform may derive from theories to do with child art (e.g., Kellogg 1969) and its legitimacy as an art form in an aesthetic where the principal (perhaps only) criterion is 'visionariness'. These ideas may, in turn, be overlaid with anarchistic concepts in the wider political sense.

It is, however, too early to say how these possibilities will develop and it might be more fruitful here to turn back to the last of those existing types of teacher whose stance may be seen a little more clearly.

This fifth group of art teachers will be called Pedagogues because this connects by the strongest implication the name of this group with values and beliefs which are essentially to do with education as well as with art and design. Where we find with other types a uni-dimensional set of values derived primarily from professional or vocational considerations of the nature of art and design or from some concept of educational management, the Pedagogue's response to the inclusion of art and design in education involves a multi-dimensional set of values and beliefs. The Pedagogue's value-stance may be derived from two principal published sources (Field, 1970, 1973). Indeed, it would not be an exaggeration to say that Field gives a clear view of the multi-dimensionality of response to which I refer.

> . . . it remains true to say that in most secondary schools the main emphasis is on practical work and the belief behind this is that the insights gained from practical work are largely sufficient, that the pupil will be able to make use of them without any further mediation than an occasional talk. It has already been suggested that this view is inadequate. For the experience of art is art seen from within; a total view of art must include art seen from without. This indicates looking at experience from outside, seeing the relationship between the doer, the process and the thing made; considering meanings and values in art and their relationship with meanings and values elsewhere and seeing art in a social context. (1970, p. 121)

Some further idea of the shift in emphasis of values away from the uni-dimensional toward a stance in which a balance or synthesis is attempted may also be gleaned from Field.

> Art education is a field of study which makes use of many disciplines. . . . For the student the study of the relationship between art and art education

provides a means of integration. He must study art as an individual and social phenomenon together with art education and must grasp the complexity of their relationships. He must use philosophy, psychology and sociology as tools. Moreover, this is not likely to be an area in which, as certain basic areas are studied, relationships necessarily become apparent; the student of art education may well discover that only through a study of relationships will the nature of the basics emerge. (1973, p. 159)

In short, the Pedagogue is concerned with the wide-ranging and complex concepts attached to the idea of personal growth through aesthetic experience, not in some junior apprenticeship scheme in the practice of art and design. The Pedagogue takes on the task of organizing the context in which such growth may occur. This he can only do through his own deep experience, knowledge, and study of art and education. Herein lie more than a few problems but I should like to deal with two of the most important and perhaps the most difficult.

The first is to do with the training and socialization of the Pedagogue. Whilst it may not be true to say of British colleges of education that:

> The educationist has, perhaps unwittingly but nonetheless effectively, seen to it that the teacher of art knows as little about the history of art and is as indifferent to the practice of art as possible. They have accomplished this, most usually, by designing curricula for prospective teachers that assure no more than a superficial acquaintance with the history and practice of art while demanding a great portion of time in education courses.
>
> This philosophy has resulted in the usual art education major being a nice young woman of unexceptional abilities and little ambition to do anything with her art on a personal level: the young man in the program is usually interested in crafts and the decorative rather than painting and sculpture and is often rather low in male hormones. (Manzella, 1963, pp. 76-77)

it is nevertheless reasonable to suggest that it is extremely difficult for even the most able and highly motivated college student to obtain, in our system, that sustained and deep personal experience of art available to the B.A. student. But, as I suggested in my discussion of High Priests, that experience is gained all too often in an environment hostile in many respects to art teaching as a career, to the nature of the studies to which Field makes reference and in which the student is subjected to irrational, even indoctrinatory pressures from which he may never recover. He may in fact hold beliefs socially originated and acquired by passive acceptance from uncriticized external authorities which postgraduate teacher training can do little to ameliorate.

This is especially disabling, as the Pedagogue, whilst continuing to practise as an artist, for this is another Pedagogic value, makes a 'separation of self', distinguishing between self-as-artist and self-as-teacher. This enables him to see the necessary connection, at the instrumental levels of creative or technical process, between himself and his pupils. For the Pedagogue attempts, as Witkin (1974) puts it, 'not only that the praxis of the teacher should comprehend the creative process, but also the process of development itself in sensate experience'. This he attempts without the corruption or contamination of that praxis by terminal values and beliefs he may hold as self-as-artist.

Szekely (1978) suggests that 'by learning to order one's experience on a canvas, one receives the best training or insight into ordering the art experiences of others'. Quite, but without what I have called 'separation of self', beliefs which inform decisions made in ordering those experiences may stem from the computer-as-self of the Designer or the ritual of the High Priest rather than from the Pedagogue's attempt to arrange for the pupil a total view of art.

The second problem lies in any consideration of what is meant by the Pedagogical value – aesthetic experience. As we see from Field (1970) this includes artistic experience – 'art seen from within' – and the Pedagogue would bear in mind Reid's (1969) suggestion that 'aesthetic insight, feeling from inside what art is – this is the central starting and expanding point for everything else'. Dewey, whose concept of growth, or something very closely allied to it, is the other twin of the Pedagogic values, writes 'the distinction between artistic and aesthetic cannot be pressed so far as to become a separation' (1934). But the Pedagogue would suggest that the aesthetic transcends the artistic and to aim only for the artistic is an essentially limited and limiting value beyond which he would wish to go. In order to do so, through 'considering meanings and values in art and their relationships with meanings and values elsewhere' (Field, 1970), the Pedagogue inevitably concerns himself with how such considerations may be carried out. This involves him in dealing in some way in the classroom not merely with what Polanyi (1967) called tacit or implicit knowledge or experience *in* art but also with explicit knowledge *about* art and knowing and experiencing *through* art.

This leads to a further problem, for explicit knowing requires a different kind of language which may be used in a different way from what is sometimes called the language of art (e.g., Klee, 1961, 1973; Arnheim, 1956) and it is likely to be verbal language which will be often most appropriate for helping pupils gain knowledge about art. The Pedagogue may therefore be differentiated from other types by his belief that some art knowledge is accessible through verbal language. This sometimes leads to conflict not only with other types of art teacher but within the area of curriculum. Many Pedagogues would claim an alliance with humanities rather than with the practical subjects with which they are most often grouped. The Pedagogue's values and beliefs may be seen to have been summarized by Barkan (1970),

> to increase the students' capacities to experience aesthetic qualities[values] in man made and natural objects and events in his environment . . . the general goal for aesthetic education can be achieved only through attention to the development of the student as a person.

These are my types of art teacher laid out, not very neatly, with what appear to be, not only to me but also largely to them, their associated values and beliefs.

In the next section I shall set out to consider the implications of what it means for the art teacher to be an authority, for unless he can be seen to be behaving authoritatively his evaluations will be questionable.

Teachers of art and evaluation

Following Peters' (1966) distinction, I am not dealing here with the art teacher as being in authority, as a legitimized agent of social control, but with the art teacher as an authority; that is, someone with the right not only to deal with or pronounce upon matters of truth or value in his 'subject' by virtue of his special knowledge and expertise, but one who also uses these truths or values as some version of an evaluatory standard. Moreover, in so doing he provides a means by which, eventually, his students or pupils may do likewise.

There are a number of difficulties associated with examining the art teacher as an authority. Not the least of these is that an art object, if it can be said to be potentially a truth, does not appear to be readily accessible as such, for we encounter difficulties of language in artistic or (as I prefer) aesthetic knowing which makes for problems in any kind of justification of the truth of that object. Hence, for example, people may say, 'Well, art . . . it's just a matter of taste really isn't it?' This is a question to which I shall return but first it will be useful to look at some less thorny circumstances in which the art teacher might be expected to be authoritative. They are less thorny because he is dealing not primarily with aesthetic knowing but with knowledge of other kinds with which aesthetic knowing is nevertheless enmeshed.

Such knowledge may be technical, to do for example with the suspension of pigment in an emulsion or with the chemical composition of a glaze in ceramics. It may be historical, to do perhaps with the impact of Proudhon on Courbet, the oriental influence on Whistler, or the development of Norman architecture. Some knowledge may certainly be sociological or anthropological in order to consider, let us say, the six principles of Hsieh Ho or the varying social/ritual function of masks. Certainly there will be knowledge which might be loosely described as scientific which will include what we know and might teach others about human perception and its operation, not merely in relation to colour or texture but to size, scale, shape, and style also. In the teaching of skills there will be part reliance on non-esthetic knowing.

Dealing with the art teacher as an authority in these areas is a comparatively straightforward and sometimes empirical matter. 'Does the glaze mature at x temperature?'; 'Is there perceptual after-effect?'; 'Do these two colours mix (physically or optically) to make the third?' Not by any means the same but illustrative nonetheless, 'Does it say in the book what he told us (about Chartres cathedral; the paintings of Seurat; the photographs of Don McCullin; etc.)?' And, 'Does this other book say the same?'

Although these examples appear straightforward or comparatively so, this is not always the case in practice. For, in the classroom, workshop, or studio the art teacher may slip, if he considers it at all, into allowing his authority as, say, a technician, to become confusedly synonymous in the pupils' minds with his authority as an art historian. To add to this existing confusion there may also be some embedded aesthetic value-judgement involved. Consider this not very subtle but reasonably typical example. 'Burnish the surface with a spoon or something – like those pre-Colombian pieces we saw the other day – it'll be OK.'

In any consideration of value, evaluation, and authority in the art department one might suggest that this kind of confusion constitutes a problem and reference to aesthetic values reintroduces the more important and difficult problem of aesthetic knowing, for this is the kind of knowledge or truth which which the art teacher is peculiarly concerned.

If we agree with our puzzled layman (or pupil) – yes, art is 'just a matter of taste really' – then we are agreeing that the emphasis, in terms of examining the legitimacy of an authority, has shifted away from some concept of knowledge, truth, or temperate certainty to those who claim to have such knowledge. Or, at least, to those who hold positions of power which enable them to arbitrate in matters of 'taste'. In short we are saying, yes, art, or what is good in art is simply a matter of social convention and I, because I am an art teacher, university lecturer, or artist, and therefore an authority, will introduce you to these conventions. The shift is from an epistemological question about some art being true, to a sociological question about the 'legitimating authorities' who say some art is true.

If, on the other hand, we say to this same layman or pupil, 'yes, what is good in art is a "matter of taste", but not simply or "just" a "matter of taste",' then we retain the emphasis in the field of epistemology. We make some claim for the possibility of aesthetic knowing ('taste') which transcends the mere social conventions of the moment, of our specific society now.

This distinction is of crucial importance in the establishment of the art teacher as an evaluating authority, for without appeal to aesthetic knowledge or truth his evaluations may appear as mere value-judgement or opinion which many, especially older, pupils will find hard to understand. One need only join pupils or students and their teachers when work is being selected for an interview folder or degree exhibition to see this problem in operation.

Only one of the types of teacher reviewed here is authoritative in the sense that his practice is shaped by this important consideration. That is the Pedagogue who, in organizing for the pupil a consideration of 'meanings and values in art' (Field, 1970), in order 'to increase the students' capacities to experience aesthetic qualities (values) . . .' (Barkan, 1970), may be seen not only to undertake with his pupils an examination of what constitutes aesthetic truth but also to offer it to them as an evaluatory standard in their own growth and development.

I therefore suggest at this point that there does appear to be some agreement in concepts and in standards of judgement, that the possibility of aesthetic knowing is a real one and that is all I am anxious to do, for it is to this possibility that the art teacher might make reference when it is suggested to him, 'Well, art – it's just a matter of taste isn't it?'

This, however much it may help to shift the emphasis from the sociological to the epistemological, is not totally satisfactory and it may well be that when we deal in aesthetic knowing we are dealing in something parallel with, even perhaps the same as, moral knowing. As Pring (1975) writes,

> Whatever the possible changes in moral judgements, resulting in different moral codes, certain assumptions must be presupposed about man for otherwise moral discourse would have no point, – viz. that he normally feels and dislikes pain, has certain desires, is generally dependent on others for survival, etc. To point these things out is to point out what I take to be 'the given' in what Wittgenstein refers to as 'the forms of life'. See Wittgenstein (1958). It is possible that there are or could be other forms of life in which the same restrictions on what might be agreed do not arise, but, given the 'forms of life', then there are limits to how one might conceptualise things, just as there are certain assumptions that cannot be changed and that make agreement possible.

Although this problem of the establishment and justification of evaluative authority is, to my mind, the most important, there are other problems of evaluation which most art teachers will find more pressing. Chief among these is one to which Perry (1973) refers:

> It [his article] draws attention to the intellectual pressure felt in all curriculum planning for formal education, namely the habit of making cognitive education the principal emphasis, subordinating other things to it and then requiring of those other things, which are apparently less cognitive, a justification for their presence in the curriculum in terms of what *cognitive* advance they can achieve. (p. 108)

But we have seen in art education that there is a coming together of beliefs and knowledge, some of which we might call cognitive, even strictly so. Some we would call by some other name, tacit or perhaps artistic. Aesthetic knowing is a fusion of artistic and cognitive and perhaps of other types, for cognitive and artistic seem to constitute poles (rather than compartments) which form a reciprocal relationship within the person. To evaluate, assess, or examine at one pole without some attention to this reciprocity is to ignore the quality of that one.

These factors, on the one hand, the pressure on teachers for some quantifiable demonstration of pupils' achievement and, on the other, a growing recognition that to ignore either the aesthetic component in cognition or the cognitive in the aesthetic, pose ethical problems of evaluation (in its narrow sense of assessing or examining) for teachers of most subjects. In art education there are the further problems of the enmeshing of aesthetic knowledge with knowledge of other types which makes authoritative evaluation difficult, the division of the subject into those value-based groupings exemplified by my teacher-types and the lack of a necessary and causal ends/means relationship within the artistic process itself. Small wonder perhaps that the responses of many art teachers have been to ignore assessment altogether; to find, consciously or otherwise, surrogate means of assessing; to patch up a compromise (within a school or on a wider front); or to find alternatives to the usual external methods by developing new examinations or assessment schemes. Most of these responses are associated with one or other of the principal types of art teacher introduced in the first section of this chapter.

Of High Priests, the Connoisseurs' preferred method of assessment, preferred because it enhances their so-called academic standing, is the external written paper, usually a G.C.E. of some kind. Connoisseurs with a leaning to Pedagogy, and this number is growing with the development of their subject at tertiary level and in other contexts such as museums and public galleries, may mediate this choice by choosing a board which allows an individual response from the candidate, perhaps a local project of some kind, as a part-submission. The response of Magicians is, as might be expected, equivocal. On the one hand are White Magicians who say to their candidates, 'Look here, forget all about art if you want an 'O' or 'A' level, just do what I tell you, draw in this style, paint in this manner and you'll stand a chance, but don't think this is art – it's just passing the exam', and, on the other, Black Magicians who regard any form of assessment or examination as irrelevant but who (usually in response to internal school pressure) will enter candidates for C.S.E. because this method of assessment will interfere least with the junior artists' 'personal development'. This strategy also has the advantage of not obliging the Black Magician actually to teach which fits his belief that art cannot be taught.

Anomics, as I have suggested, also subscribe to some form of 'O'- or 'A'-level examination although the beliefs and values underlying their subscription differ totally from those of the perhaps cynical yet benevolent White Magician. For the conservative Anomic, art in school *is* 'O'- and 'A'-level work which is synonymous with the imitation of his 'Old Master' ideal. It is perhaps the Anomic, with his vested interest in preserving the status quo, who has ensured that the response of most G.C.E. Boards to change and development in the fields of art and art education has been limited.

Logically, the Technocrats favour a rational, that is cognitive, approach. Indeed the whole development of design education may be seen not as its proponents represent it but as the outcome of a frustrated response to the problems of evaluation in art education that I have mentioned. As Witkin (1974) suggests,

> Whenever it [design education] represents an attempt to accommodate to the academic system and to justify the art process by the achievement of measurable results, it usurps the educational function of art-making. (p. 115)

Indeed, it might be more sound for a variety of reasons conceptually to separate design education from art education in schools, although the pressures that Designers exert on art teachers cannot be ignored. Given the beliefs, values, and aims of the Designer his evaluative task is comparatively simple. The Engineer, although clearly involved with art rather than design, will demonstrate his values by responding to evaluation in a way similar to that of the Designer. This will ensure that nothing will be undertaken in the art department that cannot be turned into a teaching/ learning objective, progress towards which may be 'measured'. This undoubted methodological success will bolster the Engineer's beliefs. Any syllabus and assessment scheme arranged by an Engineer will abound with 'modules', diagrams, and priority-weighted marking schemes which, although they may serve his purpose efficiently, will make him even more unacceptable to his ideological opponents.

Whatever the qualities of the Social Worker as an art teacher, a desire to evaluate in cognitive terms is not one of them. In fact, any form of assessment likely to be used by a conventional school is unlikely to meet with his approval, for the Social Worker's concept of his value of freedom may be seen to involve a rejection of evaluation altogether. However, if he can give grades for 'effort', 'attitude', or 'social adjustment', he may feel that this allows him to register the value of his subject as he sees it. The Social Worker is rarely forced to face problems of external evaluation as his pupils are very often classed, however kindly, as 'nonexam', but, if pushed, he may enter them for C.S.E.

The introduction of the C.S.E. was greeted with great enthusiasm by many art teachers. The response reported by Witkin (1974) may be regarded as typical.

> C.S.E. a great improvement! Much more valuable. The fact of an examination is a bit of a limitation I suppose. You're always finding yourself saying, 'Well, it will be nice when the exam is over'. Certainly the new C.S.E. examination seems to me really rather exciting. (p. 115)

The kind of control over the criteria of assessment which the C.S.E.

demands of teachers may be seen as either welcome or not depending on one's capacity to credit teachers in general with the professional competence to exercise the power this control gives them. As far as the C.S.E. in art is concerned, questions are being asked by some teachers about the way in which this power is used and controlled especially at the level of local consortia. One need only imagine a consortium made up largely of Magicians but including two Engineers, or another with a vocal Social Worker or two, a couple of Magicians, and some Pedagogues to begin to form some notion of the conflicts which may arise at consortia meetings. It must be stressed that the fact that conflict may arise is not in itself a measure of incompetence. Indeed it might be argued that the reverse is the case. It must also be stressed that where conflict does arise the protagonists do not necessarily behave unprofessionally. Indeed, none of the types of art teacher reviewed here behave unprofessionally or incompetently if they are judged by the standards or values to which they hold. But values are both proscriptive and prescriptive and what is proscribed by one group may be prescribed by another. Whether such conflict is the reason or not, some art teachers in some parts of the country are clearly becoming less 'excited' about C.S.E.

The Pedagogue is also in some difficulty with regard to external examinations for there is little to satisfy him about either C.S.E. or G.C.E. Both may be seen as rather blunt instruments for the evaluation of the blend of practical, historical, theoretical, and oral work that he undertakes. Indeed the evaluative procedures used in those art departments staffed by Pedagogues exceed in sophistication anything available in the wider sphere. Some of those I have seen include self-reports on drawing experiments, essays in art theory, written reports on perceptual experiments, historical and historiographical work, a consideration in simple terms of possibilities of visual response to classes of stimuli, in addition to a range of 'practical' activities. These departments are as yet few in number but the influence of Pedagogues is growing. Some evidence of this is contained in the report of the Art Syllabus Steering Group set up in connection with the Schools Council eighteen-plus research ('N' and 'F'), especially within the fine art group, and in the nature of the initial considerations being made by those involved in the DES Assessment of Performance Unit (Aesthetics). Although the former now seem most unlikely to be introduced and the latter may not come up to Pedagogic expectation, these examples are encouraging in a field in which recent developments make a review of values and evaluatory procedures overdue.

The question becomes – who would respond to such a review? Not the High Priest, for his values enable him to assure us that his is the only one true way, nor the Technocrat, for not only is his way true but it can be measured! The Social Worker meanwhile has abandoned the field in favour of paper-weaving with recidivists and the Anomic is too busy teaching a 'talented' pupil to draw an apple like Michaelangelo might have done. A Visionary Anarchist, a Semiologist, and an Ecoman argue about whether this term's work should be 'graffiti', 'the meaning of the house as a spatial statement', or 'the creative recycling of the *Daily Telegraph*'. The Pedagogue may well be free to fashion his own responses for, as a headmaster once remarked jovially to me, 'I always think of a clever boy doing art as a contradiction in terms.'

References

Adams, E. (1978) 'Art and environment', *N.S.A.E. Journal*, January.

Allison, B. (1978) 'Sequential learning in art', *N.S.A.E. Journal*, October.

Archer, L.B. (1975) Address to Design Education Conference, Royal College of Art, London (mimeo).

Arnheim, R. (1956) *Art and Visual Perception*, London: Faber.

Arnheim, R. (1970) *Visual Thinking*, London: Faber.

Barkan, M., Chapman, L.H., and Kern, J. (1970) *Guidelines: Curriculum Development for Aesthetic Education*, Ohio Central Mid-Western Regional Educational Laboratory Inc. (CEMREL).

Barthes, R. (1977) *Elements of Semiology*, New York: Hill and Wang.

Baynes, K. (ed) (1969) *Attitudes in Design Education*, London: Lund Humphries.

Bennett, D. (1978) 'The built environment: aspects of meaning', *Bulletin of Environmental Education*, (Town and Country Planning Assoc.) No. 81, January.

Cardinal, R. (1972) *Outsider Art*, London: Studio Vista.

Dubuffet, J. (1979) in *Outsiders* (Catalogue to an exhibition of Art Brut), Arts Council of Great Britain.

Eisner, E.W. (1972) *Educating Artistic Vision*, New York: Macmillan.

Eggleston, J. (1976) *Developments in Design Education*, London: Open Books.

Field, D. (1970) *Change in Art Education*, London: Routledge & Kegan Paul.

Field, D. and Newick, J. (eds) (1973) *The Study of Education and Art*, London: Routledge & Kegan Paul.

Field, D. (1973) *Art and Art Education*, in Field, D. and Newick, J.

Green, P. (1971) *Design Education: problem solving and visual experience*, London: Batsford.

Kellogg, R. (1969) *The Analysis of Children's Art*, San Francisco: National Press.

Klee, P. (1928) *Bauhaus Prospectus*.

Klee, P., (ed J. Spiller) Notebooks, (1961) Vol. 1, *The Thinking Eye*. (1973) Vol. 2,

The Nature of Nature, London: Lund Humphries.

Laing, R.D. (1967) *The Politics of Experience and The Bird of Paradise*, Harmondsworth: Penguin.

Lanier, V. (1977) 'The five faces of art education', *Studies in Art Education*, (USA) Vol. 18, No. 3.

Madge, C. and Weinberger, B. (1973) *Art Students Observed*, London: Faber.

Manzella, D. (1963) *Educationists and the Evisceration of the Visual Arts*, London, International Textbook Co.

Merton, R.K. (1968) *Social Theory and Social Structure*, New York: Free Press.

'Newsom' (1963) *Half our Future*. A Report of the Central Advisory Council for Education (England), London: HMSO.

Papanek, V. (1972) *Design for the Real World*, London: Thames and Hudson.

Perry, L. 'Education in the arts', in Field, D. and Newick, J.

Peters, R.S. (1966) *Ethics and Education*, London: George, Allen and Unwin.

Prinzhorn, H. (1972) *Artistry of the Mentally Ill*, Berlin/Heidelberg/New York: Springer Verlag.

Read, H. (1938) *Meet Kropotkin – the Master*, London: Gordon Press.

Read, H. (1943) *Education through Art*, London: Faber.

Read, H. (1948) *Culture and Education in World Order*, New York: Museum of Modern Art.

Read, H. (1965) *The Origins of Form in Art*, New York: Horizon Press.

Read, H. (1975) 'The limits of permissiveness', in Abbs. P. (ed), *The Black Rainbow: Essays on the present breakdown of culture*, London: Heinemann. (Orig. pub. *Resurgence* Vol. 8/9, 1969).

Reid, L.A. (1969) *Meaning in the Arts*, London: Allen and Unwin. New York: Humanities Press.

Rokeach, M. (1973) *The Nature of Human Values*, New York: The Free Press.

Royal Academy of Arts (1968) *50 Years' Bauhaus* (Catalogue), London.

Schools Council. 18 Research Programme Studies based on the N and F Proposals. Report of the Art Syllabus Steering Group to the Joint Examinations Sub-Committee.

Schumacher, E.F. (1973) *Small is Beautiful: Economics as if People Mattered*, New York: Harper & Row.

Stockl, M. (1974) 'Art integrated. The place of art in the curriculum', *Athene*, Vol. 15, No. 3.

Szekely, G. (1978) 'Uniting the roles of artist and teacher', *Art Education*, (USA) Vol. 31, No. 1, January.

Witkin, R.W. (1974) *The Intelligence of Feeling*, London: Heinemann Educational Press.

Zanker, F. (1971) *Design and Craft in Education*, Leicester: Dryad.

CHAPTER 11

HISTORY

Raymond Davies

Liberation from the tyranny of the present might be regarded as one of the chief benefits to be derived from the study of history. The present can be too much with us. It can limit our conceptions of the future leading us to believe that that which is to come will be another edition of today. To examine the past and witness how our predecessors' futures emerged can be a profitable undertaking for those who in their expectations of continuity in human affairs neglect the element of change. Men do not create their world afresh. Each individual, each generation is a product of history. Those who scorn the past and wish to transform the world might usefully examine the records of society. A study of past radical endeavours and the extent to which they took account of the powerful historical forces present in the situation might be worthy of their attention. Equally, the conservative who stoutly defends today's bequests from the past and seeks to prolong their existence may learn from a study of the past that hallowed antiquities were at one time upstart innovations which had to make headway against the forces of tradition.

Three hundred years ago Descartes suggested that to study history was similar to embarking on travel abroad. There, one encounters peoples whose ways of life pose contrasts to our own. The insight is still valuable. The traveller notes the differences of the host community from his own which may lead to reflections upon the particular nature of his own society and its values. He is afforded an opportunity of enlarging his perspective of the nature of mankind. In history, the student has the opportunity of examining ways of life other than those of the present which he inhabits. In one all-important respect, however, the study of history has an advantage over the traveller. He has the opportunity of studying peoples over great sweeps of time. Here the contrasting elements of continuity and change may be examined, an opportunity which is denied the traveller. Another advantage lies in the number of peoples who may be encountered in history, far greater than those whom the contemporary traveller may visit. The development of world history offers access not only to the record of groups and communities still in existence, but to many which have disappeared.

In respect of those peoples which our traveller might visit it is possible that those who are more remote and offer a greater contrast to our own ways of life might provide the most rewarding encounters. Although the remoteness and cultural distance obviously present difficulties to the visitor, the efforts involved may be outweighed by the enlargement of his conceptions of the nature of mankind.

Similarly, in respect of history it may be most rewarding to study peoples who are remote in time if one is to acquire some conception of the protean nature of man. The more remote, the more arduous the effort required, the more abundant the pitfalls of anachronism, yet the achievement of some awareness of 'otherness' derived from the disciplined exercise of imagination upon the past is one of the chief benefits of such activity. There is always the temptation to pursue those aspects of history which most narrowly reflect current preoccupations and to concentrate upon the immediate background to present passions and predicaments. Such a course deceptively exhibits the value of 'relevance' while a syllabus that does not reflect in its content a conspicuous attention to the present may be scorned as antiquated, of little utility, providing an escape from reality. Unquestionably, a course that omitted examination of the immediate antecedents of current concerns would be inadequate, yet in terms of genuine relevance it is necessary to attend to eras, areas, and situations that, though remote, may offer more insight into human possibilities than those derived from a study of immediate historical events. The preoccupations of the future, though they may be to some degree anticipated by extrapolation of current trends, may yet be markedly different from our own. E.H. Dance has noted that it is impossible to teach our pupils the history of their own times for their times have not yet arrived: our selection of themes drawn from the recent past may not be the most rewarding for those who enter upon adult responsibilities in the next ten or twenty years.

Middle aged men who were being taught contemporary history in the 1930s were being prepared by it to deal with future Hitlers and Mussolinis: they were not being taught what they need to know in the 1970s – the history of communism in China, race relations and the awakening of Africa – because in the 1930s historians were not alive to the imminence of these issues. And if the pupils of today are taught the immediate antecedents of race relations and the awakening of Africa they are almost certainly not being taught the immediate antecedents of the yet unforeseen problems with which they will be faced when they are parents of families. (Dance, 1971)

Each age requires its own history. Because it is not certain what rising generations of adults will find most useful in our current selection from the vast resources left by the past, support is lent to the contention that, being less subject to the inconstancy of time, understanding of the structures, the processes, the language, and the attitudes of historical activity should form the central part of pupils' learning, but even so the tools of historical investigation and communication must be employed upon materials and a selection of materials must be made.

In our selection syllabuses must reflect the current concerns of society, but the immediate past and immediate societies do not provide the only themes and content most relevant for the future. Such a course would unduly emphasize the element of continuity in human affairs at the expense of change. We may limit young people's conceptions of what it is to be human and limit their appreciation of the range of human potentialities if we confine their acquaintance to peoples and situations most similar to our own. What is required as much is an acquaintance with the unfamiliar, the strange, even the bizarre which more distant societies exhibit.

These unfamiliar peoples must share some common traits with ourselves or they would be incomprehensible, but the ways in which they depart from our experience provide us with contrasts that enlarge our conception of 'human nature'. An acquaintance with ancient Spartans, mediaeval monasteries, the inhabitants of Imperial China may more extend the imagination necessary for dealing with the unforeseen than a study of our immediate antecedents which merely confirms today's conventional wisdom that time inexorably renders obsolete.

The very strangeness of such remote peoples may evoke more curiosity within young people than those of the recent past. The familiar can be dull, the unfamiliar intriguing. The apparent illogicality of earlier ways of life may at first arouse scorn, but resourceful, sensitive teaching can dispel the belief that earlier necessarily means inferior. Aspects of societies that in isolation seem ludicrous may be seen as eminently sensible in terms of the totality of those societies. Works of art may differ from our own not because their creators lacked technical skills which we possess but because their vision of art differed from our own. Conceptions of justice in earlier communities and the means they sought to achieve it may upon examination make sense in terms of the underlying rationale of that society. Economic arrangements markedly different from our own may be seen as an appropriate understandable response to a particular situation. Far from being an exercise in antiquarian escapism, the examination of more remote societies may by the contrasts they afford focus critical attention upon contemporary institutions and highlight issues of enduring significance. A study of mediaeval guilds may be as fruitful in isolating the essential issues involved in economic relationships as a study of the development of trade unions during the last century, while the problems attendant upon urban development may be explored as profitably by a study of the expansion of ancient Rome as by a study of the twentieth-century city. The longer the time-scale employed, the greater the range of cases for study.

There is, of course, the danger of distance lending enchantment to the view. The purpose of study of earlier societies is not the undiscriminating praise of things past. Such an outcome would be as unwelcome as that approach to history which sees the past as no more than preparation for an ultimate present. An uncritical admiration of the past is not sought, but rather the cultivation of imaginative understanding of the varieties of human experience which may afford young people an opportunity of establishing their own identities and realizing their own values as against an uncritical, unwitting absorption of those of the contemporary world.

It might be objected that the traveller is enabled to communicate directly with his hosts and that the student of history is denied this, so that the latter's experience is inferior. This is not so. Apart from the fact that direct testimony may be misleading either by design or plain misunderstanding, the historian, on the other hand, has evidence whereby he can elicit answers from the past. He has no direct contact with the past, only with the evidence that the latter has deposited, evidence often fragmentary and incomplete, but by applying the techniques which have developed over time, but particularly systematically since the early nineteenth century, he may question the past without being at the mercy of those who have left behind the materials for examination. It is because of these means that it has been asserted that the historian may know more of the lives of peoples in the past than they knew themselves. Although the prime materials of the historian are documentary he may employ other materials – monuments and artefacts

– to aid him in his quest and he may call upon current scientific and technological techniques where it is judged that they may advance the inquiry.

Like the scientist, the historian investigates the unknown, employing disciplined and systematic methods in his search for information and its verification. They share a commitment to the intellectual values of concern for truth, validity in argument, and respect for evidence, but the natures of their subject-matter and their evidence differ. Whereas the scientist working upon natural phenomena is concerned, at least ultimately, with the formulation of general laws, the historian concerned with human experience in the past seeks to establish the truth about singular, particular events, events which cannot be reproduced for experimental verification. The unique, complex conditions in which an event had its birth cannot be reproduced, the event itself transforming the conditions from which similar future events may emerge. With regard to the social sciences, history shares a common subject-matter – man in society – but the social scientist's essential inclination towards the typical and recurrent contrasts with the historian's attentiveness to the particular and the contingent in human affairs. However, their activities are complementary, almost symbiotic, the historian frequently and fruitfully employing the social scientist's generalizations as hypotheses in his own inquiries while the social scientist finds the particular disclosures of the historian useful in framing and testing his generalizations.

If the historian in his employment of system and method has affinities with the scientist, in other respects he stands close to the artist. Sir Lewis Namier suggested that limitation and selection are essential in the historian's craft:

As history deals with concrete events fixed in time and space, narrative is its basic medium – but guided by analytic selection of what to narrate. The function of the historian is akin to that of the painter and not of the photographic concern: to discover and set forth, to single out and stress that which is the nature of the thing, and not to reproduce indiscriminately all that meets the eye. To distinguish a tree you look at its shape, its bark and leaf; counting and measuring its branches would get you nowhere. Similarly what matters in history is the great outline and the significant detail; what must be avoided is the deadly morass of irrelevant detail. (Namier, 1952)

In reporting the fruits of his inquiry the historian requires the fine discrimination of the literary artist. This need to write lucidly and persuasively is not a matter of embellishment but a requirement integral to the work itself if he is to succeed in conveying the truth of that which he seeks to portray or explain. Fine writing as such is not the goal; the demands of artistry may obscure the truth. The historian may not invent character, traits, or events to satisfy what are conceived to be the demands of art. As John Passmore remarks in his comparison of history and literature, it is both suitable and necessary to ask whether the historical narrative 'really happened like that' (Passmore, 1974).

The motto of the Historical Association 'Quid quid Agunt Homines' – whatever men do – reflects the universal concerns of the historian. His field of inquiry may be any area of past human experience and activity. In earlier times, politics, domestic and international, provided historians with their subject-matter but as newer fields of interest emerged in the wider society historians have sought to apply their perspective and techniques to each as they have arisen. Fields as diverse as engineering, art, medicine, philosophy, social organization have come under historical scrutiny. To the specialist in each field, study of its development in time may provide a valuable perspective for his appreciation of the current state of the field.

It may be argued, however, that general history is the most educative form. We may have special areas of interest and concern but they do not make up the whole of our lives however engrossing they may be. There is a danger that conceptions drawn from one field may narrow our vision and, even though we may have understanding of several fields, we may fail to make connections. Much of the recent advocacy of integration in education arose from such a realization though some proposals may have tended to neglect the distinctive contributions of the various forms of knowledge. There is undoubtedly a danger in the latter part of the twentieth century that living in the age of the specialist we may fail to see life as a whole. General history is synoptic, affording the opportunity of seeing life as a whole, comprehending the entirety of man's experience, all that he has uttered, undertaken, or endured. Past societies may be observed laterally just as much as sequentially and of any epoch the student may examine the interrelatedness of all aspects of life – politics, religion, technology, arts, economics. The current concerns of any society will be reflected in the demands laid upon each field of disciplined knowledge and history is not exempt. At the present time assertions that the significance of science and technology in our lives has been neglected in the education of young people are justified. If, as many fear, 'Things are in the Saddle and Rule Mankind', then an investigation into the nature of these rulers and their domains is an immediate need and history can play a part. However, a course which solely concerned itself with internal developments and failed to relate them to their interaction with other aspects of human experience would prove of little value.

Richard Pring has argued that young people bring to schooling a practical knowledge of the world in that they have learned to speak, how to argue, how to find their way about, and how to relate to people (Pring, 1976). Their skills in these areas may be unrefined but they provide the context for education. The opportunities for reflection and criticism of their day-to-day activities which the various modes of disciplined thinking and activities afford should issue in greater mastery over themselves and their environment, so that they may act more effectively. The teacher's task should be to make that which the pupil is already engaged upon more effective, pleasurable, and imaginative through an introduction to the particular skills, practices, and understanding which his discipline offers.

Several historians have suggested that the practices of the historian constitute the refined, disciplined, systematic employment of methods employed by the layman from an early age. According to J.H. Hexter, we get so much rigorous training in historical explanation from the time that we develop any facility for talking; everyone works at history every day out of sheer necessity, seeking to provide reasons, convincing accounts, and explanations of the events of everyday life (Hexter, 1972). Similarly, G. Kitson Clark has suggested that any attempt to describe what has happened before the actual moment of narration presents some of the problems which are common to all historical work and may be subjected to the same critical techniques as that to which historical works are subjected (Kitson Clark, 1970). Much that is encountered in the ordinary business of life poses the same problems as professional history – the records of words spoken and actions reported for which the testimony is uncertain or plainly insufficient. The critical layman and the critical historian employ the same fundamental procedures of posing the questions 'What is your authority for saying this?', 'How do you know that this happened in the way you say it happened?'

In a world abounding in the slanted, partial message, be it explicit or (even more dangerous) covert, the acquisition by young people of the habit of critical appraisal, saving them from the pitfalls of cynicism and gullibility, is not among the least of the values that a historical education can provide. In its treatment of the humanities 'The Proper Study of Mankind', the Newsom Report of 1963 stressed that knowing what evidence is and what it will prove is central to work in this field, suggesting that pupils should study problems where only some of the facts are known but where a decision has to be made (Newsom, 1963). For the authors of the report cynicism seemed to be a greater danger than gullibility. They noted that pupils of quite poor academic ability were markedly suspicious of that which purported to be the truth, tending to disbelieve everything, and concluded that 'a more hopeful defence would be provided by an elementary training in evidence and how to handle it'.

There has been a growing use of evidential approaches in school history over the last decade and an enthusiastic employment of historical materials in the classroom. The mode of inquiry of the historian has provided the structure for several schemes but at times enthusiasm may not have been tempered by a proper appreciation of the context in which evidence is employed. G.R. Elton has asserted, admittedly of the adult professional student of history, that he 'does not grasp the true meaning of his material until he has thoroughly acquainted himself with the organization that produced it, the purpose for which it was produced and the difference between common form and the exceptional', but it is noteworthy that Dickinson, Gard, and Lee in their recent examination of children's historical understanding emphasize that some context of historical knowledge is a condition of understanding evidence and that the gradual development of children's understanding must go hand in hand with the acquisition of knowledge of the historical context which produced the evidence (Elton, 1967; Dickinson, Gard, and Lee, 1978).

Several writers have suggested that the historian, though seeking truth like the scientist, differs from the latter in his employment of common sense. J.H. Hexter has remarked that of all the learned disciplines history is 'the least mysterious, the least removed from common experience', while Fritz Stern asserts that even after it became a discipline history preserved its immediacy to life, 'and of all the intellectual concerns of man, save art it remains closest to a sense of life'. Sir Isaiah Berlin suggests that, whereas the scientist, the external observer, takes as little for granted and abjures common sense, the historian in his inquiries of historical actors, as an actor himself, appeals to his own experience and imagination. He employs his knowledge of what social relationships have been and might be, his awareness of his situation in respect of other people and of the physical environment. It is this quality of common humanity that the student of history employs in examining the remains bequeathed by earlier men (Hexter,

1972; Stern, 1956; Berlin, 1978).

The historical enterprise is a dialogue between the historical remains and the historian's own accumulated experience. The broader, the deeper that experience, the more fruitful will be the inquiry. The more limited the experience, the more inadequate and partial the quality of the investigation and exploration, a point made by Berlin and G. Kitson Clark, who observes that conceptions of what is probable in human affairs are narrowed if personal experience is limited and not extended by reading or a lively interest in other people. The wider the acquaintance with the diversity of humanity, the less the likelihood of imputing to historical figures and societies conceptions, valuations, motivations, reactions that anachronistically reflect the preoccupations of our own age. The deeper the acquaintance there is with the particular society studied, an acquaintance derived from many sources including recognized secondary sources, the greater the likelihood of individual historical materials making sense to the student in terms of the realities of the age in which it was produced. Elton points out that historical research consists of an exhaustive and exhausting review of everything that may conceivably be germane to a given undertaking rather than the pursuit of some particular evidence which will answer a particular question (Elton, 1969). This is, of course, advice to the adult professional aspirant, but it is a statement that might be borne in mind by those purporting to employ the historian's methods with children. What accompanying knowledge and understanding do the pupils bring to the examination of an item that is proffered as evidence? Anachronisms can be as easily perpetrated through misinterpretations of primary materials as through the misunderstanding of a textbook statement.

The stress laid upon the need to initiate pupils into the acquisition of the skills and their active employment of the procedures involved in historical inquiry, undeniably one of the most valuable suggestions of the 'new history', along with the equally undeniable realization that there is no corpus of knowledge fundamental to a history course may lead to enormities equal to any committed by fact-ridden students of the 'old history'. Knowledge still matters. 'Content-free' misconceptions which have led some to suggest that pupils' understanding of the historian's use of evidence might be examined by their responses to 'unseen' passages unrelated to a subject they have studied reflect a failure to appreciate that history is essentially concerned with substance – particular people and societies at particular times in particular places. A pupil who encounters 'the king' in a fifteenth-century document and whose conceptions of kingship are derived soley from his understanding of contemporary monarchy is not likely to achieve much success in his interpretation of the document.

To emphasize the crucial significance of knowledge and context in the acquisition of historical understanding is not to reject the skills approach to history teaching in schools. The move away from courses dominated by factual content which failed to employ more than a narrow range of skills, which disregarded pupils' existing if unrefined capacities to infer and deduce has been welcome. Efforts made over the last twenty years to go beyond formal statements of aspirations in history teaching and to proffer a range of more specific learning objectives, procedures for their achievement, and appropriate evaluative instruments have borne fruit not only in G.C.E. and C.S.E. examinations but in the day-to-day practice of increasing numbers of classroom teachers. While retaining their conviction that historical knowledge is an essential aspect of historical understanding, they have sought to enlarge that understanding by activities which demand critical thought and judgement of their pupils.

To many history teachers, who encounter the technical terms of the educational evaluator for the first time before appreciating the underlying rationale, the objective approach may smack too much of the scientific, positivist, systematizing spirit which encroaches upon many areas of late twentieth-century life. In its particular application to historical education, it may be viewed as an immoral invasion of a subject which is proudly regarded as teaching its students what it is to be human in an age that witnesses the dehumanizing results of efforts to measure, to predict, to control. This initial reaction is not only understandable but welcome. It guards against the danger of prizing evaluative procedures above the purpose which they are employed to serve – the acquisition of a deepened understanding of the nature of history. If, however, it is acknowledged that some appraisal of success has always been demanded legitimately of any learner, such teachers may examine without prejudice what wider-ranging and more refined modes of assessment may offer their own particular discipline, modes sensitive to the essential qualities of the subject.

To such teachers, objectives would constitute a guide, a check-list, an *aide-memoire* in devising pupils' learning experiences, but not a mechanism dominating the ensuing activities to the extent that valuable unforeseen objectives emerging spontaneously from pupils' responses to the unfolding situation are treated as of secondary importance if not dismissed out of hand. The recognition that response to learning involves an affective as well as a strictly cognitive engagement would ensure that much more is sought than pupils' acquisition of a collection of particular intellectual skills. Only a minority of pupils will become professional historians; for the majority, even though their acquisition of some of the elementary skills involved in historical investigation and communication will prove valuable both now and after school, if the unimaginative pursuit of techniques destroys their enjoyment of the vital, if vicarious, experiences of life which history affords, then the teaching of history would stand condemned. Ben Jones, an eminent practitioner of the 'new history' and one who stresses the value of a framework of aims and objectives, points out the dangers lurking in the approach, particularly that of seeking our historical materials solely for the purpose of revealing a particular skill whereby the course becomes little more than a series of exercises each measuring a little item.

> In this way if you seek too much to isolate individual skills you may end up in a worse state than even old-fashioned History would have served you. Clio's robe is seamless: there is no harm in showing how it is woven but it is not to be divided. (Jones, 1976)

An abiding enjoyment of history that will enrich the pupil's life long after school is as cherished a goal of those who espouse the 'new history' as it is of traditional history teachers, but there is a danger that in the pursuit of objectives, whether drawn from general education taxonomies or from particular subject disciplines, an insensitive, unremitting training of pupils in the use of discrete skills may result in the atrophy of enjoyment. What would be thought of a student of art who acquired a battery of techniques both of painting a picture and of appraising another's canvas but by the time that his course was concluded had no desire either to produce or look upon another work of art?

History certainly presents problems for examination and explanation but it should present at the outset human situations that engage the feelings. Without involvement of this kind the curiosity that poses questions and seeks explanations will not emerge. Even when it does, the teacher needs constantly to check that, though planned sequential exercises are being followed according to the logic of objectives, the initial involvement is sustained.

What are the particular skills that teachers of history most value and wish their pupils to acquire? They include the ability to pose and recognize historical problems and to employ the appropriate methods to seek solutions, to be able to recognize what constitutes relevant evidence, recognizing omissions or deficiencies in such evidence, and to be able to structure a convincing valid conclusion for communication to others. The teacher is not seeking to produce mini-historians. Pupils lack both the academic equipment and the experience of life of the adult historian. They are, however, guided in their acquisition of skills by a teacher who because of his own training is both familiar with the fundamental skills and techniques required for the pursuit of history and with the developmental stages of his pupils. The teacher's historical competence is as important as it was in more conventional, content-grounded courses. Indeed, the need is greater.

> As long as the role of the history teacher was to impart knowledge of historical facts, the reading of history books was probably sufficient to keep him informed of new knowledge and to maintain a commitment to historical study. However, as soon as the teacher is expected to instruct his pupils in 'historical thinking' it becomes necessary for him to be constantly involved not just in reading historical books but in practising all aspects of historical thinking, including the creative thinking of the research historian. If pupils are to learn history by 'doing it', then the teacher must keep himself professionally fit by 'doing it' too. (Garvey and Krug, 1977)

The same point is forcibly put by Richard Pring. Teachers of specific disciplines employ ways of thinking located in various traditions of thought and activity in which they should be deeply involved. Unless they are so involved and sustained by their discipline then they have little to offer their pupils.

> A teacher of history who is himself in no way completely transformed by historical reading and research will have nothing to communicate to the pupils. He will simply underline to them the worthlessness of the subject. (Pring, 1976)

How may the teacher evaluate the student's progress in historical understanding? The deft and sensitively timed question, whether in the course of exposition, during pupil investigation of materials, or at the conclusion of an exercise, is one of the most valuable techniques. A variety of questions can help the student's own critical approach to materials presently encountered from which will grow fruitful habits with respect to those met in the future. Questions which go beyond those requiring recall but demand comprehension, interpretation, extrapolation, invention, and evaluation can be employed. Students can be asked to translate that which is seen or read into another medium, to relate and compare that which is seen with their existing knowledge of the topic, to infer and to proffer hypotheses, to propose possible personal responses to particular historical situations, and to attempt the evaluation of the credibility of a particular piece of evidence. Greater employment of open-ended questions and sequenced inquiries with the youngest pupils, employing approaches appropriate to their stages of development, would render less arduous the transition from 'what' to 'how' and 'why' questions when public examinations techniques require more than recall.

Questioning, of course, may be abused. Constant and unremitting questions by teachers can be dispiriting to pupils. The questions posed by pupils are often the most fruitful in giving clues to that aspect of the topic which they find most interesting, or to their capacity to grasp crucial stages of the process which might otherwise remain unknown until written material is examined at a later date. Questioning, particularly that which is undertaken to encourage discussion, may not be successful with the more self-conscious if employed on a class basis. Questions might best be addressed to groups where the more reticent may be readier to participate with a smaller audience. In all cases however, questioning, in addition to stimulating pupils' learning, can serve as a valuable informal means of assessing students' progress in achieving the skills and attitudes necessary for historical understanding.

Apart from oral appraisals of students' work drawn from questioning and discussion, more structured methods may be employed. The objective test has its place. By this means, not only may a broad range of content knowledge be tested but particularly by means of multiple-choice questions understanding and knowledge of the processes of historical study may also be measured. Selection of individual words and phrases is required of the pupil and, if ambiguity is avoided in the framing of questions, high reliability may be achieved. To many traditional teachers of history, accustomed to the essay as the prime means of appraising students' mastery of the subject, the multiple-choice question may arouse suspicion if not hostility. To them the ability to frame historical argument fluently and coherently is the hallmark of the historian and the requirement of the objective test which demands no more than recognition and selection is an illegitimate importation of a scientific methodology which lays emphasis on precision and economy. Were multiple-question exercises the sole assessment pattern the charge would be upheld. History is indeed a literary discipline, but the essay or any other discursive activity, if employed alone, may reward eloquence at the expense of both knowledge and understanding. The fluent writer may avoid discussing important issues of which he is uncertain and where the student knows that he may choose optional essays he may not give due attention to all aspects of the course, which presumably are of equal importance in developing his knowledge and understanding. As to multiple-choice questions themselves, not only may knowledge of facts and events be tested, but understanding of concepts, principles and methods of inquiry, and the ability to handle conflicting interpretations may be appraised.

The skills of comprehension, analysis, and interpretation of historical material fundamental to courses that seek to make the pupil conversant with the nature of historical evidence are best acquired by pupil response to historical materials themselves. They need not be primary sources. Secondary passages, statistical data, pictures, cartoons, charts, and diagrams may all be employed. If pupils, as part of their course, are trained to pose the types of questions that may be usefully addressed of specific types of material, then terminal assessment by means of interpretive exercises will genuinely test skills learnt rather than an aptitude for straightforward comprehension. Unseen passages describing or appraising an event may be followed by questions that test the pupils' capacity to interpret, translate, draw inferences, and test hypotheses. Prior knowledge of the topic is required of the pupil if he is to embark upon the exercises, but it is his analytical skill in employing the knowledge upon the material that is being examined. By defining the nature and delimiting the length of the responses sought, it is possible to pin-point the degree of skill achieved and avoid the inappropriate fluency which hopes to mask lack of understanding.

The historical essay as a form of assessment has several advantages. It is creative, allowing and indeed encouraging pupils to organize their own ideas and express them freely, employing information from their own background knowledge and understanding. The student may use and organize evidence from a variety of sources to present a coherent, sustained narrative or explanation. The abilities to select, synthesize, and generalize are exercised while a command of literary skills is necessary for the presentation of lucid, coherent, and convincing argument. The essay cannot answer all the demands required for assessment. It does not measure purely factual knowledge efficiently. It can only cover a selected field of knowledge: in so far as essay questions take a long time to answer only a few may be tackled within the confines of a particular session. The freedom afforded students in the organization of materials renders the task of the assessor more judgemental than that of marking an objective test. Nevertheless, the value of the essay in assessing pupils' abilities to use historical knowledge in a truly historical way outweighs the disadvantages outlined above and with respect to the latter it is possible to minimize the defects. Apart from the accompanying employment of objective tests to ascertain the students' knowledge, the avoidance of options, and the stipulation of the length of compulsory questions, it is also possible to specify the particular skills required in defining the tasks set the student. The problem of unreliability in assessment may be countered by multiple marking.

The individual project is the activity which approximates most closely to the work of the professional historian. The student determines the topic and identifies the means most appropriate to answering the question he poses. The exercise requires a search for and assessment of materials that might provide evidence for his thesis and an ability to communicate his conclusions. To achieve any competence at the level of project work requires the acquisition of a great number of subordinate, prerequisite skills. The ability to find information by the proper use of indexes, tables of contents, and library catalogues, to translate the substance of literary, graphic, and other media, an understanding of the basic vocabulary, terms, and concepts peculiar to historical work are required, in addition to the capacity to infer, hypothesize, and generalize. Although literary presentation is most frequently employed, reports may serve as alternatives or as supplementary forms of presentation, while graphic communication of findings may also be appropriate. The criteria applied by the evaluator will include the following: ability to recognize a historical problem and to choose the most appropriate means of solving it; to select, use, and interpret relevant materials, showing therein the capacity to recognize omissions or deficiencies in the evidence; the ability to draw justifiable conclusions and to present them lucidly and coherently.

Where the student may be examined orally upon his project, it is possible to escape the constraints imposed by written submission alone. The evaluator can check more searchingly particular aspects of the project, affording the student the opportunity of disclosing the depth of his understanding and the degree of involvement and enjoyment which accompanied the task. The individual interview is time-consuming but, where questions have been carefully prepared and the basic rules of interviewing technique are observed, the exercise can prove a fruitful supplementary form of evaluation.

Whatever attention is addressed to the acquisition of discrete, contributary skills, the evaluator's ultimate concern is the student's perception and apprehension of the attitudes and values of peoples living in the past, the prime goal of historical study. Courses which include as a component the examination of particular eras in all their aspects, political, economic, social, religious, and cultural, offer students an opportunity of extending their understanding by studying the ways of a society in depth. Hegel remarked that the brief all-encompassing history 'must give up the individual presentation of reality and abridge itself by means of abstraction'. The era-approach offers details for examination which present reality. Whether fourteenth-century Florence, fifth-century Athens, or the Incas be chosen, pupils are able to appreciate the interplay of the various activities which made up a particular way of life. An extended understanding of a society in its own terms may be essayed while comparisons and contrasts with contemporary society may be continually employed.

Static studies of societies however are insufficient. Development of time is a basic concept of history. D.G. Watts has noted the static treatment of topics which fail to show that people and societies change over time, citing patch histories such as 'The Romans' or 'The Anglo-Saxon Peasant' which can neglect the transformations that take place over several hundred years (Watts, 1972). It has been remarked that the processes of change are tortuous and usually quite unpredictable rather than linear and regular. If pupils are to achieve some understanding of these processes, then studies of development should feature prominently in a history course. Family history and the contemporary landscape offer materials for an introduction to the fundamental processes. Studies of the development of language, of human activities such as transportation or medicine may similarly serve to illustrate the ways by which change takes place yet elements from one age survive into another. Attention can be drawn to periods of marked transformation and those when dramatic innovation was largely absent and some attempt may be made to account for the contrasts in terms of the interaction of contemporary cultural phenomena which might have impeded or stimulated change.

Studies of the development of societies and institutions over time provide material for an appreciation of the moral issues posed by the tension between freedom and necessity in human affairs. Are men the authors of their own actions? Are they prisoners of circumstance? To what extent are historical events the product of men's desires and intentions, to what extent their unintended consequences? What degree of freedom was enjoyed by the actors on the stage of history and in what measure were their actions constrained behind the scenes by forces of which they may have been unaware but which succeeding generations have sought to disclose?

History provides a rich field of case studies for those who wish to examine in concrete terms the issues involved in the perennial argument of free will versus determinism. The concern of the teacher here is not to elicit the snap judgement on historical actions, precipitate pontifical awards of culpable and laudable, but rather to seek an appreciation by his pupils of the complexity involved in appraising the nature of human choices and decisions.

This does not entail a covert denial of the demands of moral obligation nor, for that matter, of the existence of eternal ethical principles, but represents an emphasis upon some understanding of the bounds to freedom imposed by situation and circumstance. What is rejected is the unprofitable, presumptuous, and indeed immoral attempt to sit in judgement upon the dead whose innermost nature can never be wholly known to other men, living or unborn. We cannot, nor should we attempt, to adopt a value-free approach in history, however impartial as technical historians we may strive to be. There are historical deeds which may be praised or condemned as good or evil, whatever allowances be made the variation of moral codes or the particular situation in which the deeds occurred. Massacre is still massacre whether it be termed 'execution', 'liquidation', or 'taking out', but the prime concern of the student of history is learning how and why things happened, not the erection of a moral tribunal for the prosecution of individuals. What we can do for our students is to provide as representative a range of sources for historical topics, primary and secondary, that display the tangled strands that need to be unravelled in seeking to explain any human action – historical or contemporary. History cannot render its students moral but it may heighten their moral awareness by making them more sensitive to the ingredients that enter into any human decision, the interplay of reason, will and emotion, the interaction of individual and society and man and his physical environment.

> Were those who followed Hitler necessarily worse than those who rallied to Churchill? Why did they do it? Might we have done the same? How did some of his own people stand out against him?

This passage from a section of the Newsom Report calling for an education in empathic awareness, 'an ability to enter imaginatively into other men's minds', catches the required spirit (Newsom, 1963). Preordained conclusions are not being sought. The approach is one of helping pupils pose appropriate questions which demand an appreciation of circumstances and situation, yet do not suggest a knowledge of all excuses all – some of Hitler's own people did stand out against him.

To learn to live with the ambiguities and contradictions inherent in human life, such as those posed by the conflicting demands of freedom and necessity, is an essential part of education. Young people need to learn that in addition to those problems for which there can be, in principle, complete solutions there are others which by their nature are insoluble because they are the manifestation of what it is to be human. There are dilemmas and quandaries that must be endured, the sources of comedy and tragedy. The student of history is made aware of the eternal antinomies of human existence, the unremitting tension of such polarities as past and present, the universal and the particular, absolute and relative, science and humanities. Such a discipline not only offers information and techniques but the subtler and more profound knowledge of humanity derived from insight and understanding.

References

Berlin, I. (1978) 'The concept of scientific history', in Hardy (1978).
Dance, E.H. (1971) *History for a United World*, London: Harrap.
Dickinson, A., Gard, A., and Lee, P. (1978) *Evidence in History and the Classroom*, in Dickinson and Lee (1978).
Dickinson, A. and Lee, P. (eds) (1978) *History Teaching and Historical Understanding*, London: Heinemann.
Elton, G.R. (1967) *The Practice of History*, Sydney: Sydney University Press.
Gardner, P. (ed) (1974) *The Philosophy of History*, Oxford: Oxford University Press.
Garvey, B. and Krug, M. (1977) *Models of History Teaching in the Secondary School*, Oxford: Oxford University Press.
Hardy, H. (ed) (1978) *Concepts and Categories: Philosophic Essays by Isaiah Berlin*, London: The Hogarth Press.
Hexter, J.H. (1972) *The History Primer*, London: Allen Lane.
Jones, B. (1976)'Practical approaches to the new history', in *History in School*, No. 3, University of Leeds, School of Education.
Kitson Clark, G. (1967) *The Critical Historian*, London: Heinemann.
Namier, L.B. (1952) 'History', in *Avenues of History*, London: Hamish Hamilton.
Newsom Report (1963) *Half our Future*. A Report of the Central Advisory Council for Education (England), London: HMSO.
Passmore, J. (1974) 'The objectivity of history', in Gardner (1974).
Pring, R. (1976) *Knowledge and Schooling*, London: Open Books.
Stern, F. (1956) *The Varieties of History*, Cleveland and New York: Meridian Books.
Watts, D.G. (1972) *The Learning of History*, London: Routledge & Kegan Paul.

CHAPTER 12

SCIENCE

David Malvern

Man is but a reed, the weakest thing in Nature. But he is a thinking reed.

Blaise Pascal

This passion for our kind
For the process of finding out
Is a fact one can hardly doubt,
But I would rejoice in it more
If I knew more clearly what
We wanted the knowledge for,
Felt certain still that the mind
Is free to know or not.

W.H. Auden

The view that science is free from values is surprisingly widely held. The argument which is usually given to support this opinion is straightforward. Scientists in their research provide descriptions of how the universe does what it does. They make no attempt to find explanations as to why things are, nor to prescribe what ought to happen. This act of describing what is there to be seen is viewed as being independent of values. The chairman of the British Humanist Association would go so far as defining science thus: 'Science: a body of knowledge and understanding concerning matters of fact not of value' (Stopes-Roe, 1979).

Despite the attraction of its simplicity, however, such a view will not do, for in the words of Barara Ward: '. . . the painful divorce between how and why, between facts and values, between science and religion, between secular aims and ethical systems, may in fact be ending, precisely because of the scholarship and scientific research of which we are the heirs' (Ward, 1978).

No matter how temporary the separation between science and the humanities may be, it cannot be denied that in many minds it existed and is of long-lasting consequence in education. In evidence to the Clarendon Commission, Dr. Temple accounted for the lack of science teaching at Rugby School because it 'did not have any tendency to humanise, such studies do not make a man more human but simply more intelligent' (Clarendon Commission, 1864); and in 1880 Thomas Huxley complained: 'How often have we been told that the study of physical science is incompetent to confer culture. In the belief of the majority of Englishmen culture is obtainable only by a liberal education and a liberal education is synonymous with one form of literature . . .' (Huxley, 1880). A decade earlier Huxley and other members of the scientific fraternity who formed the 'X-Club' had been represented on the Devonshire Commission which marks the beginning of the entry of science teaching into the school curriculum. It was a slow beginning, a fact perhaps made more understandable when we realize that Gladstone, whose administration set up the Devonshire Commission, had himself little time for its findings. Lecky, in *Democracy and Liberty*, a contemporary account, informs us that there were 'wide tracts of knowledge with which he [Gladstone] had no sympathy. The whole great field of modern scientific discovery was out of his range!'

Almost half a century after the Devonshire Commission the Thomson Committee began its report of 1918 by noting 'Not for the first time educational conscience has been stung by the thought that as a nation we are neglecting science' (Thomson Committee, 1918). By then, however, there were significant numbers of teachers of science with experience to have founded in 1901 an association of science masters (SMA) which could command attention, and in 1912 the Association of Women Science Teachers (AWST) came into being (the two finally amalgamated as the Association for Science Education, ASE, in 1963). These associations have played a major part in determining the character of science education.

In submitting evidence to the Thomson Committee, the associations presented a two-part justification for teaching science. The first had to do with science as a disinterested exploration of truth; its study would lead to a respect for evidence freed from external authority and combine imaginative qualities with operational skills. The second concerned the usefulness of science in its applications, both those which afford an understanding of the natural world and those which release greater benefits for mankind. It is the first of these, however, which has come to dominate curriculum design in science education.

Two important examples of the associations' thinking serve as evidence for this. They can both be found in Mary Waring's detailed and absorbing case study of the Nuffield Science Project. At the annual meeting of the SMA in 1942 reference was made to Sir Richard Livingstone's book *The Future of Education* and its proposal that the twin pillars of education be Christianity and Hellenism. To the associations, science as a search for truth could be seen as a third 'fundamental principle in the development of high ethical standards'. The subsequent policy of the associations incorporated this idea in the more general form of beauty, goodness, and truth, and although there was no segregation of the three values to separate parts of the curriculum, in Waring's words: 'From then on, however, the association of science with truth features in all official statements by the Science Masters' Association' (Waring, 1979).

In 1958 there began a series of meetings by the chemistry panel of the two associations. The resulting policy statement became the springboard for the Nuffield chemistry 'O'-level project. Its first meeting presented the principal justification for teaching chemistry as:

(a) its contribution to general culture . . .
(b) its uniqueness as an example of inductive logic . . .
(c) the understanding chemistry affords of many substances of everyday importance . . . (SMA/AWST, 1958)

It was the second of these which became uppermost in the minds of the panel, and Waring has traced a note pencilled into the minutes of the panel's second meeting. In this note, which Waring attributes to the chairman E.W. Moore, is carried a key phrase. It refers to the pupils experiencing 'the science of the scientist', before going on to record a decision taken to put scientific method at the core of the proposed course.

That science is more than a body of knowledge is not merely recognized in modern science teaching; it has become one of its fundamental and characteristic assumptions. 'Nuffield Science' set out to bring about a broad education through participation in and experience of the procedures of scientific investigation. It is not an emphasis on participation or experience which characterizes the Nuffield approach, for science teaching has a long history of promoting learning through activity. Unlike many of its predecessors which saw 'doing' as an effective way of gaining understanding, this modern view holds it as an essential process, important in its own right as an induction into science as practised, an initiation into the science of the scientist. For those involved in school science, as teacher or examiner, thinking about 'what science is' and 'what do scientists do' has become a necessary first step in thinking about what science education has to offer.

Inextricably included in the notion of science are its methods of working, and the community of scientists who do that work. Their activities do not always conform to searching out merely what is, but frequently prescribe what ought to be. What is more, although at any one time science can go no further in saying what is than to describe what is known or thought to be the case at that time, what is known or thought to be known is not fixed. In order for more science to come about, scientists must either focus their attention on hitherto unstudied phenomena or shine new light on old data. To do this decisions are made as to what ought to be included in researches. In other words, deciding what science is to become may well be value-laden. These arguments deserve some attention.

To begin with the first point, science, broadly speaking the study of natural phenomena, is both the canon of what such study has to tell us about the universe and the method of study itself. Science is a way of looking at the world as well as what can be seen. Among the characteristic procedures of scientific investigation are commonly held to be observation; data-collection and tabulation; biassociation of various sets of such data; hypothesis-forming, testing, and rejecting; theory-building; prediction; law-making and acceptance. It is also normal to demand that these activities are undertaken in some sort of humility, reported honestly, and open to scrutiny. Replication is essential, and on occasions cooperation is encouraged over competition. The proper performance of these procedures can be considered as virtuous. That is to say, precision in measuring, for example, is a virtue in a scientist in that the application of such skills expresses a worthiness in the pursuit of truth. The overall aim of these activities is to bring about an objective search for truth, which is seen as a value in its own right.

But two recent views question not just whether or not the search has always been objective or has always unearthed truths, but whether or not it can be objective or ever obtain truth. The two views differ in the importance to understanding science they ascribe to the different kinds of activities scientists undertake. One, that of Popper, is concerned with problems in the creation of general statments from accumulated observations of specific instances, the bringing into being of new theories. The other follows Kuhn in noticing that the most common scientific activity is the exploration of the implications of general laws, and it is through this deductive process that science bears its fruit when theories are used to solve problems.

In this 'normal' science of Kuhn, the scientist has established paradigms as the framework of his or her activities. It is because there is an acceptance of a set of theories that much progress can be made; the success and relative efficiency of such work comes about because the scientists 'take the foundations of their field for granted' (Kuhn, 1970) and get on with the patient, almost remorseless business of exploring their implications and applications methodically. It would be a mistake to assume that because such activity is methodical that it is also always orderly. Medawar has described how the conventions for reporting scientific work obscure just how untidy a process it can be. An example of how the untidiness can also obscure the underlying method can be found in the account of the researches into the function of the pineal gland, which J.Z. Young describes as follows: 'We know approximately what it does, and the sequence of the discovery makes an interesting case of scientific procedure. So far as I can see it does not conform to any clear schedule of method such as proposed by Popper or Kuhn' (Young, 1973). But Ormell, using Young's paper as a source, sets out the main steps in the researches and demonstrates how '. . . a series of fairly routine exploratory researches gradually led to the accumulation of a total body of information which could be interpreted in one specific way.' (Ormell, 1979). As Ormell points out, the interpretation is a tentative answer to the question 'What does the pineal gland do?' Throughout the investigations, then, it was assumed that the pineal gland has a function, and that the function would be reflected in the chemistry of extracts from the gland, in the reaction of organisms to the presence or absence of those chemicals, etc. In other words, it conformed to the prevailing paradigm to do such things as treat tadpoles with extracts from the pineal gland, to remove the pineal gland from lampreys and observe the effect on colour changes, and all the otherwise strange activities involved. To anyone not familiar with the typical procedures of biochemistry, and in particular ignorant of the care and responsibility exercised in deciding to do such experiments, these activities must seem bizarre; and it will come as surprising indeed that they may contribute to an understanding of puberty in man and possibly, one day, have important consequences for our social systems. What is of importance here is that this example of normal science shows just how successful a collection of apparently routine investigations can be when guided by a potent paradigm. It is precisely because the vehicle is not coasting in neutral through a wilderness of experience but is firmly in gear, and because there is at least some idea of the route, that progress is perceived.

If not wholly objective, the search is also not subject to the idiosyncracies of individual scientists. It is an organized and collective enterprise. Even though the perception of progress depends on a bias in the perception, it is the bias of consensus. To be perceived to be true in science means that it is generally agreed to be true among scientists; and scientists have developed an elaborate system of communication, checking, and criticism of each other's work. The importance of this system, which is both social and intellectual, cannot be overestimated. The necessity of replication before acceptance in scientific work not only puts a value on being open to the criticism of others to the extent of encouraging and welcoming it, but also determines that what a scientist does cannot be unique to an individual. Many of the greatest scientists have, of course, shown startling originality, and the history of science is full of inspiration and intuitions and on occasions the rarer qualities of genius, but in every case we can all follow in the steps of the innovator. When Newton acknowledged that, if he had seen a little further than had been seen before, it was because he stood on the shoulder of giants, he would have been justified in noticing that in so doing he provided a 'back' from which we might gain an even greater perspective.

It would also be true to say that the mechanisms which allow the community of scientists to cooperate, like any institution, entail problems particularly when current orthodoxies become dogma. The work of Crane and his associates provides an instructive warning. Between 1950 and 1967 at the University of Michigan they carried out a series of experiments aimed at a direct measure of the g factor of the electron (the index of the ratio of the electron's magnetic moment to its spin angular momentum); a measurement which has had far-reaching implications in quantum mechanics. Serious doubts as to the validity of these experiments stemmed from a lecture given by Bohr in 1920. Bohr demonstrated unequivocally that the two methods for making this measurement proposed *at that time* offended Heisenberg's uncertainty principle, which states that there is a natural limitation on the precision with which the position and the linear momentum of a particle can be known simultaneously. Mistakenly this was generalized by others to say that *no* experiment to measure the magnetic moment of the free electron could succeed. This mistaken generalization found its way into the textbooks and in Crane's words 'became, one might say, gospel'.

Crane's successful experiments were unlike the earlier proposals and did not offend the Heisenberg principle, but he and his colleagues had considerable difficulty in persuading their fellow scientists out of this dogma.

> I can recount an incident that is amusing in retrospect to show the firmness of the conviction that experiments on the magnetic moment were not possible. At the meeting of the American Physical Society in Washington in April 1958, Louisell presented his first successful measurements and two theorists in our Department, Kenneth Case and Harold Mendlowitz presented proof that the concept of the experiments was in harmony with quantum mechanics. Yet the evidence was not persuasive to several physicists in the audience, who rose to cite the Bohr proofs to us. The person who voiced the strongest objection said later that when he was half way home on the airplane he satisfied himself that there was no conflict between our experiments and what Bohr had shown! (Crane, 1968)

The obvious danger is that, as time goes by, few if any experiments are performed which bring into question the orthodox theories and methods which make up paradigms. Perhaps no experiments are designed to do so, as such questions are not asked. For the most part the chance of an experiment 'accidently' raising them is small for not only are experimenters virtually blind to the event but the experiments which are performed emphasize in the design the successful application of the paradigm in hand. If such a state of affairs were to continue, most if not all the work would be being done by scientists who had never seriously experienced experiments testing the accepted theories. These theories would then take on the role of dogma, and the authority for them become vested solely in the transmitted beliefs of a scientific community whose members are selected by their ability to accept successfully these beliefs.

Fortunately, even when such things happen all is not lost. In the first instance the dogmas are born in the perceived truths of their day and are far from arbitrary. Moreover, if theories lack power, there will be no extended exploration of their applications and they will not become dogma. As Kuhn himself tells us: 'History suggests that the road to a firm research consensus is extraordinarily arduous' (Kuhn, 1962, 1970). By and large the dogmas of the scientific community only become so because they do provide description, are fruitful, and fulfil many of the usual reasons for theory choice. But perhaps more importantly, although theories become dogma because the authority for their acceptance as truth rests on the authority of established scientists, the authority for their being true does not. For the ultimate arbiter of truth the scientist looks to empiricism.

It is on the occasions when established theories fail the test of empiricism that revolutions occur in science. It is at this point that the inductive nature of science becomes apparent. In originating a theory of universal applicability the scientist must generalize from his or her necessarily limited experience, and it is open to judgement as to when he or she is prepared to do that. How many apples have to fall to earth before we are prepared to say that all apples fall? After such an hypothesis is made, however, it will only take one apple to ripen and then rise from the tree to destroy the generalization. How can we say that this will *never* happen? We cannot. The power of empiricism lies in the ability to falsify theories, not to verify them. The consensus views of established science are always open to refutation by experiments, but can never expect to be proved by them. We arrive at the apparent paradox that the experimental method which allows scientists to build theories so powerful in description and fruitful in application reserves its true cutting-edge for their destruction, yet in so doing provides the constructive evidence for further progress. When a theory's predictions are refuted by experiment, what delights the scientist is not that the theory has been destroyed by ugly facts, but that our knowledge of the applicability of that theory is enhanced. Nowhere is the scientist's position better expressed than in the opening sentence of H.A. Bethe's important paper on 'The Electromagnetic Shift of Energy Levels': 'By very beautiful experiments, Lamb and Retherford have shown that the fine structure of the second quantum state of hydrogen does not agree with the predictions of the Dirac theory' (Bethe, 1947). The community of scientists is always held in check, for however dogmatic its theories become, it can never know if it has an absolute truth, nor claim to do so. Because the certain knowledge of absolute truth is beyond the methods of science, the scientists are prevented from making too dogmatic or too arrogant a claim for what they know.

We are left, however, with the problem of whether absolute truth exists? Roughly speaking there are three possible ways of beginning to answer this problem for the scientist: that knowledge of such truths is impossible and all knowledge including scientific knowledge is relative; that all knowledge is human and fallible but to be able to say that we must have the *idea* of absolute truth which acts as a standard; and that the balance of probabilities would have it that absolute truths exist even though we cannot know if any are included within our knowledge.

Kuhn does not accept the last of these. 'One often hears that successive theories grow ever closer to . . . the truth. Apparently generalisation like that refer to . . . its [a theory's] ontology, to the match, that is, between the entities with which the theory populates nature and what is "really there". Perhaps there is some other way of salvaging the notion of "truth" for application to whole theories, but this one will not do. There is, I think, no theory-independent way to reconstruct phrases like "really there"; the notion of a match between the ontology of a theory and its "real" counterpart in nature now seems to me to be illusive in principle' (Kuhn, 1970). But he also counters the charge of relativism made by a number of critics: '. . . applied to science it [Kuhn's position] may not be [relativistic], and it is in any case far from *mere* relativism . . .' (Kuhn, 1970 – his italics). Kuhn is primarily concerned with science as 'puzzle-solving', and the dominant criterion which scientists apply in choosing between theories is the power to solve problems presented by nature. The progress to be seen in science is towards better and better ways of solving puzzles within a changing environment. A different, but related, argument against relativism can be illustrated by considering the following statements which all include the relationship 'weaker than'. (a) Nation M is weaker than nation N; (b) Women are weaker than men; (c) Bridge, type X, is weaker than Bridge, type Y; (d) Chemical bond P is weaker than chemical bond Q. Let us suppose that in each case, by selecting particular instances or a relevant context, we know the statement to be true. Obviously what is meant by 'weaker than' is arrived at by stipulation and is different in each case, but we can put that difference to one side, and concentrate on the implication for action of, say, ignoring the 'truth' of these statements.

Does universal agreement as to the truth of (a) prevent Nation M going to war with Nation N even when (a) refers to military might? Clearly it does not, and history has many instances of just such acts. What is more, universal agreement need not prevent nation M winning the 'trial of strength'. As Tolstoy noted: 'Sometimes, when there is no coward at the front to cry "we are cut off" and start to run, but a brave spirited lad who leads the way . . . a division of five thousand is as good as thirty thousand, as was the case at Shöen Graben, while at other times fifty thousand will fly from eight thousand, as happened at Austerlitz' (Tolstoy, 1869).

Again in (b) we can point to societies which would agree with the proposition but make no attempt to acknowledge its truth in social action, either by so arranging affairs that variations in strength cause no discrimination, or in some cases by demanding that women do all the physical labour.

Statements (c) and (d) are similar in that ignoring their truth could lead to otherwise predictable disasters – a collapsed bridge or an untimely chemical decomposition or whatever. If we take (c) in a technological context, however, that X-type bridges are weaker than Y-type bridges does not necessarily result in an expensive replacement of one by the other. The more important questions are 'do type-Y bridges do the job expected of them safely', and if not 'what is the best thing to do about it' – where 'best' can include economic, social, and aesthetic considerations.

But when we come to statement (d) can scientists, having decided what the stipulation means and agreed as to its truth in a particular instance, subsequently act as though its truth did not matter? No, for all our theories relevant to this particular measurement must either include it in their foundations or predict it in their applications. It is as though nature has a kind of veto over our actions. For although 'is weaker than' remains a human stipulation, and the propositions which contain it are not verifiable but carry no more than potentially fallible, perceived truths, we are forced by the experimental evidence to act in certain ways. In this sense, science cannot be *merely* relativistic.

The third way of approaching absolute truth is to take the idea of it as a standard. In this case the existence or not of an absolute truth is irrelevant. But what is meant by a standard is not, and nor is the means by which standards are set. These problems are considered at length elsewhere in this book, but it is appropriate here to mention one argument given by R.G.A. Dolby and others: namely that the standard can be set as assertions 'about which all societies or groups, actual or possible, past, present or future may agree'. This has the advantage over any relativistic consensus as it excludes assertions which we may all have agreed to be true yesterday, but today agree to be false. But it fails to take us further in solving the problem of induction, for even if such an agreement were obtained *we could not know it*, and we are back in the same dilemma.

Nonetheless, it is a useful notion, and goes a long way in describing what scientists are trying to do when gathering experimental evidence. The demarcation that makes an experiment scientific is not simply that it is testing the falsifiability of theories but also that it is repeatable. It is the insistence on replication in the collection of experimental evidence which provides scientists with a substitute for universality. The requirement of replication ensures that the authority for scientific evidence is wider than any individual, however powerful, and increases the opportunity for nature to exercise its veto – although the interpretation of the evidence remains solely the product of human minds. In this way we make shift around the problem of absolute truth, by settling for knowledge which is as reliable as we can make it.

Underlying all this activity is the assumption that the natural world is consistent in its observable behaviour. Or to put it another way, science can only be cognizant of those parts of nature which are open to observations of the kind described and which respond consistently to our observations. The gaining of new knowledge, then, depends on the techniques of observation available and on decisions as to what to observe.

In deciding what is to become scientific knowledge the researcher is both within a tradition and forced to look outside it. The researcher is a part of the scientific community, and the tradition of that community can tell us where its work has got to. But it is the researcher's imagination or intuition, vision or inclinations which prompt as to where he or she is to go next. The scientist has a choice as to what is to be put forward. Even though each proposal will be subject to criticism, and open to test and modification by the community as a whole, the process of forming the proposal is an act of individual creation and the choice involved is an expression of values. It is this point which leads Magee to say in his discussion of Popper: 'The scientist and the artist, far from being engaged in opposed or incompatible activities, are both trying to extend our understanding of experience by the use of creative imagination subjected to critical control, and so both are using irrational as well as rational functions. . . . Both are seekers after truth who make indispensable use of intuition' (Magee, 1973).

It is important to realize that science cannot go on separated from society in general. So deep is the inclusion of values in our science, and so power-fully can science express them, they cannot be ignored by the scientist nor forgotten by those with the responsibility for using science, as Benn reminds us: 'You cannot discuss technology in isolation from the values of society. We must choose to which values we wish to attach ourselves. It is the values of a society which shape its very nature.

'Scientists and technologists . . . must inject them [social and political values] directly through their own work, and the choices they make in their work' (Benn 1979). This is in Benn's own words 'a solemn warning' stemming from growing anxieties during his experience as Secretary of State for Energy as to the unthinking application of technology.

Problems to do with nuclear power plants will serve as one example of the sources of his anxiety. It is not the problems of safety, formidable though they may be, which cause concern; for man has been playing with fire to

198 Values and Evaluation in Education

good effect for generations and will continue to do so. Rather it is the implications for the organization of society which give rise to worry, and the failure of the scientific and technological community to take them into account. The technical and associated managerial systems of a nuclear power plant cannot ignore the possible military implications nor the potential security risks. The result of uncaring technological decisions may well be that the terms of employment within such a plant, the policing around it, and the conditions for residency in its vicinity are all different from those elsewhere in the country; and moreover of a kind unacceptable to the rest of the community.

Benn is not alone in voicing concern over such issues. The Bishop of Durham has made much the same point, reporting an emphasis on 'the need for scientists and technologists to see their work in a broader social and moral context. The old picture of the remote academic scientist pursuing his research, uninfluenced by anything going on around him, and driven by only the pure love of truth, now bears less and less resemblance to what actually goes on' (Durham, 1979).

Writing on science education, Bullock acknowledges that science is too important an activity for scientists any longer to be left alone with their work, and sees science education in need of improvement 'because we must ensure its full contribution to man's survival' (Bullock, 1976). Jevons also claims 'we may need all the power over nature that they [the branches of natural science] give us in order to survive the dangers and uncertainties that face mankind as a whole' (Jevons, 1975). It is of interest to compare these recent declarations with the thoughts of Francis Bacon, who is at the beginning of the development of modern philosophy of science: 'Upon a given body to generate and superinduce a new Nature or new Natures is the work and aim of Human Power . . . the true and legitimate goal of the Sciences is none but this: that human life be enriched with new discoveries and wealth' (Bacon, 1620).

Despite our own age being overwhelmingly more rich in material terms than in Bacon's time, it may be the uncertainty which surrounds us that is responsible for the shift in emphasis from the creation of wealth to a fight for survival. We have come to realize, however, that man is not destined for the governing of a separable universe for the plunder it affords him. What is important is that science, while being the study of the natural world of which man is a part, is also the determinant of our association with nature. In both its reflective mode searching to understand nature, and in its applications interacting with nature, science is as dependent on values as all other activities. Because science is, as we have seen, a kind of contract between man's imagination and nature's ways, its authority stems from the harmony it achieves between man and nature. It is not power over nature, but power within nature that science puts within our grasp. In seeking to understand nature, science establishes a relationship between man and his environment. It is our values which will decide how harmonious that relationship will be.

The 'science of the scientist', then, is a complex interplay between various methodologies, attitudes, and responsibilities. It is not an easy thing to find a reduction suitable for teaching in schools. One of the key voices in the formation of the Nuffield approach to science teaching is H.F. Halliwell, the organizer of the 'O'-level chemistry project. The contribution to science teaching of Halliwell and his colleagues in the various Nuffield projects is enormous, and no one can deny the value of it. In particular by making experimental practice an integral part, even giving it the central role, of school teaching they provoked a revolution in the design and provision of apparatus in schools. Above all they presented a real and successful challenge to moribund and arid teaching styles. Nonetheless, the emphasis of the projects has come to be the promotion of the 'science of the scientist' as a pedagogical model, and this has led to serious difficulties in applying it to the role of science in general education.

How have these difficulties come about? In 1960 Halliwell discussed the 'human activity known as science' and identified two distinct characteristics:

1 Arising from curiosity and 'a wondering if. . .', it [science] searches for patterns of behaviour, and offers explanations for them in terms of models which *not only* explain, but also co-ordinate and are, therefore, suggestive . . . the patterns that we see change with the years. . . . The model used for explanation is that which is good enough for the moment, and the criterion of acceptability is effectiveness within a framework of logicality. It is, however, man's disciplined speculation and creative imagination that fathers it. . . .
2 Such activity has been found to give power – power to do good or to do evil – but it does not supply the means of distinguishing between these alternatives. (Halliwell, 1960)

To Halliwell the explanatory activity of science is separate from the morality of its applications, the social implications having moral issues not to be found in the 'scientific' problems. He advocated that school science teaching should include both characteristics, and in Waring's words, 'it should therefore aim to give pupils an understanding, first, of what it means to approach a problem scientifically and, second, of when it is appropriate to do so. Nevertheless, he warned, the way in which this new educational opportunity might be provided in the classroom had not yet been worked out. In his view it depended quite fundamentally upon an approach which stressed the interplay of speculation and fact finding' (Waring, 1979). In effect, although he himself saw both characteristics as important ingredients of science education, a wedge was driven between the science and the morality of the scientist and the stress allowed to fall on the former. Whatever the original intention, the outcome has been that in the minds of most science teachers Nuffield science is identified not with learning about science but with teaching pupils to do science.

The science that pupils do is a simple science, but it will have to have a methodology. The methodology adopted in the chemistry project was amplified in the 1961 report of the chemistry panel. It stressed that theory-making was an imaginative process and 'the product no more than a corrigible human creation', before going on to take the Popperian line that theories can never be proved but are provisional, good enough for the job in hand, open to modification, and ultimately open to rejection. The model for the scientist whose science the pupils are to do is the research scientist creating new science, for 'It is in this way that the bounds of knowledge have been extended' (SMA/AWST, 1961). What emerged from the early deliberations of the Nuffield team was the centrality of the 'inquiry' or 'discovery' approach to science teaching.

In general terms the pedagogic aims of this approach are best summed up by Bruner:

> Finally, a theory of instruction seeks to take account of the fact that a curriculum reflects not only the nature of knowledge itself but also the nature of the knower and of the knowledge getting process. It is the enterprise par excellence where the line between subject matter and method grows necessarily indistinct. A body of knowledge, enshrined in a university faculty and embodied in a series of authoritative volumes is the result of much prior intellectual activity. To instruct someone in these disciplines is not a matter of getting him to commit results to mind. Rather, it is to teach him to participate in the process that makes possible the establishment of knowledge. We teach a subject not to produce little living libraries on that subject, but rather to get a student to think mathematically for himself, to consider matters as an historian does, to take part in the process of knowledge getting. (Bruner, 1966)

It is instructive to compare this theory of instruction with Popper's views on knowledge, as it is a Popperian view of innovatory inquiry in science which underpins the curriculum platform. Popper postulates three 'worlds'. World 1 is the world of material things, World 2 the realm of subjective minds, and World 3 is the world of objective structures which are the products of minds. Knowledge is not in World 2, the private state of minds, but is of World 3 and is often recorded in things of World 1: books, films, etc. As Magee puts it, 'most human knowledge is not "known" by anyone at all. It exists only on paper', and what is more: 'Although all World 3 entities are products of human minds, they may exist independently of any knowing subject. . . . (Hence the crucial difference between the knowledge in peoples' heads and the knowledge in libraries, the latter being far and away the more important)' (Magee, 1973). To use Popper's terms, the theory of instruction for the most part gives a greater emphasis to World 2 and underestimates the relative importance of World 3 to be found in the philosophies which have in part been used to form the base of the curriculum platform. This difficulty is particularly sharp in science, because as we have seen, to be scientific knowledge the means of getting it have to be replicable – it cannot be scientific unless it becomes independent of the private state of mind of any individual knower. The science teacher has to consider what it is that is to be discovered as well as the process of discovery.

The research scientist bringing about new knowledge is employing empirical evidence and reasoning to be creative. The principal activity demanded of a school pupil in science lessons is the learning of previously encoded knowledge, at best a re-creative activity. We could, of course, if we so wished make the science education of school pupils a prolonged series of discoveries and encourage their revisions of science. This would result in other problems. For example, no teacher could guarantee his or her pupils' knowing any particulars of established science. We would also be in the unfamiliar position of being able to cover less ground with the more able students, as presumably their imagination would require a greater number of more thorough investigations to settle each point. For good or ill, however, even the Nuffield science courses seek to ensure that pupils learn an important subset of established knowledge, although they have tried to move away from an authoritarian presentation of that knowledge and to emphasize the process of establishing knowledge. The pupil, therefore, is seeking to rediscover our science, not to create his or her own. At best the teacher has to make certain that, in creating their own science, the pupils' creations inevitably reduce to ours – a process normally known as 'guided discovery'.

The guidance begins to destroy the discovery from the beginning. The teacher not only decides what is to be studied next; he or she builds the framework of the discussions. Elsewhere I have referred to a pupil of mine who formed his own 'explanation' of bodies falling under gravity (Malvern, 1977). He proposed that bodies went faster as they fell because there was a growing weight of air above them pushing them down. I had asked the class to observe the motion of dropped masses as they got *nearer and nearer to the ground* (answer: they fall faster and faster). Had he been the teacher, he could well have asked: 'What happens to the motion of the masses as *more and more air gets on top of them?*' The point is we should both have felt we were encouraging the pupils, in the words of one of the objectives of Nuffield secondary science, 'to observe phenomena accurately'.

Later on the teacher's guiding hand has to weed out the inappropriate hypotheses put forward to explain such 'observations', before allowing the usually already prepared experiment to support the appropriate one. It soon becomes obvious that what the teacher knows represents a virtually unchallengable authority, quite distinct from and normally more powerful than the all too fallible experiments of the pupils. Even the gifted teacher will find it difficult to prevent the potential excitement of following in the footsteps of the great from becoming an intellectually bankrupt game of guessing the 'right' answer.

The problems are further compounded when we add, to those of method and content, consideration of the context in which 'discoveries' are made. A mature scientist is at one end of a long and powerful tradition with which he or she is fully acquainted. He or she makes decisions as an active and important member of society, and has cause to consider the purposes and to be responsible for the implications of his or her actions. In contrast, pupils are only partially aware of that tradition, and as their awareness is growing what they see and respond to is changing continually. By and large, their role in society is passive and relatively insignificant, the responsibility they do have is for themselves, and the test of how successfully they apply that responsibility is the teacher's approval or approbation. The pupils are given the methods of a research scientist, but in the absence of the values, purpose, and responsibilities which inform that method. What they are left with is the 'corrigible human creation' without its sense of purpose and power to solve immediate and important problems. In some older and more able pupils can be observed a sense of frustration as they come to realize that the industry and effort they have invested in 'doing science' has no more reward than if they had been told it in the first place.

This is not to say that pupils do not gain in other respects, albeit in ways which they will be unable to appreciate. The quality of their understanding may well be different from what it would have been had they merely been told about science, their chances of remembering what they have learnt may have been improved, and as not the least of its merits learning through activity usually goes on in a more pleasant ambience for pupil and teacher alike. The evaluation of the Nuffield secondary science project, for example, notes that although the trial group's attitude towards science deteriorated in much the same way as the control group's, the secondary science pupils' attitude towards their teachers improved (Alexander, 1974).

It would seem, however, that the simple methodology of school science is not robust enough to compete with the more obvious importance of the prescribed content of the courses. The Association for Science Education's consultative document published in 1979 compares the outcomes of eleven school science schemes to their intentions. It is noticeable that, although five schemes intended an emphasis on method over content, only two were judged to have achieved it. Perhaps not surprisingly these two are the primary projects and the only two where the knowledge to be taught is negotiable, not prescribed. Without such negotiations the methodology of school science becomes as prescriptive as the content. The pupil is left with no more than a set of procedures which at best disguise the lack of contention about the subject-matter under investigation, and at no point invest the activity with personal meaning or a socially relevant context.

Nowhere is this more noticeable than in assessments which require that the pupil knows this or that, or can apply certain skills and knowledge to arbitrary problems. Examiners confront the pupil with a particular problem and ask 'Can you do this?' They do not appear to ask 'What can you do?' The writers of well-constructed examinations would refute this, and not without some justifications. It is assumed that the performance of the candidates as a group over the particular subset of the syllabus found in any given examination is an accurate reflection of their potential performance over the whole syllabus, could it be measured. The assumption is based on a statistical inference which is probably sound as far as it goes. That is to say, relatively few candidates appear to benefit or suffer from the sampling of the contents and, although there are some who do, both kinds come in about equal numbers. In this sense most examinations are fair, and the examiners could claim what they are trying to find out is the answer to 'How well can you do?' By introducing techniques such as pretested objective tests, examiners can cover more of the syllabus in the limited time available, and every effort is always being made to improve methods of testing. Nonetheless, from the pupils' point of view what is at stake is 'Do you know this?', and not 'You have studied science for five years or so, what have you got out of it? What do you know?'

In most school examinations any considerations as to how the pupil came by the knowledge or skill are noticeable only by their obvious absence. It is as though the pupil is being told it matters not who you are, what your history is, nor what inclinations you may have, at a given point in time you must come round to thinking in a certain way. This is not to say that the thinking required is not of a high level, nor important, nor useful, nor that the opportunity to display that skill cannot be challenging and stimulating. But it is not always obvious that examinations represent a public acknowledgement of the acquisition of a kind of mental tool-kit of little worth unless it allows the owner greater choice in the ways he or she can manage his or her life.

Of course any assessment imposed by someone else serves needs wider than those of the pupil; the information gathered may help the teacher decide what to do next, or aid an employer select entrants to particular jobs. These needs, which are important, can often lead to a conflict between the necessities of the assessment and the nature of the work being assessed. As we have seen, the dominating pedagogic model in science education has placed the aims of the course into the methodology of learning, but examinations tend to reflect them only in the content. The limited range of tried techniques of assessment is partly to blame for this, and the Schools Council Examination Bulletin 27: *Assessment of Attainment in Sixth Form Science*, particularly records with regret the lack of alternatives to the single-occasion test of practical work. Until new forms of practical examinations are developed, Bulletin 27 recommends that internal assessment by teachers is preferred to the traditional practical examination, while recognizing difficulties in reconciling the demand for an examination to be a reliable account of an individual with the usual practice in schools where most practical work is done in pairs or larger groups.

Bulletin 27 acknowledges that assessment interferes with 'the normal co-operation which takes place in the laboratory between students and between students and teachers'. In part, the difficulty is caused by examining boards being reluctant to be seen to be dictating teaching methods, the choice of which is held to be the professional prerogative of the teachers. The teachers' concern for and response to the pupils in their day-to-day work is thought to make them unwilling or unable to take a dispassionate view of the pupils' achievements. The conclusions of Bulletin 27 recommend not relying on an independent assessment by the boards, and suggest a three-part assessment:

i) The assessment of a common core curriculum . . . by a national external authority. . . .
iii) The assessment of an alternative syllabus by an external authority.
iii) An element of internal assessment by the teachers . . . confined to practical and project work. (Schools Council, 1973)

The results would be presented as a profile.

This does not, however, necessarily answer the point that in modern science teaching the method of acquiring knowledge is no longer a means to an end; it is valued in its own right. Perhaps the partnership between the teachers and the examinations boards can be taken a stage further, although it would mean a compromise on some aspects of the choice of teaching methods in practical work. There could be an agreed list of important experiments, and each pupil could be required to carry out so many of them during the course. A laboratory notebook could be kept. The essential thing is not to make fine distinctions between the performance of different pupils, but for the board to check simply that the work had been done in a satisfactory manner. If it is the experience of doing the experiment which is worthwhile, it ought to be sufficient that the examiner and teacher together ensure that it has been done.

The key words in this proposal are 'satisfactory' and 'worthwhile'. To explain them attention should be drawn to the innovation of the proposal, i.e., the replacement of a terminal practical test by a series of monitored experiments within the course. The traditional single-occasion practical examination seldom involves the candidate in doing any experiment, let alone an important one. It usually consists of a set of laboratory procedures which may involve the establishing of the conditions which allow some phenomena to be observed, measurements to be taken and displayed, or an analysis leading to some sort of identification. For the most part it is a test of skills and organization: dissection skills, titration skills, or whatever. The importance of such skills should not be lost, and it is in everyone's interest that 'satisfactory manner' includes care, accuracy, patience, organization, and the rest. What the proposal has to say is that their public display as well as their acquisition should not be isolated from important experiments. Important experiments are those which provide evidence of nature and help us to understand and evaluate our theories about nature. It is the first-hand experience of these while learning which is 'worthwhile'.

One way of going about this is to select crucial experiments from the historical development of given theories, and to ask the pupils to repeat them. For more advanced pupils in some instances, it will be possible to compare their own apparatus, procedures, and results with the original work. It is vital that this replication is not seen as confirmation of one hypothesis, but as a test which falsifies one and allows another to remain on continued probation. One of the rewards for the time and effort spent becoming a skilled practitioner in the laboratory is to be able to stand at the crossroads in the thoughts of great scientists and to see what they have seen, to know for oneself why one road was preferred.

This alone would require such work to be part of teaching and not solely examining, for the teacher can choose when and how to introduce it as well as what to do next. Each teacher can adopt a sequence and style to suit his or her particular class, taking into account the logical constraints of the subject and the development of the pupils' notions. For example, in one school the availability of certain apparatus may make one experiment a vehicle for discussing the changes in measuring techniques, limits of accuracy, and sources of error, while in another it may be more appropriate to do the experiment as an examplar of seeking empirical evidence for choosing between or among alternative theories. In a third school it might be preferred to use the experiment as a starting point for the pupils designing different experiments testing the same hypothesis, and so on.

Another thorough approach to an assessment which combines the processes involved in learning science with the content has been prepared by the science group of the Assessment and Performance Unit (APU). The APU team has drawn up a set of categories of scientific activities which have a validity for those involved in science education. The categories include using apparatus and measuring instruments, observation tasks, design of investigations, and other classes of activity of a like kind. It is intended that this assessment should monitor pupils' abilities to perform these activities when related to a variety of scientific concepts and in different contexts. The main concern of the APU team is to develop test questions for the assessment of the 'science processes' because the ultimate justification of the process list 'is that it defines the main aspects of school science teaching' (APU, 1979).

Unlike the examining boards, APU is not charged with the assessment of individuals. It is to monitor the overall achievement of pupils in schools, to identify areas of underachievement, and to relate the results to circumstances in which children learn. It is appropriate, therefore, for the science team to include the assessment of the work of groups engaged in a cooperative exercise. It is to be hoped that the techniques which are developed to do so will be made generally available and result in more direct associations between the ways of learning and the manner of being assessed.

Although APU emphasizes the processes, each test item will be described in terms of three characteristics: *scientific process, science concept,* and *context.* The last of these accepts the importance of the pupil being able to act like a scientist in a variety of circumstances. Three broad areas have been chosen to categorize the contexts in which the pupils' performance of the processes will be tested: 'contexts of science teaching, contexts of teaching in other subjects, contexts in every day or out of school situations'. The example given in the 1978 progress report to illustrate what is meant by these categorizations is disturbing. In considering how things are kept hot or cold by insulation, questions might be asked about the conductivity of different substances (a science lesson context), about home insulation (an everyday context), or of the ways used to keep food cool before the invention of the refrigerator (a nonscience lesson context). It is to be greatly regretted that the application of simple scientific knowledge to reduce the fuel bills at home, and the appreciation of the systems and ingenuity of a past age using the same principles to preserve food, are not seen as being part and parcel of science lessons.

Materials for teaching and assessment which contain case studies of industrial and social applications of science have been prepared for use in schools. The Schools Council Integrated Science Project deserves credit for including some of this work in its course. Also available to the teacher are extended simulations which immerse the pupils in many of the aspects of siting a steel works, say, or running a farm. These exercises allow the pupils to come to decisions and to form plans for action on the basis of social as well as scientific information. One example is the 'Ridpest File'; it is of interest because using it with postgraduate students as part of their training for teaching affords an insight into the thinking of those who have been inducted into the 'science of the scientist'.

The 'Ridpest File' is a teaching package which seeks to introduce pupils to the idea of a pest as being something growing in the wrong place or an animal whose population is excessively large and leads to interference with the production of foodstuffs. It suggests that pests are not necessarily evil in themselves to be eradicated at all costs, but that the farmer is trying to control them to bring about a balance which does not undermine his livelihood.

The first part of the package looks at the problem of bracken taking over pasture land. It contrasts the understandable attitude of a sheep farmer wishing to get rid of the stuff, with the equally understandable desires of the local community wishing to continue to enjoy the beauty of bracken-covered countryside. The pupils are asked to plan a strategy for the control of bracken over the landscape of a particular farm with given resources. They can seek the sorts of information normally available to a farmer. To do this they may ask the teacher specific questions and if able to reply he or she does so by giving over the appropriate card from a collection representing the sources open to the farmer. Among these cards is one outlining the effects on the environment of the different means of removing bracken. It is very noticeable that newly qualified graduates in science, playing the part of the pupils while practising the techniques of this kind of teaching, do not usually ask for this card. Having tried it with over one hundred PGCE students, I have only ever known one seek this information. On being asked none of the others knew it already. They become so fascinated with looking for the most technically efficient way of removing the bracken that they are blind to the real optimization of sound economy within an attractive countryside. These students are not uncaring people. When given a task to do, however, they respond by making full use of the mental tool-kit they have so painstakingly learnt to use throughout their education. It is the tool-kit which is not flexible enough.

There is not enough experience of using these materials to judge how effective they will be. It is clear, however, that the direction will be the right one provided that the intention remains to offer youngsters some opportunity to use their knowledge by practising the solving of problems in which the apparently most effective technical solutions must be measured against less tangible considerations such as social policies, community preferences, or an individual's sensibilities. It is not always easy to find good examples suitable to all levels, and the teachers involved in trial public examinations incorporating project work have found the extra workload hard. The Sixth Form Mathematics Project's Alternative Ordinary-level examination in applicable mathematics has had to drop the requirement that each candidate produces a mathematical essay modelling some aspects of real life chosen by him or herself (fortunately not before demonstrating that more or less reliable mark schemes could be devised for this work).

Some pupils are already so motivated for one reason or another that they can be bored by an application which requires lengthy introduction; they want to get on with the 'real' science. Others, however, are only too happy to extend a general discussion of wider issues, and put off the moment when they may have to do some work. The bigger the issue the more exaggerated these responses become. There is no easier way to elicit polite conversation or encourage opinionated, coffee-time chat than talking in abstract terms about policies for the conservation of the environment, energy distribution, or the social effect of the microcomputer. Through their work both groups of pupils need to learn what David Eccles had to say, quoting the inspectorate: '. . . "the qualities, both moral and intellectual, which go to make the devoted scientist carry with them much of great value for a liberal education".

'This must be our aim in teaching science. For although it is good to know how machines work, it is better still to know to what use to put them' (Eccles, 1960).

The intention is for all pupils to recognize that no matter how general the matter under consideration, informed opinion can only be founded on knowledge from particular evidence, and responsible opinion requires reliable knowledge. To teach and to examine this needs examples where attention switches from the application to the science and back again quickly. At point after point the application should demand that some science is done before progress can be achieved. The science should be seen to inform specific decisions within the application leading towards a solution.

The development of appropriate material is time-consuming, and there seems little sign at the moment of the two most obvious solutions to this problem – more science teachers and less crowded, though still challenging, syllabuses. There are two approaches to finding good material. The first is to look at work already being done as part of a science lesson and to present it in a relevant context. For example, simple paper chromatography is a routine school laboratory exercise. Different inks are dropped onto damp blotting paper, and the constituent parts of the inks separate by spreading through the blotting paper at different rates. Instead of just looking at blots, two signatures with different inks of the same colour can be used. The pupils are asked to spot the 'forgery', and a routine exercise becomes an introduction to forensic science.

The second is to ask simple questions about things common to the pupils' experience. It is noticeable, for example, that the small, oblong first-aid plaster strips used to dress small cuts begin to come unstuck first at the points of the corners. One way to prevent or delay this is to use a stronger adhesive. Another is to cut the corners so that they are rounded. A third method is to produce slightly longer strips with rows of perforations at intervals along the strip so that as one edge becomes loose it can be ripped off leaving a progressively smaller plaster. To choose between these, and any others they can think of, involves the pupil in considering how people like or react to having things stuck on their skin, as well as the more direct problem of keeping the wound covered.

The important thing to aim for is that on occasions, during their collecting of scientific knowledge and understanding, pupils have to face up to simple but real problems in which people, including themselves, will care about the outcomes. It ought to be made clear that the technically most efficient solutions may not be the best, that most problems have many sides to them, that there can be more than one solution and to arrive at them requires more than knowledge. Above all the choice between solutions may be contentious and a matter of debate between designer, producer, and user.

Both ASE and the inspectorate have outlined proposals for including work towards a more general education through science. As the inspectorate has it: 'No one disputes the irrefutable case for basic skills and techniques; equally there is a case for cultural experiences and an introduction to values. . . . Any scientific subject can have three components, namely, science for the enquiring mind, science for action, and science for citizenship' (H.M. Inspectorate, 1977). ASE adds to these a further three 'appropriate and legitimate contexts within which science can be explored and developed', and they are Science as a Cultural Activity, Science and Leisure, and Science as Survival. But even in what is admitted to be the most radical model for future science teaching these elements continue to be taught separately, so that the pupils will first learn some science, then learn to apply it, and only afterwards place that science into an 'historical, social, and personal context' (ASE, 1979, see Model 3).

This will not do. What the experience of the curriculum developments of the last twenty years has to teach us is that we can no longer afford to allow the learning of science to go on isolated from how we came to create it and considered separately from how it continues to influence what we are and what we will become. This is not solely because we would wish to improve science's contribution to an education in values.

Science, any science, is not a series of isolatable truths. The science of the past came into being to solve problems, both social and intellectual, peculiar to its day. If we continue to retain some of that science it is because it remains relevant to our times, and along with the science we are creating it is part of the fabric of our outlook on the universe. The next generation will need to know that, and will need to understand how of necessity their values will be reflected in their science and the uses they make of it. In the words of Barbara Ward:

> We have always known that man cannot live without the Good, the Beautiful and the True. What we have learnt in our own day is that the supposedly rationalistic and materialistic systems and experiments of the last 400 years end by saying exactly the same thing. (Ward, 1978)

References

Alexander, D.J. (1974) *Nuffield Secondary Science – an Evaluation*, London: Macmillan.

APU (1979) *Science Progress Report 1977-78*, London: HMSO.

ASE (1979) *Alternatives for Science Education*, London: ASE.

Bacon, F. (1620) *Novum Organon* translated by G.W. Kitchin.

Bath University School of Education/British Agrochemicals Association (1976) *The Ridpest File*, London: BP Educational Service.

Benn, A. (1979) 'Technology's threat to parliament', *The Guardian*, 19 February, 1979.

Bethe, H.A. (1947) 'The electromagnetic shift of energy levels', *Physical Review*, 72.

Bruner, J.S. (1966) *Towards a Theory of Instruction*, Boston: Harvard University Press.

Bullock, Lord (1976) 'Presidential address: science – a tarnished image?', *School Science Review*, Vol. 57.

Clarendon Commission (1864) *Report of Her Majesty's Commissioners 'Appointed to inquire into the Revenues and Management of certain Colleges and Schools and the studies pursued and instruction given therein'*, London: HMSO.

Crane, H.R. (1968) 'The g factor of the electron', *Scientific American*, Vol. 218, January.

Durham, Bishop of, Rt. Rev. J.S. Habgood (1979) *The Bishop's Letter, Diocese of*

212   Values and Evaluation in Education

Durham, No. 197, September 1979.

Eccles, D. (1960) Foreword to *Science in Secondary Schools: Ministry of Education Pamphlet No. 38*, London: HMSO.

H.M. Inspectorate of Schools (1977) *Curriculum 11-16 Working Paper by H.M. Inspectorate – A Contribution to Current Debate*, London: DES.

Halliwell, H.F. (1960) 'Atoms and atomic structure of material: the educational challenge', in *Birmingham Institute of Education Report on a Course of Science Teaching in Secondary Modern Schools* held at Dudley Training College, 5-12th April, 1960 (mimeo).

Huxley, T.H. (1902) 'Science and culture', Address at the opening of Sir Josiah Mason's Science College, Birmingham, 1 October 1880, in *Science and Education*, collected essays, Volume 3, London.

Jevons, F.R. (1975) 'But some kinds of knowledge are more equal than others', *Studies in Science Education 2*.

Kuhn, T.S. (1962) *The Structure of Scientific Revolutions*, Chicago: University of Chicago, Enlarged 1970.

Magee, B. (1973) *Popper*, London: Fontana/Collins.

Malvern, D.D. (1977) 'Science education: its image and imagination', *Cambridge J. of Ed.* 7: 3.

Medawar, P.B. (1963) 'Is the scientific paper a fraud?', *The Listener*, 12 September, 1963.

Ormell, C.P. (1980) 'Mathematical models and understanding in science', *Schools Science Review*, 41.

Popper, K.R. (1963) *Conjectures and Refutations: The Growth of Scientific Knowledge*, London: Routledge & Kegan Paul.

Schools Council (1967) *Teachers Experience of School Based Examining (English and Physics): Examinations Bulletin No. 15*: London: HMSO.

Schools Council (1973) *Assessment of Attainment in Sixth Form Science: Examinations Bulletin No. 27*: London: HMSO.

SMA/AWST (1958) *Chemistry Panel: Minutes*, 25 January, 1958.

SMA/AWST (1961) *Chemistry for Grammar Schools*, London: John Murray.

Stopes-Roe, H.V. (1979) Letter, *The Guardian*, 18 October, 1979, p. 25.

Thomson, J.J. Committee (1918) *Report of the Committee Appointed by the Prime Minister to Enquire into the Position of Natural Science in The Educational System of Great Britain*, London: HMSO.

Tolstoy, L.N. (1869) *War and Peace*, translated by R. Edmonds, Harmondsworth: Penguin Classics, 1957.

Ward, B. (1978) 'What is this thing called the world? – science and values on a small planet', *New Era* 59: 4.

Waring, M. (1979) *Social Pressures and Curriculum Innovation*, London: Methuen.

Young, J.Z. (1973) 'The pineal gland', *Philosophy*, Vol. 48.

CHAPTER 13

MATHEMATICS

Christopher Ormell

Introduction

In 1957 the Russians launched their Sputnik I. In retaliation the Americans launched the 'new maths': an attempt at instant reform of their system of mathematical education, which had evidently fallen into a somewhat moribund state. In fact it was not so much a case of 'instant reform', more a case of 'revolutionary experiment'.

What happened might be described in very simple terms as follows: the politicians were upbraided by the American public for their neglect of scientific and mathematical education. So they turned to the country's ablest mathematicians, and asked for help in bringing US mathematical education up to date. The ablest mathematicians in the United States were almost all pure mathematicians. Moreover pure mathematics in the previous half-century had been drifting further and further away from any kind of concern with the real world. Its conception of itself had become formalistic, autonomous, isolationist. John von Neumann was one of the few to speak out against this trend. Mathematics, he remarked, 'was becoming more and more pure aestheticizing, more and more *l'art pour l'art*' (Von Neumann, 1956). Dieudonne, the leading French pure mathematician, even went so far as to boast that 'modern mathematics . . . constitutes an intellectual discipline, the "utility" of which is nil' (Dieudonne, 1964).

The credibility of the eminent pure mathematician in 1957 was very high. The computer had just arrived: the public were dazzled by the almost magical applicable power of the new machine, and this awe transferred itself, in a great degree, onto the mathematicians. After all, was not the new machine initially invented by mathematicians for the use of mathematicians? (No, but the mistake was easily made.) In 1957 the convention still held that the ordinary person was very respectful of the mathematician; perhaps because he was the possessor of a special expertise which one might need in a fix, and for which there was no available substitute. People were nice to mathematicians much as people are nice to plumbers. (Incidentally, now that people can buy scientific calculators for a few dollars, much of this instant respect seems to have disappeared.)

Of the fraternity of professional mathematicians the most able, it was generally agreed, were the pure mathematicians. And it was mainly on the basis of their judgements that a completely new kind of 'school maths' began to be promoted. It embodied for the first time some of the characteristic terminology, concepts, and values of late twentieth-century pure mathematics.

When intellectual values change, teachers begin to encourage their pupils to try to achieve different kinds of cognitive development. In the case we are considering the newly admired type of cognitive development involved at least five shifts of emphasis:

1 The use of more technical and classificatory terms than had previously been attempted: also an earlier introduction of the characteristically timeless syntax of mathematical language. (For example, when we speak of the 'solution set' of an equation as 'existing', when it has not yet been solved.) On the increased linguistic learning load, see Kaner (1972).

2 Greater pedantry of statement.

3 A more rapid introduction of highly generalized formulations.

4 A sharply decreased interest in problems arising in the real world: for example, under the influence of 'new maths' many countries cut out of their syllabuses the very Newtonian mechanics of which Sputnik I had been a triumph!

5 A decreased use of problem-solving strategies based on the visual imagination, physical analogies in the real world, and intuition.

If questions of values are invariably associated with preferred patterns of relationships, it is evident that the emphases listed above point to two major changes: (a) a reduction of links between mathematics and other subjects, (b) a strengthening of links within mathematics. In a word, after the change in values mathematicians were less likely to talk to, and to discuss common problems with, their colleagues in other subjects. And they had to tread more carefully within the subject itself; since in the absence of external motivations, rigour became a nearly total preoccupation.

This, then, was the essence of the idea of 'new maths'. Eminent research mathematicians saw it as cutting out so much lumber, and bringing the average student much closer to the knowledge, concepts, and values currently accepted in research circles. We have no record of any doubts being entertained about this process: whether, for example, they ever asked themselves whether the 'knowledge, concepts, and values' involved would fit better, or perhaps *less well*, to the needs of the ordinary person. It was widely assumed, indeed, that this question was inappropriate: that if school children were to be taught 'mathematics', it must be the mathematicians who decided what was taught. Many said that if school mathematics was to be in a healthy condition it must *a fortiori* reflect the state and style of the subject as seen by the most eminent practitioners. Later Allanson (1968) observed that '. . . mathematics is too important to be left to the mathematicians', but this was a thought which would have seemed all but incomprehensible in the heady days of 1957-1958.

New maths diffused at faster or slower rates to most of the advanced countries of the world in the following decade; leaving only the USSR and Japan among leading countries comparatively unaffected by it. It generated great enthusiasm. This was the result, no doubt, of various factors. There was massive support from parents, industrialists, etc., who felt very strongly that the more up to date the mathematics taught in schools, the better. It appealed greatly to the ordinary mathematics teacher who received a powerful stimulus from the new ideas. (The exercises, though more formal, were also more straightforward.)

The fact that the US Government spent many millions of dollars on promoting this development was also a potent stimulus. The fact that eminent professors of mathematics were taking an interest in school mathematics, often for the first time, was another. As 'new maths' spread, it was modified, diversified, adapted, softened, to try to meet the actual psychological and social conditions of the average school. In the primary school, it was recognized quite early on that the new ambitious cognitive targets would require a stronger foundation in concrete experience, if they were to stand a chance of success. In England SMP (the School Mathematics Project, set up in 1962) introduced a relatively undoctrinaire interpretation of the new curriculum, and managed to include a somewhat higher proportion of real-life problems than was customary in the USA, France,

Sweden, etc. But in spite of having a relatively undoctrinaire syllabus, SMP was promoted in the early days with all the zeal of an evangelical church.

The main factor which was probably responsible for the 'new maths' movement having the confidence, even the arrogance, to move ahead, was the feeling that it had a virtually unanswerable case. How could anyone seriously oppose a movement which consisted, essentially, merely in an updating of the mathematics curriculum to bring it into line with modern knowledge? 'New maths' would surely inexorably succeed! This, incidentally, was the main 'argument' advanced in its favour by the report *New Thinking in School Mathematics* (O.E.C.D., 1959); and this was the main plank in the case for the dozens of new projects which proceeded to spring up and try to exploit the new idea.

With the passing of the years this feeling of historical inexorability has gradually disappeared. It has come to be widely seen that it is not simply a case of more up-to-date mathematics superseding more old-fashioned mathematics. It is, rather, a case of more up-to-date mathematics, taken in conjunction with certain values trying to oust more old-fashioned mathematics taken in conjunction with different values.

'New maths' has been toned down still further to enable it to blend more harmoniously with the main body of knowledge teachers have inherited from the past. And many of those who opposed 'new maths' have tried to bring their methods and ideas up to date, whilst still reflecting the values which the 'new maths' seems to deny. (Some of the new topics such as computer programming, flow charts and linear programming actually seem to relate more closely to 'old maths' than to 'new maths'.)

So the issue, which seemed at first to be that of 'modern' versus 'traditional' method (or of 'highbrow' versus 'lowbrow' mathematical language) has finally resolved itself into a conflict between two modern views of the nature of mathematics; between the different values these views reflect, and between two accounts of the alignment – or nonaligment – of these values to the general aims and purposes of education.

Some readers may be surprised that so much rethinking has been taking place in school mathematics since 1957 – that 'new maths' has been less than universally triumphant. This may be partly a result of the hit-or-miss coverage of the issue in the press; for the term 'new maths' – as used in the press – can mean a surprisingly wide range of different things. And the underlying conflict of values gets rather confused when the press uses the same term for protagonists supporting opposite sides of the argument!

The first signs that the so-called 'revolution in school mathematics' was not going to be a quite straightforward affair came in the early 1960s. Morris Kline wrote an article in the *New York Alumni News* (1962) bitterly attacking the assumptions underlying the new curriculum. And a group of sixty-five eminent mathematicians working in the United States (including Birkhoff, Courant, Coxeter, Kline, Morse, Pollak, Polya, Rado, Sawyer) issued a joint memorandum, which was published in the *American Mathematical Monthly* (1962), urging caution and the need to maintain continuity with the methods of the past. Shortly afterwards the present author, in conjunction with Frank Budden, wrote a book (1964) which subjected the whole prospectus of 'new maths' to a sustained critical examination. Later Hammersley (1968) and Scott (1969) published articles which criticized 'new maths' on the grounds that it presented too little problem-solving challenge, and too much confusing jargon. In 1972 Rene Thom's paper 'Modern Mathematics, does it exist?', delivered at the second I.C.M.E. at Exeter, caused a sensation; including the sudden exit of the French delegation from the hall. (This paper was published in 1973 in the Convention Proceedings, *Developments in Mathematical Education*.) Since 1973 many others have joined in, and the situation is now that the 'new maths' movement and its critics are probably represented in higher academic and educational circles in roughly equal strength. In the schools 'new maths' has not suffered any sudden dramatic decrease in influence, but its grip on the curriculum has been gradually reduced as a result of a multitude of small adjustments and revisions. (For example, it is hardly mentioned in H.M. Inspectorate's 'Green Paper' on the primary school, 1978.)

Many ordinary mathematics teachers still blink and find it hard to understand how the glorious revolution of the early 1960s has somehow come unstuck. What went wrong? How did it come about that a change in the school syllabus, which looked so utterly irreversible in the early 1960s, has gradually been reduced to the state where it is having to fight rearguard actions to maintain its presence in the curriculum?

The answer lies, of course, in terms of the values embodied in the 'new maths' curriculum.

One might be tempted to add that it also lies in the evaluation of the 'new maths' curriculum, but the situation in relation to evaluation is very strange. At first many experts did not consider that any detailed evaluation of the main tenets of new maths was necessary; the new curriculum must, obviously, supersede the old. In effect there was 'no contest', because there were no other candidates in the field. A number of educationalists also felt a certain reluctance about using traditional yardsticks to evaluate the new curriculum. How could one compare two systems based on such markedly different principles? Later various piecemeal evaluations of the work of the projects were undertaken. It appears that most of these gave unexciting, neutral, or negative indications. This led to a reluctance on the part of some schemes to submit themselves to the kind of comprehensive evaluation which would be commensurate with the importance of the problem.

At last an alternative to the original 'new maths' paradigm has begun to appear. It is often called 'applicable maths', and signs of its emergence may be seen in various projects around the world. The Schools Council Project, *Mathematics Applicable*, which the present author directed for ten years (1969-1978) was one of the first off the mark. M.M.C.P. (directed by Peter Kaner), the Ontario Project (Peter Waygand), the Wattle Park, Adelaide Project (John Gaffney), and U.M.E.S. in the United States are among those which have contributed to this movement. In England initiatives at the Open University, Cranfield Institute of Technology, the Shell Centre, Nottingham, Atlantic College, and the Polytechnic of the South Bank have also strengthened this development.

So now the argument that there is no alternative to 'new maths' has faded out.

Our purpose in this chapter is not, however, to give a blow-by-blow account of an episode in education which the social historians of the future are likely to find of absorbing interest. It is, rather, to take a look at the role of values in a subject like mathematics, which appears, at first glance, to be an entirely objective, dry, formal, value-free affair. How do values manage to emerge in such a context? In what aspects of the mathematics curriculum may these values be most clearly seen? Where do they impinge on the evaluation process?

Evidently, in view of the twenty-year saga of 'new maths' it would be hazardous not to take the presence of values into account. Yet the problem of disentangling values is one which few mathematics teachers, mathematical educationalists, or evaluators are positively equipped to handle. As Warwick Sawyer says (1966):

> In some countries, at an early stage in the educational debate, mathematicians have been asked what they thought important, and it seems to have been assumed that their answers would automatically provide material relevant to the problems of industry and attractive to teach young children. But the

evidence for this mystic harmony is hard to find. Indeed, there is considerable evidence in the opposite direction. For specialists differ not only in what they know; they differ in their philosophies of life and in what they regard as important. To ignore this is to run the kind of risk you would take if you bought a car on the advice of a friend, and only afterwards discovered that, while you judged a car by the power of its engine and its mechanical performance, he judged it by its colour and artistic appearance.

What Sawyer is saying is that eminent mathematicians, who have been consulted in many countries about the proper content of the school curriculum, have brought a certain 'philosophy of life', and view of what they 'regard as important', to bear on the question. But this is not the only 'philosophy of life', or view of 'what is important', which is held by experts. There are two schools of eminent mathematicians, not one. It is by no means clear that the values of the specialists who promoted 'new mathematics' in the early years were more appropriate to the proper aims of education (i.e., the needs of the child in society) than the values of those who queried this.

And the reason why this is 'by no means clear' is that little attempt was made to demonstrate that the 'new maths' curriculum was appropriate to the proper aims of education. Little inclination was displayed, indeed, to admit that there *were* questions of changes of values involved in the 'revolution in school mathematics' at all. It was presented as a purely technical change; an irreversible step from the obsolete to the efficient, from the out of date to the modern. As I have argued elsewhere (Ormell 1969, 1973), the innovators preferred to pitch their proposals in an ideological, rather than in a reform, context.

The origin of values in mathematics

If it appears odd that values should emerge in controversies concerning mathematics, this can only be because a certain view of the nature of mathematics, in which values seem to play but a minor part, is widely held. There are various ways of stating such views on the nature of mathematics. Sometimes it is said that mathematics consists of 'glorified calculations', or 'endless logical distinctions for their own sake', or 'a body of tautologies: more and more roundabout ways of saying that $A = A$'.

These deflationary views of the nature of mathematics are quite common: they seem to express a certain aversion to the essence of the subject.

Needless to say, such views are not held by mathematicians themselves.

But some mathematicians (e.g., Zeeman, 1962) have come close to saying things which echo the 'endless logical distinctions for their own sake'. And a scientifically minded positivist, Sir Alfred Ayer, did claim (Ayer, 1935) that mathematics consisted of tautologies. So perhaps the unflattering judgements of the mathematically averse layman are not so very wide of the mark, after all!

The surprising thing is, perhaps, that mathematicians often seem prepared to countenance definitions of their subject which not only effectively remove the possibility of finding values in it, but which also remove the possibility of it having any discernible social purpose. An extreme instance is Hilbert's view that pure mathematics consists in moving meaningless marks about on paper, i.e., that it is a meaningless formal game. Are such views supportable, and if not, how does it come about that mathematicians holding such views seem, in fact, to be able to mobilize considerable social support? One can only conclude that it suits many people in society to believe that the premier intellectual discipline should be impotent in relation to the problems of the real world. That rationality, raised to the nth degree, should finally turn out to be useless, is a thought which clearly gives a lot of pleasure – especially to those whose encounter with mathematics at school was less than happy, and who cling jealously to their right to think irrationally on the strength of this!

There is a different kind of view about the nature of mathematics. It is that mathematics is a very useful subject, particularly in relation to industry, organization, development, science, and technology.

Sometimes people in ordinary life go further than this and form the view that mathematics is *only* or *mainly* a very useful subject. Such views can easily appear to have been shown to be absurd. It is only necessary to have a sketchy, outline view of the history of mathematics to see that much of what happened in the past does not fit well into so neat a theory.

However 'useful' mathematics may be, it is also, clearly, a rather tricky subject. And it is evidently necessary, on this account alone, that a large number of people should specialize in the internal logic and organization of the enterprise. One could no more cut out the role of the specialist pure mathematician in this than one could cut out the staff officer in war, or the administrator in any business organization. Applicable mathematics without pure mathematics would be a headless beast.

Indeed we may see mathematics as a many-layered subject, like an onion with many skins. The outer layers are visibly applicable, but as one plunges more and more deeply into the onion one finds that the questions being discussed bear less and less relation to the problems of the outside world. Now most eminent mathematicians are concerned in their teaching and research with deep problems in mathematics far removed from the outer skins. That this is so poses an occupational hazard, because the pure mathematician can so easily lose contact altogether with the problems of the outer layers. This leads to the extraordinary situation in which eminent mathematicians are less aware of the potency of their own subject in relation to the outside world than less talented mathematicians whose work happens to lie on the real world-mathematics interface. Indeed it is stranger than this: because some *laymen* are more aware of the potency of mathematics in the real world than some eminent mathematicians.

So there are two main ways to interpret mathematics. As a form of activity which is an end in itself at all levels, or as a form of activity which is extremely useful on the outer layers, and which only gradually becomes more and more an end in itself as we move down to deeper layers in the onion. We may call these two interpretations of mathematics the 'structured intrinsic' interpretation of mathematics and the 'structured applicable' interpretation of mathematics.

Mathematicians who see pure mathematics in the 'structured intrinsic' way can hardly dispute the existence of a body of applicable mathematics, though they are more likely to describe it as 'applied mathematics'. Many different views are possible of this additional wing of mathematics. A common view would be that it is a fairly limited body of concepts and methods involving heuristic rules and nonrigorous arguments, which in so far as it has any validity, is merely an addendum to, and wholly dependent on, the main body of 'structured intrinsic' (pure) mathematics.

We may therefore show the difference between the two views of mathematics on a diagram (page 222). The degree of shading shows the degree of involvement in applications.

The basic difference between the two schools of thought hinges on whether one regards mathematics as a unity embracing applicable and intrinsic elements, or as polarized into two quite separate enterprises, the intrinsic (pure) enterprise being the significant member of the pair. In other words, we may distinguish the mixers from the separators: the integrated and the bifurcated schools of thought.

It is the coexistence of these rival views of mathematics itself which gives rise to conflicts of values in the classroom.

Figure 13.1

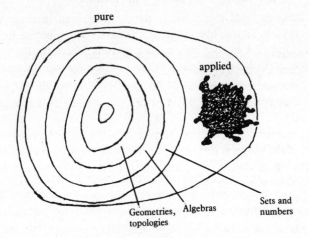

The Structured Intrinsic and
Applied or Bifurcated Interpretation

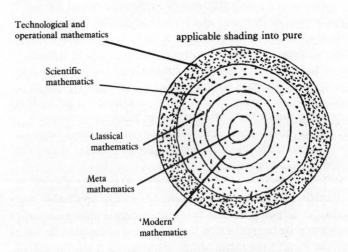

The Structured Applicable or
Integrated Interpretation

The expression of values in the classroom

We saw in Chapter 6 that talk about values is talk about motivation: '. . . the rhetoric of scorn and admiration, of encouragement and discouragement'. How does the difference between the bifurcated and the integrated interpretations of mathematics manifest itself in values? How do these values, having emerged, inform the character of the teaching exposition, the classroom dialogue, the worksheet, the homework assignment?

Do they really make a difference? Isn't is still, in the end, *mathematics* after all?

The answer is that they make an enormous difference to the texture and colour of the classroom experience. They also imply great differences in the sequencing of topics. For example, in one new mathematics textbook designed for eleven-year-olds, we reach problems on page 205 of the following kinds:

Calculate 87.8 + 9.4, Calculate 3.25 − 2.20, Calculate 5.51 − 4.5

and this seems to be quite traditional, unremarkable, even dull. But the conceptual preparation for this work, as expressed in the sequence of topics in the book, includes: set, cardinal numbers, subsets, orderings, infinity, multiples, divisors, invariance, symmetry, open sentence, rays, open segment, closed segment, modulus, X-, Z-, and F-angles.

The bifurcated interpretation of the school mathematics curriculum, then, places its emphasis on the introduction of a multitude of precise definitions, the point of which is to try to inculcate habits of precise expression and precise thought. As we saw earlier this is one of the main characteristics of the new maths: a preoccupation with linguistic and symbolic expression. An attitude frequently expressed in these books is one of scorn for the old quasi-intuitive definitions of numbers, angles, lines, etc. What is admired is the use of new and apparently baffling symbols, particularly to state results or create distinctions which were overlooked in the previous generation of mathematics textbooks. Whether the use of these books actually does increase the precision and power of thought of the intelligent or average child at the end of the day is, however, quite another question. There are signs that it is less effective in this respect than the old curriculum; that the sheer mass of jargon the child is expected to learn serves as a barrier to vigorous thinking, and that the antimotivation produced in this way does more harm in the long term than the short-term gain in 'instant rigour' might suggest.

There are many variations between different books. Generally speaking, those books which have emphasized exploratory work involving semi-geometrical systems of rules seem to have fared best. It is also important to add that very few books stick consistently to the pure side of a bifurcated interpretation of mathematics. Most books mix in a few sections on things like probability, statistics, physical vectors, and hence flip towards applications (often treated quite summarily) for at least part of the time.

If one adopts an integrated view of school mathematics, the pattern of work which seems to be appropriate to the school curriculum is rather different. There is more emphasis on formulating and solving problems taken from the outside world; on envisaging new situations as potential responses to current problems; on analysing these situations into their main elements, and modelling their implications; on interpreting the results, graphically, diagramatically, and verbally.

On this interpretation much of the work done in the 'new mathematics' books looks rather colourless, since relatively few real-life problems cross the page (and even fewer solutions). The degree of formalistic rigour adopted seems quite inappropriate, since it gives the average child the jargon of modern research mathematics without developing the high problem-solving ability, to complement which the jargon is (eventually) needed. What is admired, from the integrated point of view, is not a precocious fluency with the scholasticism of modern abstract mathematics, but a degree of spirit, zest, and stamina in tackling problems of all kinds; translating into and out of mathematics; looking for optimum frames of reference; and diligence in following through accurately to tangible conclusions. In other words, the work done by the child should make sense on various levels simultaneously, not just on the level of specialist terminology and symbolism.

So the two schools of thought about school mathematics offer quite distinct patterns of development to be admired. They encourage the development of different kinds of ability. The following table summarizes some of the differences, i.e., contrasts in the emphases:

Table 13.1

Bifurcated interpretation of school mathematics	Integrated interpretion of school mathematics
Knowing definitions	Problem-solving
Precision of terminology	Realism
Formal expression	Practical imagination
Use of symbolism to replace words	Abstraction from the real

Possessing formal concepts	Interpretation to the concrete
Hyper-generalization	Comprehension of ordinary language
Scepticism concerning intuition	A robust kind of rigour

It is evident that mathematics in the first style is more inward looking, isolationist, academic; whereas mathematics in the second style is more outward looking, interdisciplinary, practical. Richard Pring in his *Inaugural Lecture* (1978) distinguishes the 'respectability' and the 'relevance' schools of thought in education. The difference between the two schools of thought concerning school mathematics may be seen as a clear-cut reflection of Pring's distinction.

Educational values in mathematics

We argued in Chapter 6 that the characteristic feature of educational values is that they consist of motivations to encourage features of development of an overall kind, which *distribute* across the ordinary values. The primary educational values are those concerned with the encouragement of wholeness, balance, life, coherence, comprehensiveness, general understanding, general awareness, constructivity, and creativity.

Bifurcated mathematics encourages all these things, mainly on the pure side. (The applied side is regarded as an amorphous mass of heuristic methods and nonrigorous ideas within which there is much less scope for the exercise of the 'wholeness, balance. . .', etc. mentioned above.) Integrated mathematics on the other hand offers a chance to apply the educational values across the gamut of mathematical thinking.

Put like this, the issue may appear rather marginal. That it is not, may be seen when we consider the content of first-order values (i.e., roughly, stable motivations) over which the educational values operate. Bifurcated mathematics hives off all the purposive connections and relevancies of mathematics into a rag-bag of applications, leaving the teacher free to wax eloquent on the unity, coherence, balance, etc. of pure mathematics. The result is to drain the major part of the work of nearly all the values which emerge from the boy's or girl's own experience. This is the great problem about the bifurcated interpretation of mathematics: it tries to educate in a context almost devoid of first-order values.

At first sight from a Hirstian point of view (Hirst 1965), the pure side of the bifurcated interpretation of mathematics may seem to be tailor-made to meet the criteria for being considered to be 'educational'. Here, surely, is one of those basic 'disciplines of knowledge' into which it is an essential part of the job of a liberal education to initiate the child. If this did not count as a case of 'initiation into a form of intrinsically worthwhile intellectual culture' whatever would? I think it would not be unfair to say that, through all the difficulties involved in trying to introduce the pure side of the bifurcated interpretation of mathematics into the schools, its protagonists have taken comfort from this thought: that what they have attempted is manifestly much more *educational* than the curriculum it superseded.

Why, then, has the pure side of the bifurcated interpretation of mathematics so often been a disaster when introduced into the ordinary school? Could it be that a philistine population do not want their children to be initiated into a form of intrinsically worthwhile intellectual culture? Could it be that what we call a 'liberal education' is a commodity only suited to a minority of the school population?

Such a conclusion would, of course, be absurd. For, almost by definition, the job of education is to 'draw out' the full powers of the minds of all the children in the schools; and a 'liberal' education should do that job more fully than an 'illiberal' education would. Some exponents of the bifurcated interpretation of mathematics in the schools, sobered by their new-found awareness of the poor 'teachability' of bifurcated mathematics to the average child, have queried whether it is really necessary to inflict such mathematics onto all the children on virtually every day of the school year. Perhaps the proper level for the pure side of bifurcated mathematics in the schools is as a minority 'appreciation' subject for the average child, and as an option for the abler child. Such thoughts are quite widely entertained. But if so, what has become of the argument that bifurcated mathematics has a unique claim to be considered 'educational'? If the pure side of bifurcated mathematics is not intrinsically worthwhile material for inclusion in the curriculum, whatever is?

The problem seems to reduce to this: that the average child fails to see the value of the pure side of bifurcated mathematics in the school curriculum. And this leads us to wonder whether the values of the pure side of bifurcated mathematics have been properly established. Do the values of the pure side of bifurcated mathematics really exist? And if so, what are the necessary preconditions for anyone to 'see' them?

To 'see' the values of the pure side of bifurcated mathematics one needs various things:

a   a capacity to suspend one's disbelief at the uselessness of the activity;

b   an appreciation of the importance of rules, in general, in any area of
   life;
c   an appreciation of the importance of the rigorous observance of rules;
d   a capacity to remember abstract rules which are wholly unconnected
   with ordinary life;
e   a degree of mental agility and stamina in searching for solutions to
   difficult problems;
f   an awareness of the 'state of the game' in relation to the presumed
   difficulty of different problems;
g   a desire to do well in this form of competition.

Given these conditions, the value of the activity of pure, bifurcated
mathematics becomes almost self-evident. It constitutes a kind of game in
which the participant achieves feelings of satisfaction by doing better than
the other players, or merely by bettering his own past achievements in the
game. And by 'better' we mean solving problems involving more rules,
rules which are more confusingly tangled together, to achieve more
generalizable results, more swiftly, via neater, more elegant pieces of symbolic manipulation and verbal argument.

The reason why the average child fails to 'see' the values of pure bifurcated mathematics is now clear: the average child fails to meet conditions a
to g above. The average child tends to be unwilling to pay the entrance fee to
this particular game.

It appears, therefore, that pure bifurcated mathematics is not experienced as being 'intrinsically worthwhile' unless one has first managed to
suspend belief in its nonvalue. And this raises awkward problems, if
accepted widely as a principle. For what is there to prevent any group of
people from inventing a form of totally useless, referenceless, ritualistic
activity, and then claiming the unique satisfactions to be gained from doing
it well? Must we, by definition, accept all such claims at face-value? Is any
activity which can be said to be 'intrinsically worthwhile' to be regarded as
being 'educational', regardless of its relationship to other things and the
entrance or exit fee? The answer must clearly be no. If pure bifurcated
mathematics is to be regarded as 'educational', it must be possible to make a
stronger case on its behalf than chess, which also constitutes a demanding
intellectual game, with its own intrinsic satisfactions. But, many
mathematicians will exclaim, 'mathematics is much more important intellectually than chess!' Precisely so: mathematics has a central role to play in
science, technology, organization, and development. It is an integrative

subject which illuminates the possibilities of scientific explanation, technological planning, organizational development. It provides a training in logical thinking which is valuable, not merely in relation to its own intrinsic challenges, but in relation to these wide areas of application. In other words, many mathematicians who regard themselves as supporting the bifurcated view might change their mind if they took into account the full range of their feelings about the subject. The great strength of the bifurcated point of view is the clean basis it provides for *rigour* deep in the structure of mathematics. Draining the subject of meaning produces an instant improvement in rigour; germs can hardly live in a vacuum.

To provide a sound epistemological basis for integrated mathematics we principally need two things: (a) an integrated view of the *content* of the subject, and (b) an integrated view of *method*. The first may be found in a neo-Peircean interpretation of mathematics as 'the science of possibility' (see Ormell, 1972). The second may be found in mathematical modelling, the method of approach which, as Atiyah has pointed out (Atiyah, 1977), is used at all levels of mathematics. It is used, of course, in applications; but it is also used in axiomatics: for example, in producing an arithmetical model of propositional logic. Indeed modelling is implicit in the very idea of abstraction: noticing and representing certain features of a situation, and not noticing and not representing others.

So mathematics, regarded as a modelling, possibility-exploring activity, may be construed, not just as another subject, but as a whole dimension, of curriculum. (See Morrison, 1979.)

This is a relatively new point of view, which seems to be rapidly gaining ground. It is ironic that the pendulum which, previously tilted heavily in favour of bifurcation, is now beginning to tilt the other way. It is coming to be widely seen that the values of pure bifurcated mathematics, far from guaranteeing the subject a place in the pantheon of 'educational' activities, actually reduce its status to that of a game, and, with this, risk reducing its place in the curriculum to that of a minor activity like music, or an out-of-school activity like chess. To be 'educational' a subject must not only involve an initiation into a worthwhile form of activity, but this worthwhile activity needs to be one which does not involve a suspension of disbelief, and therefore, in effect, a cutting off of other thoughts. Whether education is uniquely and fully specified by Forster's famous phrase 'only connect . . .' may be open to reasoned doubt, but that there is something odd about a claim which bases the status of being 'educational' on the condition 'first disconnect . . .' is fairly plain.

References

Allanson, J. (1968) 'Mathematics for the majority', *Journal of Biol. Education*.

Atiyah, M. (1977) *Proceedings of the 3rd I.C.M.E.*, Karlsruhe, 61-74.

Ayer, A.J. (1935) *Language, Truth and Logic*, London: Gollancz.

Budden, F.J. and Wormell, C.P. (1964) *Mathematics through Geometry*, Oxford: Pergamon.

Dieudonne, J. (1964) 'L' Ecole francaise moderne des mathematiques', *Philosophia Mathematica*, 1, 2.

Hammersley, J. (1968) 'On the enfeeblement of mathematical skills', *Bulletin of the Inst. of Mathematics*, 4, 4, 3-22.

Hirst, P.H. (1965) 'Liberal education and the nature of knowledge', in *Philosophical Analysis and Education*, R.D. Archambault (ed).

H.M. Inspectorate (1978) *Children in their Primary Schools*, London: HMSO.

Kaner, P. (1973) 'Mind your language', *Newsmaths* 8.

Kline, M. (1962) 'New high school math imperils U.S. technical progress', *New York Alumni News*.

Morrison, P. (1979) *Termites and Telescopes*, London: B.B.C. Publications.

Ormell, C.P. (1964) see Budden, F.J.

Ormell, C.P. (1969) 'Ideology and the reform of school mathematics', *Proc. Philosophy of Education Society Gt. Brit.* III, 37-54.

Ormell, C.P. (1972) 'Mathematics science of possibility', *International Journal Mathematical Education in Sci. and Tech.*, 3, 329-341.

Ormell, C.P. (1973) 'The problem of curriculum sequence in mathematics', in Langford and O'Connor (eds) *New Essays in the Philosophy of Education*, 216–233, London; Routledge and Kegan Paul.

Polya, G. et al. (1962) 'On the mathematics curriculum of the high school', *American Mathematical Monthly*, 69, 3, 189-193.

Pring, R. (1978), *Inaugural Lecture*, Exeter.

Sawyer, W.W. (1966) *A Path to Modern Mathematics*, Harmondsworth: Penguin Books.

Scott, D.B. (1968) 'The modish maths', *The Advancement of Science*, 44, 135-142.

Thom, R. (1973) 'Modern mathematics, does it exist?', *Developments in Mathematical Education*, Cambridge, 194-209.

Von Neumann, J. (1956) 'The mathematician', *The World of Mathematics* IV, 2053-2063, New York: Simon and Schuster.

Zeeman, C. (1972) 'Mathematics and creative thinking', *Mathematics in School*, 2, 3-5.

AN OVERVIEW

The original idea behind this book was simple and yet appealing. Philosophers working in educational fields frequently take part in debates about values, and such discussions are central to any consideration of the aims and practices of education. Likewise, educational researchers and curriculum developers spend much of their time in thinking about the problems of evaluation, and in actually evaluating the fruits of curriculum development. Evaluation has become so all-pervading that an unkind critic might refer to the activity as an evaluation industry.

Two things struck us about these developments. First, there seem to be experts in each of the fields of evaluation, psychometrics, and examination research, but despite the obvious links between these activities little communication takes place between the practitioners in these fields. Psychometricians contribute to the development of psychological and educational tests; examination board researchers are fully occupied with problems of the comparability, the reliability, and the validity of public examinations; and evaluators confine their attention to discussing methodology and to assessing the quality and the effects of development projects. Secondly, many evaluators, and most psychometricians, seem rarely to consider underlying values. Value-judgements clearly underline almost all evaluations – yet seldom are such value-judgements made explicit.

We believe that the underlying message of the essential link between values and evaluation has emerged in the various chapters of this book and that the link between the various aspects of the measurement and evaluation process is also clear. Wynne Harlen in particular (in Chapter 5) discusses the complex nature of a comprehensive evaluation, mentioning the importance of pre-evaluation activity. It is at this point particularly that value-judgements are involved. She mentions 'new mathematics' and refers to Christopher Ormell's chapter in which he argues that advocates of the early 'new mathematics' materials did not consider evaluation necessary 'because there were no other candidates in the field'. We would put the point differently. The early curriculum developers in mathematics in the 1960s (particularly those concerned with SMP) were indeed confident in their own beliefs and values and they were capable of producing *acceptable* new curricula in mathematics – acceptable that is to the decision-maker, in school, university, examining boards, and offices in local and national Government. The SMP group employed thorough evaluation procedures of a formative kind, designed to improve the quality of the product. The consequent assessments, G.C.E. examination results for example, were all in terms of the original SMP goals and SMP mathematics. No attempt was made to evaluate performance on the new syllabus in terms of the old one. So there *was* an evaluation, but it was under the control of, and influenced by, the developers, and it was entirely within their own value-system. At that time, the freedom to evaluate original curriculum development within its own terms was a precious one, by no means to be taken for granted. Much the same happened with Nuffield science, as David Malvern makes clear in his chapter. Such self-controlled, intrinsic evaluation and assessment of the new methods and content within their own terms was permitted because of the authority and respect ascribed to the developers. University mathematicians and scientists accepted 'A'-level grades in SMP mathematics and Nuffield science, not because of some mythical belief in the comparability with grades in traditional mathematics and science, but because they trusted the developers. No clearer example of the link between values and evaluation could be found – yet the link has rarely been made explicit.

Two other examples of present-day activity exhibit the values/evaluation link in a clear fashion. First, the development of C.S.E. Mode 3 procedures, that is, of an internal examination set in the school and moderated externally by an examination board. John Wilmut, in his chapter, reflects contemporary worries about C.S.E. Mode 3. But, in Mode 3, the link between values and evaluation is seen very clearly – if the teacher makes his own assessments on his own terms and in his own school, then *his* values and *his* evaluation are closely linked. The intensity of effort needed to achieve this integration is one reason why Mode 3 has always been the preoccupation of a minority. It is easier and safer to work to a Mode 1 external syllabus and to other people's values, worked out in advance and presented on a plate, so to speak, for the teacher and pupil. When Mode 3 does operate effectively the external moderation element is an important aspect of the work. This external moderation acts as a check on the standards of the local school and the individual teacher. It not only adjusts the level of marks to make the local standard comparable to the national standard, but also takes account of the values of the individual teacher or school as compared with the more general values of the informed public as seen by the moderator. This is the reason why the act of moderation is such a complicated one.

Similarly, and secondly, the work of the Assessment of Performance Unit (APU) at the DES, touched upon by several of our contributors, is another example of the link between values and evaluation. Much effort is being expended by the APU to make sure that, in English, mathematics, and science, what is assessed or measured is important and worth assessing from a subject-content point of view. In determining what should and can be monitored, value-judgements are made all the time. Only after considerable discussion and thought about content are tests and instruments constructed. In this latter process the sometimes rather vague notions associated with discussion on aims and objectives are sharpened. Once again we are involved with a complicated process. The consideration of possible evaluations sharpens the discussion of values, and the discussion of values is an essential precursor of the consequent evaluation.

One of the clear messages of this book is that it is not possible to make useful generalized statements in the realms of values, aims, and objectives without the essential discipline of the subsequent evaluation and measurement. This is no doubt partly what Lord Kelvin had in mind (quoted by Rob Morrison in his chapter) when he said that when one could measure what one was talking about and express it in numbers we knew something about it. The interaction between precision and ambiguity is an interesting one. Discussion in the immediate future about a common curriculum, or a framework for the curriculum, especially if associated with the monitoring aspects of the APU work, will no doubt also exemplify this interaction.

Those of our colleagues who have contributed to the second half of this book have each found it necessary to write, in part, a justification of their own subject. Eloquent pleas are made by Raymond Wilson for the value of literature and poetry, by Raymond Davies for the uniqueness of the historical contribution to thought, and by David Malvern for the distinctive nature of science. Christopher Ormell for mathematics and Desmond Vowles for English language are perhaps able to take the importance of their subjects for granted, but they make clear that values greatly affect attitudes to their subject and hence affect the content and method of teaching. So we see the need for a thorough-going discussion of the nature of any particular subject discipline as a prelude to, or perhaps as an integral part of, the study of its value, and certainly as a precursor of any evaluation or measurement within the subject.

One general question emerges with regard to evaluation for all the arts subjects of the curriculum – how 'subjective' is this activity?

We have had some difficulty with the words 'subjective' and 'objective', as they are capable of bearing a variety of meanings and so causing mis-understanding – particularly between philosophers and psychologists! Many philosophical problems surround the notions of 'subjectivity' and 'objectivity', but this is not the place to plunge into these complexities. We need to make it clear, therefore, that the terms are being used here in their (fairly) straightforward, psychological sense: i.e., a subjective evaluation being one which depends upon personal judgement and an individual point of view, and an objective evaluation being one which is based upon com-monly agreed, impersonal features of whatever is being evaluated. In this sense, then, evaluating a child's mathematical ability, for example, will be a *more* objective matter than evaluating his artistic ability. But it does *not* follow from this, we must emphasize, that no impersonal standards what-soever can be applied to artistic work (see Fraser Smith's comments in Chapter 10 on the possibility of 'aesthetic knowing'), nor that within the arts everyone's opinions are of equal worth.

It matters very much *who* is doing the evaluating here. Raymond Wilson in Chapter 9 refers to the clerisy, that group of informed individuals described by Coleridge, as the only people capable of making informed judgements to be handed down to the multitude. Similarly, Fraser Smith writes of those art teachers who are 'High Priests' and of 'Connoisseurs' as evaluators. One of the editors (Jack Wrigley) once claimed, in an unguarded moment, to be able to evaluate and measure anything. When challenged he took refuge in an imaginary group of twenty men, or women, or both. They would cast their votes or make their assessments, perhaps on, say, a 5-point or 7-point scale on any issue, topic, activity, or event. The subjectivity of their opinions would be ironed out either by the necessity of agreement, like a jury in a criminal trial, or by the use of averages, like judges in an

234 Values and Evaluation in Education

ice-skating competition. Many of the more obvious difficulties concerned with the evaluation of examinations, events, and creations in the arts can be minimized by the application of some version of Coleridge's clerisy, Wrigley's twenty people, or some kind of connoisseurship. The use of multiple marking of English essays or of using two or three examiners for research theses are variations on the method. Some problems remain though. How do we select the clerisy, the connoisseurs, or the twenty people? How do we refresh the group so that it is not too self-satisfied, self-opinionated, or self-perpetuating? How do we allow for the fact that in taking an average view, admittedly a more reliable and more objective view, we may miss the essence of genius? Would the connoisseurs recognize the genius of an original innovator? What if all the clerisy are wrong?

There are of course no complete answers to these questions. Common to all arts subjects are questions of fashion and taste. To evaluate the worth and quality of a Haydn symphony is a complex affair. The musical equivalent of the clerisy can determine if and when the general public can even hear Haydn adequately performed. Only then can the general public accept or refuse that opportunity. The popularity of composers rises and falls with time in a complex fashion, and in any case the judgement of the masses may not coincide with that of the connoisseurs. Then there is the question of originality. If a modern composer were now to write the equivalent of Beethoven's Tenth Symphony he would probably get little credit for it from the connoisseurs of today. Similar considerations apply to art and to literature. Why is Titian regarded as an artist's artist? How do the innovations of modern art become generally accepted? In passing, one might note that in art we have a most fascinating value-system, that of money itself. Could one evaluate a work of art simply by its market value? Obviously not fully, as can be seen by considering the case of forgeries of Old Masters. And yet the financial aspect of works of art is one interesting measure of an aspect of value. In literature how do we compare T.E. Lawrence with D.H. Lawrence, the importance of George Eliot as compared with Jane Austin, or of Kingsley Amis with his son Martin? Perhaps such comparisons are simply odious. Yet they are made by some combination of the opinion of the clerisy and the common reader. Market values can be applied to literature as well as to art. Raymond Davies in his justification of history gives us some clues about how works of art become classics when he points to the importance of the historical dimension.

Let us admit that our clerisy, our connoisseurs, or our twenty people will not solve all our evaluation problems. But some such similar group (it might be as small as two or three) can make an acceptable start in our efforts to make our evaluations more objective. The existence of such groups would ensure that possible conflicts of value were considered when evaluations were made; the resulting judgements would certainly be more consistent, and very often the consequent assessments would also be more valid. This method of judgement by replication or averaging is of course often employed in marking English essays and in evaluating content in arts subjects generally, although Desmond Vowles in Chapter 8 draws attention to the dangers of producing a combined 'averaged' assessment of different qualities within the same piece of work.

Do not, though, let us fall into the common trap of believing that evaluation in mathematics and science, being less subjective, is therefore easy. A careful reading of the chapters by Christopher Ormell and David Malvern will show that this is not so. In fact, mathematics is deceptive in the apparent ease with which performances can be judged. Once a person has committed a particular piece of mathematics to paper it is easy for a number of different examiners to agree on the standard of worthwhileness of the performance. Such agreement is much easier than the corresponding task in English, art, or history. But the actual performance in mathematics is easily altered by relatively slight variations in the form of the question. For example, if a pupil is asked to add 23 to 15 it might make all the difference if the question is asked in words or in either of these two forms:

$$
\begin{array}{r}
23 \\
+\ 15 \\
\hline
38
\end{array}
\qquad \text{or } 23 + 15 = 38
$$

So even simple changes in notation can affect performance as well as the more large-scale changes in values of the kind mentioned by Christopher Ormell. No wonder the questions concerned with rising and falling standards are so complex!

Our final points then are as follows:

1 Evaluations always depend upon values, either explicit or implicit, and there is much to be said for making as explicit as possible the underlying value-judgements. The very act of, and attempt at, evaluation may clarify our thoughts. Consideration of aims and objectives,

and the development of guidelines and frameworks for the curriculum, are sharpened, not only by a consideration of the underlying values, but also by the attempt at evaluation.

2 There is less agreement in arts subjects than in science and mathematics over what constitutes rightness or wrongness, merit or inadequacy, success or failure. Attempts to make evaluation of performance in the arts more 'objective' (in the sense of achieving a greater degree of consensus among the evaluators) are certainly possible and should be attempted by means of replications involving connoisseurs of some kind. Whilst such methods involve a risk that the genius will not be spotted, they are less dangerous than methods which involve a pedantic analysis of only the more mechanical, easily assessed elements within a complex subject like English or art. It would follow that it is preferable, for example, to make a number of holistic assessments of English essays and to average them, rather than to use an analytical scale of the so-called skills of essay-writing. The great advantage of the use of a clerisy, or connoisseurs, or even a group of like-minded colleagues is that value-judgements can be preserved, articulated, and discussed before, during, and even after the evaluation process takes place.

3 Evaluation in science and mathematics is not so simple as is often assumed. Value-judgements are still necessarily involved and a false accuracy and reliability is often assumed.

4 In assessment, examining, testing, and evaluating there are common problems. Some of these problems are technical, to do with the act of measurement, and some are to do with the underlying value-judgements. Sophisticated measurement techniques, although occasionally necessary, are rarely possible in matters concerned with education. The underlying data is too rough and the consensus on values not great enough to justify the use of sophisticated research techniques. The interaction between simple measurement and evaluation techniques on the one hand and an explicit consideration of values on the other is much more important.

5 Christopher Ormell coins a new word in his chapter on values – exomotivation; he says, 'The idea behind the concept is that it is a case of exporting a motivation which one has oneself, to others.' We think this very important. It bears on the question that bedevils most discussion on values – the gap between ideals and practice, between

motivation and performance. It is the interaction between values and evaluation which might help narrow this gap between theory and practice, between ideals and reality, especially if teachers can be encouraged to think more clearly about what they want to achieve, why they want to achieve it, and whether their actual results bear any relation to their aspirations.

R.S.
J.W.

AUTHOR INDEX

References in italics are to bibliographic details

SUBJECT INDEX

References in italics are to the tables and diagrams

The Harper Education Series has been designed to meet the needs of students following initial courses in teacher education at colleges and in University departments of education, as well as the interests of practising teachers.

All volumes in the series are based firmly in the practice of education and deal, in a multidisciplinary way, with practical classroom issues, school organisation and aspects of the curriculum.

Topics in the series are wide ranging, as the list of current titles indicates. In all cases the authors have set out to discuss current educational developments and show how practice is changing in the light of recent research and educational thinking. Theoretical discussions, supported by an examination of recent research and literature in the relevant fields, arise out of a consideration of classroom practice.

Care is taken to present specialist topics to the non-specialist reader in a style that is lucid and approachable. Extensive bibliographies are supplied to enable readers to pursue any given topic further.